CW00458382

# EAST OF INDIA, SOUTH OF CHINA

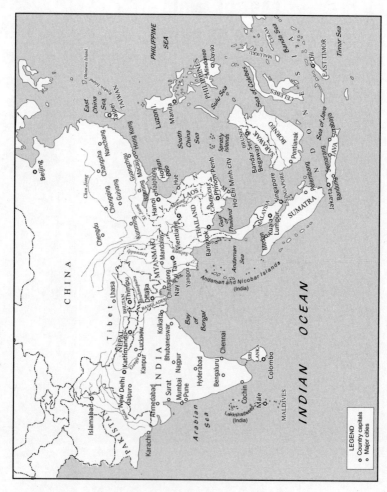

Southeast Asia

*Source:* Based on the author's inputs.

AMITAV ACHARYA

# EAST OF INDIA, SOUTH OF CHINA

Sino-Indian Encounters in Southeast Asia

OXFORD
UNIVERSITY PRESS

# OXFORD

UNIVERSITY PRESS

Oxford University Press is a department of the University of Oxford.
It furthers the University's objective of excellence in research, scholarship,
and education by publishing worldwide. Oxford is a registered trademark of
Oxford University Press in the UK and in certain other countries.

Published in India by
Oxford University Press
YMCA Library Building, 1 Jai Singh Road, New Delhi 110 001, India

© Oxford University Press 2017

The moral rights of the author have been asserted.

First Edition published in 2017

All rights reserved. No part of this publication may be reproduced, stored in
a retrieval system, or transmitted, in any form or by any means, without the
prior permission in writing of Oxford University Press, or as expressly permitted
by law, by licence, or under terms agreed with the appropriate reprographics
rights organization. Enquiries concerning reproduction outside the scope of the
above should be sent to the Rights Department, Oxford University Press, at the
address above.

You must not circulate this work in any other form
and you must impose this same condition on any acquirer.

ISBN-13: 978-0-19-946114-1
ISBN-10: 0-19-946114-7

Typeset in Garamond 3 LT Std 12/14.5
by The Graphics Solution, New Delhi 110092
Printed in India by Replika Press Pvt. Ltd

# Contents

# *Acknowledgements*

*I* thank C. Raja Mohan for encouraging me to write this book. It would not have been possible without the support of the ASEAN Studies Center at Chulalongkorn University, Thailand. I am especially grateful to M.R. Kalaya Tingsabadh, the former vice president for academic affairs, and Professor Suthiphand Chirathivat, the executive director of the ASEAN Studies Center, for encouraging me to complete this project. My commissioning editor at Oxford University Press, India, took on the publication of this manuscript with considerable enthusiasm. I thank Nidhi Prasad for her editorial work on the final manuscript and Allan Layug for the valuable research and editorial assistance that helped in the completion of this book.

# Abbreviations

| | |
|---|---|
| ACFTA | ASEAN–China Free Trade Area |
| ADB | Asian Development Bank |
| ADMM Plus | ASEAN Defence Ministers' Meeting Plus |
| AEC | ASEAN Economic Community |
| AIIB | Asian Infrastructure Investment Bank |
| APEC | Asia-Pacific Economic Cooperation |
| APSC | ASEAN Political-Security Community |
| ARC | Asian Relations Conference |
| ARF | ASEAN Regional Forum |
| ASCC | ASEAN Socio-Cultural Community |
| ASEAN | Association of Southeast Asian Nations |

| | |
|---|---|
| ASEAN-PMC | ASEAN Post Ministerial Conference |
| BIMSTEC | Bay of Bengal Initiative for Multi-Sectoral Technical and Economic Cooperation |
| BJP | Bharatiya Janata Party |
| BRICS | Brazil, Russia, India, China, and South Africa |
| CBIC | Chennai–Bengaluru Industrial Corridor |
| CECA | Comprehensive Economic Cooperation Agreement |
| CENTO | Central Treaty Organization |
| ChiJIA | China–Japan–India–America |
| DMIC | Delhi–Mumbai Industrial Corridor |
| DRV | Democratic Republic of Vietnam |
| EAEC | East Asian Economic Caucus |
| EAEG | East Asian Economic Grouping |
| EAS | East Asia Summit |
| ECAFE | Economic Commission for Asia and the Far East |
| ESCAP | Economic and Social Commission for Asia and the Pacific |
| FDI | Foreign Direct Investment |
| FTA | Free Trade Agreement/Free Trade Area |
| ICC | International Control Commission |
| ICWA | Indian Council on World Affairs |
| MGC | Mekong–Ganga Cooperation |
| NAFTA | North American Free Trade Agreement |
| NAM | Non-Aligned Movement |
| NATO | North Atlantic Treaty Organization |
| NEFOS | new emerging forces |
| OBOR | One Belt, One Road |
| OLDEFOS | old established forces |
| PAFTAD | Pacific Trade and Development Conference |
| PBEC | Pacific Basin Economic Council |
| PECC | Pacific Economic Cooperation Council |
| PRC | People's Republic of China |

| | |
|---|---|
| RCEP | Regional Comprehensive Economic Partnership |
| ReCAAP | Regional Cooperation Agreement on Combating Piracy and Armed Robbery against Ships in Asia |
| SARS | Severe Acute Respiratory Syndrome |
| SCO | Shanghai Cooperation Organization |
| SEATO | Southeast Asia Treaty Organization |
| SLD | Shangri-La Dialogue |
| TPP | Trans-Pacific Partnership |
| USSR | Union of Soviet Socialist Republics |
| Western DFC | Western Dedicated Freight Corridor |
| ZOPFAN | Zone of Peace, Freedom and Neutrality |

# Introduction

The first important ideas about constructing Asia's regional architecture after the Second World War came from India—more precisely, Jawaharlal Nehru. It was India's first prime minister who articulated the earliest vision of a regional order that emphasized Asian unity, advancement of decolonization and anti-racialism, and rejection of great-power intervention. He hosted two of the initial intra-regional gatherings of Asian leaders, called Asian Relations conferences (ARCs), in 1947 and 1949. He was perhaps the most influential ideational force behind the holding of the Asian-African Conference in Bandung, Indonesia, in 1955. Nehru's India was not only the dominant voice in Asian interactions but also played the chaperon to communist China (People's Republic of China [PRC]), as it sought acceptance from sceptical and fearful Asian neighbours.

Things changed rapidly after Bandung, and especially after the Sino-Indian War in 1962. India's leading role in Asian diplomacy quickly faded. From being the major champion of Asian regionalism, India almost became a political and diplomatic non-entity—if not a pariah—particularly in Southeast Asia by the 1980s. Several factors contributed to this. Not only did India lose territory and face to China in the 1962 confrontation, it also lost respect among Asian neighbours for its leadership. India was also distracted by myriad domestic problems, including conflicts and insurgencies. Wars with Pakistan in 1965 and 1971 distracted it from its eastern horizons. More importantly, India's pro-Soviet stance during the Cold War and its support for Vietnam on the Cambodia conflict (sparked by Vietnam's invasion and occupation of Cambodia between 1979 and 1989) caused misgivings and even animosity among its East and Southeast Asian neighbours. The Association of Southeast Asian Nations (ASEAN), formed in 1967, did not invite India to join the group—a far cry from the Bandung era when India was a co-convener of the Conference of South East Asian Prime Ministers. India's lack of economic openness limiting foreign investment and lacklustre growth rate, especially when compared with the rapidly growing economies of the 'Asian Tigers', was another factor that contributed to the drift between India and East Asia. India remained outside of the East Asian production networks created by a massive flow of Japanese investment in the 1980s and the 1990s. It was also excluded from the first Asia-Pacific regional organizations that emerged in this period, notably the Asia-Pacific Economic Cooperation (APEC, formed in 1989) and ASEAN Regional Forum (ARF, formed in 1994, which India joined two years later).

But did India's loss mean China's gain? To some extent it did—but with a qualification. What many observers do not realize is that China's triumph at Bandung was short-lived. The goodwill achieved at Bandung by the 'charm offensive' strategy of Chou En-Lai, the first premier of the PRC, dissipated quickly due to China's aid to communist insurgencies in Southeast Asia. While India suffered a loss of prestige in Southeast Asia on account of its humiliating defeat in the 1962 Sino-Indian War, China did not necessarily win the diplomatic–political relations contest in Southeast Asia either. Its support for the communist movements challenging Southeast Asian governments invited mistrust and isolation. At the same time, both got mired in domestic problems: China through the upheaval caused by the Cultural Revolution and India with its myriad internal conflicts. Further, India was also bogged down with its conflicts with Pakistan, fighting successive wars in 1965 and 1971 (the latter over the liberation of East Pakistan).

Post-Bandung, however, China did gain incrementally. The spectacular results of China's economic reforms under Deng Xiaoping since 1979 and its more moderate policy towards the ASEAN countries, combined with its common cause with ASEAN against the Vietnamese occupation of Cambodia, helped it reverse the decline of its influence in Asia. Although neither India nor China could claim the leadership of Asia, China moved ahead in terms of gaining recognition and respect from its Asian neighbours.

India, for its part, has since made inroads into the Asian diplomatic stage. Its own economic reforms since 1991, while not as dramatic and wide-ranging in their scope and consequences as China's starting over a decade earlier, were still a crucial turning point. India gradually found its way into the Asian regional fora as a full-dialogue partner of ASEAN, and a member of the ARF and the East Asia Summit (EAS), although it is still not a member of APEC. Moreover, the end of China's post-Cold War 'charm offensive' around 2009 and the fear of growing Chinese power in East and Southeast Asia, fuelled by its territorial claims in the East and South China seas, have created some strategic appeal for India, at least as a potential 'regional balancer'.

Yet there is little question that it is China that has emerged as the pre-eminent Asian economic and military power. Whether viewed with admiration or suspicion—and often both—China dominates the Asian diplomatic stage. It is seeking new friends and allies, even at the expense of ASEAN's solidarity. There are also growing fears in Asia and the West of a Chinese Monroe Doctrine over Asia, or a rerun of the traditional Chinese tributary system.

In this book, I do not pretend to offer a comprehensive stage-by-stage narrative of Asian interactions. Nor is this a book about India–China relations. Rather, it explores the role of India and China in Southeast Asia. It brings together a series of reflective and research chapters, highlighting some of the key events and turning points in the evolving India–China–Southeast Asia relations—an important triangular system worthy of investigation to deeply understand the evolution of Asian and global order.

It is also not a book about Indian policy towards China or Asia, nor is it written from an Indian perspective. But it places India at the centre stage of Asian security dynamics. Lately, it has been rare in non-Indian writings on Asian security and international relations to see India having anything but a peripheral role in the Asian security architecture. Most writings and policy debates on Asian security have more or less ignored India—instead focusing on the idea of the Asia-Pacific (without India).[1] This book brings India back into the picture. It does so by looking not at India's role in Asia from what C. Raja Mohan has aptly described as a 'Curzonian' geopolitical perspective, but from an ideational and normative perspective. While not dismissing the importance of geopolitics, I do not focus on it exclusively or independently of ideas and norms. Ideas and norms are the places where India played a central role in building an Asian order. It may do so again in the future.

In short, while India has been 'missing in action' in the Asian order since the Bandung era, its pivotal role in the post-war Asian interactions combined with its re-emergence as a 'rising' power makes it pertinent and justifiable to approach Asian security from an Indian vantage point or by giving India an important, but not dominant, place. This, I believe, is the essence of my approach. In this book, some of the discussions focus directly on India with a view to explain its re-emergence as a player in Asia in general and Southeast Asia in particular. At the same time, the other parts of the book, such as the discussion about the ideas of Asia, Asianism, and the 'rise of Asia', while not directly dealing with the Indian policy towards China or Southeast Asia, cover it or have India as part of the story.

Although this book is not directly about Southeast Asia or ASEAN, I give a prominent place to Southeast Asia. This is not as surprising as it may seem to those who are used to thinking about regional order in Asia in terms of the policies and interactions of the major Asian powers such as China, Japan, and India. Southeast Asia is the true crossroads of Asia, where India and China meet; hence, the expression 'East of India, South of China'. I do not imply at all that Southeast Asia is a cultural or political appendage of China or India, as will be clear in chapters 1 and 2, but a meeting place of the two civilizations and powers. Moreover, Southeast Asia was the historic diplomatic core of postcolonial Asia. Today, it is the 'fulcrum' of the Asia-Pacific regional architecture, to quote the former US Secretary of State Hillary Clinton. While much has been written about China–Southeast Asia relations, and on a lesser scale about India–Southeast Asia relations, there is really very little literature available on the interactions among the three with Southeast Asia. Indeed, the Bandung drama unfolded on a Southeast Asian stage, and ASEAN today is a major hub of interaction between China and India. This three-way understanding of regional order is, therefore, another aspect of this book's novelty.

The first chapter is about the idea of Asia, Asianism, and the 'rise of Asia' discourse. Although they cover many different voices, the Indian voice is among the most prominent, especially in the early stages of their life histories. Although Japan might have invented the notion of pan-Asianism in the later Meiji era, it was, with some exceptions, a mask for Japanese hegemony presaging the nation's subsequent turn to imperialism. The Indian idea of Asianism was unabashedly emancipatory: it stressed on Asia's emergence from the dark ages of colonialism, called for the restoration of its traditional civilizational ties, and set an agenda for economic progress and political rejuvenation at the world stage. To be sure, India, after dominating discourses about Asian unity in the early post-war period, faded away from the picture due to its internal and external distractions. But Chapter 1, as well as chapters 2, 3 and 4, establish beyond doubt that the first major visions of Asian order came from India. Chapter 1 also shows the fragility of 'Asianism' and the 'rise of Asia' discourse. This is partly because coming from the big powers, some of these regional projects lacked legitimacy since, among other things, they raised fears of big-power dominance over the weak. Another lesson is that the rise of Asia discourse of the 1990s is not the same as the Asianism idea of the early post-war period (up to Bandung); the former was about Asia's power ambitions, the latter about Asia's weakness and re-emergence.

Chapter 2 explores India's present relations with Southeast Asia in the light of its past. India's 'Look East' policy was initiated in the 1990s by the Narasimha Rao government and was a by-product of the nation's economic liberalization as well as its growing concerns about a rising China. But a dispassionate view of the past is an important factor in making that policy viable. Rarely does an Indian leader visiting Southeast Asia or at an Indian event concerning that region fail to include in their speech a homage to India's civilizing mission in the region, as seen in the case of the Inter-Asian Art Exhibition at the 1947 ARC in New Delhi (Chapter 1). What may seem natural or necessary for the Indian dignitary or scholar visiting Southeast Asia is perceived as cultural arrogance and has been a major irritant to the Southeast Asian elite, an annoyance compounded by foreign policy differences between India and Southeast Asian countries and the latter's intrinsic suspicion of big powers.

Just as ignoring India's monumental contribution to the classical civilization and politics of Southeast Asia would be an error, so would be the tendency to exaggerate the nature and scope of that contribution. The truth is that there is little evidence of Indian 'colonization' of Southeast Asia even in the sense of large-scale Indian migration to the region, or what Indian classical texts referred to as 'Suvarnabhumi', or Greater India, as the nationalist narrative of the Greater India Society of Calcutta (now Kolkata) implied. Nor is there any evidence of an Indian military conquest apart from the raids carried out by the Chola kingdom of South India on the maritime empire of Srivijaya in the eleventh century AD. It was neither colonization nor conquest but commerce that defined India's interaction with Southeast Asia. From the Southeast Asian perspective, evidence points to Southeast Asians selectively borrowing Indian religious and political ideas and localizing them to fit their context and suit their need. The Dutch economic historian Jacob van Leur's 'idea of the local initiative' (discussed in Chapter 2), which suggests the manner in which Southeast Asian rulers 'called upon Indian civilization to the East', offers a more plausible conjecture about India–Southeast Asia relations than Bengali historian R.C. Majumdar's Indian 'colonization thesis'. Against this backdrop, the recognition of Southeast Asian autonomy and agency is critical to the success of India's 'Look East/Act East' policy.

Chapters 3 and 4 examine the role Southeast Asia played as a crucial stage for India's and China's post-war approaches to regional and world order. Their role in the Asian-African Conference held in Bandung in 1955 is explored. The Bandung Conference marked the high point of India's post-war engagement not only with Southeast Asia but also Asia as a whole. It was also the point of the decline of that engagement. Chapter 3 takes a critical look at Nehru's role in the Bandung Conference that was marked by triumph, bitterness, and tragedy. At Bandung, Nehru pursued two closely related objectives. The first was to frustrate the American Cold War strategic design in Asia, as represented by the Southeast Asia Treaty Organization (SEATO), which he felt was a genuine threat to Asia's security. His second goal was to engage the PRC, which he believed to be more Asian than communist. While Nehru had an extremely visible presence at Bandung, his performance, though intellectually superb, was marred by a style that was perceived to be arrogant and somewhat heavy-handed. At the same time, Nehru, contrary to the claims made by his Western and pro-Western Asian critics at the conference, might have succeeded in delegitimizing the SEATO with the conference urging countries to abstain from collective defence pacts that serve the 'particularistic interests of any of the great powers'. Nehru's vindication lay in the fact that SEATO failed to attract any new members after the conference (which was one of the Western objectives at the conference).

Nehru, however, was far less successful in achieving India's other major objective at Bandung—that is, the rebranding of China as an Asian power rather than a communist bloc member. Chapter 4 looks at how India's relationship with China evolved prior to, and during, the Bandung Conference and the role of the conference in fuelling Sino-Indian mistrust, although the Nehru–Chou rivalry at Bandung was clearly exaggerated by Western media and spies (there were supposed to be more spies than delegates at this historic gathering). By and large, as the key player in Asian regionalism at this stage, Nehru succeeded in the goal of 'introducing' communist China to the rest of Asia—something that would have taken the new Chinese regime enormous effort and concessions had it tried the same without India's initiative. But Nehru did so at a great cost to India's credibility and position. In the contest of the 'charm offensive', Chou En-Lai clearly outperformed Nehru despite the latter's immense intellectual prestige. Even Nehru had to concede this, in remarkable self-deprecating good humour, when he wrote to Edwina Mountbatten confessing about his tendency towards irritability.

Bandung was the high point not only of India's but also of communist China's diplomatic engagement in Southeast Asia. And it went downhill thereafter for both powers. The 1962 war between Asia's two largest nations put paid to any residual hopes for pan-Asianism and gave Southeast Asian countries an opportunity to assert their own voice and role in regional organization. This they did on a sub-regional basis—minus India and China—by creating ASEAN in 1967.

It was not until the 1980s that China and India returned to the centre stage of Asian diplomacy. In both cases, economic reform and growth paved the way for their diplomatic activism (in the case of China, a 'charm offensive') in Southeast Asia. Chapter 5 addresses the vital question: what is the place of China, India, and Southeast Asia in the Asian order? It specifically asks whether China's rise might return Asia to a Sino-centric regional order, something akin to the tributary system that had marked East Asia's regional order before European colonialism, or whether China's own version of the Monroe Doctrine is already active in shaping Asian order in general and Southeast

Asian order in particular. I reject the view advanced by some analysts that Asia's Sino-centric past will be its future. Instead of the cultural–historical precedent, one might look at the more modern forces of economic interdependence and multilateral institutions as holding the clue to a new Asian regional order. History can teach us about the past, but the past will not return to us. Also, a Chinese Monroe Doctrine would not materialize because it will be vigorously resisted by the US and others, particularly India and ASEAN as co-builders of Asian and global order.

Just as the Chinese tributary system will not reappear in contemporary Asia, the extreme Indo-centric versions of the 'Indianization' thesis are also not likely to define India's new engagement with Asia. My analysis of the rise of India in Chapter 5 shows that while China may have more comprehensive power generally and in Southeast Asia more specifically, India has a potential for exercising influence over Southeast Asia. To a much greater extent than China's, India's rise is cheered, not feared by Southeast Asians and the international community. While the growth of Indian military and economic power is more limited than China's, the latter's geopolitical role is a mixed blessing at best, depending on how much restraint it chooses to exercise, especially towards its Southeast Asian neighbours. Also, in Chapter 5, I offer some thoughts on how the lessons from India's past involvement in Asia, including its mistakes and pitfalls, might apply to its current 'Look East/Act East' policy. And in addressing the key question of the chapter—the role that China and India play in Asia in general and Southeast Asia in particular, as well as the latter's contribution to Asian order-building—both competition and convergence, mainly in economic, geopolitical, and strategic arenas, will define the fulfilment of such important roles.

It is one thing for India and China to find accommodation in Southeast Asia, and it is another for them to provide a leadership to the world commensurate with their rising-power status. Thus the underlying question 'can Asia lead?' in Chapter 6 answers itself largely in the negative, at least for the foreseeable future. Despite the hype of Asia rising, Asian powers are yet to meet the expectations of their contribution to global governance. The argument here is that Asian powers are largely of a status-quo rather than revisionist orientation in that they are more interested in 'rising'—that is, fulfilling their national power ambitions—than in contributing to global governance. Part of the reason for this failure is their mutually competitive relationship and the lack of regional legitimacy. One answer to the deficient role in global governance is to have more committed regional engagement. Regionalism can be a useful launching pad for their role in global governance. This challenge is especially crucial for India, which, after decades of isolation and estrangement, has a major opportunity to re-embrace Asia. In addressing their leadership deficit, both Asian powers can learn from Southeast Asia, specifically ASEAN's approach of mutual restraint and accommodation through regional cooperation and legitimization.

To sum up, this book not only spotlights the historic encounters between two ancient and enduring civilizations, but also discusses the issue of their legitimacy and role as major players in the twenty-first century world order. As a key point of connection between India and China, Southeast Asia has been central to Sino-Indian encounters, especially in the initial decades after the end of the Second World War. But then, both powers flunked the test of offering leadership or even co-existing in Southeast Asia. They not only failed to keep peace with each other and thereby provide a model for the rest of Asia, but also failed to convince their Southeast Asian neighbours of the importance of building a regional political and economic framework with their own inclusion. Will they fail the test again?

This book presents an unconventional and challenging argument: Asia's future depends as much on India–China–Southeast Asian interactions as on the much-written-about China–US–Japan relationship. While the latter is of immediate geopolitical significance, it is the former that is integral to the cultural and geopolitical crossroads of Asia, past and future. Hence it deserves far more attention than it has received until now. This book is a contribution towards redressing that neglect.

## Note

1.  This may be changing now with the new concept of an 'Indo-Pacific' region, but it remains to be seen if this seemingly Indo-centric notion can really hold. The Indo-Pacific idea may get help if Southeast Asia resumes its historic role as a meeting point between India and China.

# 1.

# The Ideas of Asia*

*T*here are two powerful myths about Asia that plague any debate over whether it exists as a region. One myth sees Asia as essentially an outsider's invention. The other conflates it with

\* This chapter is based on an essay originally published as 'The Idea of Asia' in the roundtable 'Are We Adequately Training the Next Generation of Asia Experts', *Asia Policy*, no. 9 (2010): 32–9. *Asia Policy* is a journal published by the National Bureau of Asian Research (NBR). The NBR retains the rights to this material in all languages. Reprinted with the permission of the publisher. The chapter also draws from Amitav Acharya, 'Asia Is Not One', *Journal of Asian Studies*, vol. 69, no. 4 (2010): 1001–13. Reprinted with permission.

the 'rise of Asia'. Both are misleading or misguided, the latter even more so than the former.

The term 'Asia' was first used by Greek historian Herodotus to designate Anatolia in modern Turkey in the context of the Greek–Persian wars. But Asia was in many ways an invention of colonialism. François Godement, a French scholar of Asia, associates 'Asia' (and 'the East') with 'a fantasy seemingly woven from a Baudelaire poem, a melody by Ravel, a short story by Somerset Maugham and a James Ivory film'.[1] When the *Economist* magazine launched a new weekly column in April 2009 called 'Banyan', it reminded readers that the magazine itself had, as recently as in 1987, written about Asia as 'a geographic accident'. While today there might be a growing 'search for an Asian identity', the 'suspicion lingers on that Asia is a Western construct'.[2]

Then there are those who speak of the 'rise of Asia' or 'Rising Asia' or 'Asia rising', and even of a growing Asian identity but still predict a future of rivalry and strife. Consider a recent book on Asia by Bill Emmott, a former editor of the *Economist* magazine.[3] Emmott recognizes Asia's economic integration and even an emerging sense of regional identity based on the overlapping interests of its principal powers—China, Japan, and India—across the region. But he nonetheless foresees rivalry, rather than cooperation, as the dominant trend; hence the title of the book, *Rivals*.

To compound the problem, Asia also has had multiple names and identities. I can count at least 13 different ways in which Asia has been described with various prefixes and suffixes, namely (a) Asia, (b) Asia-Pacific, (c) Asia Pacific, (d) Asian Pacific, (e) Asia and the Pacific, (f) Asia/Pacific, (g) East Asia, (h) Eastern Asia, (i) Far East, (j) Greater East Asia, (k) Pacific, (l) Pacific Asia, and (m) Pacific Rim. Power, prosperity, and identity have determined which of these names are in vogue. Hence, terms such as the Far East, Greater East Asia, and the Pacific are associated with British, Japanese, and American power respectively. Hegemons are especially fond of naming regions after their own interests and spheres of influence. By contrast, Pacific Rim, Pacific Asia, Asia-Pacific (as in APEC), and Asia Pacific (a Canadian preference) are linked to rising economic interdependence and prosperity. Not long ago the idea of 'Asia Pacific' was distinguished from the idea of the 'Indian Ocean'. While the former connoted prosperity and progress, the latter was associated with poverty and underdevelopment. Yet in the past few years, the idea of an Indo-Pacific region has gained currency.

Asia is, of course, not a given. It is constructed, as most regions tend to be. There are powerful forces working against the concept. Diversity (geographic, cultural, and political), rivalries, and the lack of EU-style regional integration are chief among them. Yet to view Asia simply as a Western construct is misleading. In a wonderful little booklet called *Narratives of Asia,* Brij Tankha, a Japan specialist at the University of Delhi, and Sinologist Madhavi Thampi compare Indian, Chinese, and Japanese discourses about Asia to assert that 'while "Asia" is in many ways a colonial construction, it is important to remember that it has an earlier genealogy that continues to find expression in ways (*sic*).' As they see it, 'ideas about the region are a complex of premodern and modern developments'.[4]

Although the myriad peoples and cultures of what is loosely known today as Asia did not name themselves as such, that is, as Asians, the 'idea of Asia', far from being simply the invention of westerners, was also robustly imagined from within. Asia's first generation of nationalist thinkers and leaders such as José Rizal of the Philippines, Sun Yat-sen of China, Jawaharlal Nehru of India, and Aung San of Myanmar were among those doing the imagining. Although some of their ideas were self-serving and the colonial context was important, they were Asians recognizing Asia's emerging place in the international system. They used a Western term to articulate a changing local awareness and context, just like banyan (a variant of the Bodhi tree) that (as the *Economist* pointed out) was so named by the Portuguese after Gujarati merchants (*bania*s) who used to conduct business under the tree. In other words, naming a region is not the same as constructing a region. The term 'Asia' may be outsiders' but the *reality* of Asia is not.

Before proceeding further, let me briefly comment on the concepts of region, regionalization, and regionalism—the three central pillars of any meaningful discussion on the contemporary idea of Asia.[5] First, our understanding of what makes a *region* has undergone a major change. There is a growing agreement in the literature that (a) regions are not just material constructs but also ideational ones; (b) regions are not a given or fixed but are socially constructed—they are made and remade through political, economic, and social and cultural interactions; and (c) just like nation states, regions may rise and wither.[6]

In his discussion of the pre-Second World War period, Duara sets 'imperial regionalism' against the 'anti-imperialist regionalization project in Asia'. While I agree, I also believe that the anti-imperialist project, which persisted well into the post-war period, was not singular as a source of 'Asianness' and Asianism. The trajectory of Asian regionalism had varied underpinnings that need to be recognized. While Duara focuses on Tagore, Tenshin, and Zhang Taiyan, I bring in José Rizal, Ho Chi Minh, and Aung San. The richness and diversity of the Asian idea cannot be fully captured without looking at these Southeast Asian proponents, for it was in Southeast Asia that Asian regionalism took its most decisive shape.

## Contested Visions

Asia is not 'one', as Okakura Kakuzo had once argued, and there is no singular idea of Asia.[7] Asia is of multiple (although not always mutually exclusive) conceptions: some drawing upon material forces such as economic growth, interdependence, and physical power; others having ideational foundations such as civilizational linkages and normative aspirations. Some of these varied conceptions of Asia have shaped the destinies of its states and peoples in meaningful ways. Moreover, they have underpinned different forms of regionalism, which in turn has ensured that Asia, despite its fuzziness and incoherence, has remained a durable, if essentially contested, idea.

While 'Asia' has not lacked protagonists for the past century and half, they have differed widely in terms of their normative beliefs and political goals. Looking at the champions of Asia and their ideas, at least four different conceptions of Asia can be identified in the early post-Second World War period. These may be termed as *Imperialist Asia*, *Nationalist Asia*, *Universalist Asia*, and *Regionalist Asia*. A fifth conception, *Exceptionalist Asia*, though already incipient, would emerge later as a major political force. These categories are not mutually exclusive. Moreover, elements and impulses within these categories may be present to different degrees in a single proponent of Asia. Thus, while Jawaharlal Nehru of India belonged primarily to Nationalist Asia, he also identified with Universalist Asia (or at least an internationalist) and Regionalist Asia. Moreover, these impulses can shift during the course of a political career and a lifetime.

## Imperialist Asia

The first conception, Imperialist Asia, is tied to the hegemonic purposes of great powers, both Western and Asian. While the term 'Asia' did not originate with it, Western colonial rule, even though it severely disrupted the existing intra-regional commercial traffic and helped divide Asia into different spheres of influence, did contribute to the reification of the concept.

It thereby furthered the cultural and political dichotomy that had developed between Europe and Asia through the centuries, well before the 'consciousness of an Asian identity originated [within Asia] largely in reaction to the colonial system and in the common denominator of anti-Western sentiment'.[8]

But it was in the hands of an Asian power—Japan—that the imperialist notion of Asia assumed a peculiar prominence, as imperial Japan and its apologists sought to invoke a discourse of pan-Asianism to legitimize its dominance in a way that Western powers in the region had not and other Asian powers such as China and India would not. The dual role of Japan as Asia's saviour and its hegemonic leader was clearly illustrated in the Japanese notion, nay, ambition, of a Greater East Asia Co-Prosperity Sphere. Encompassing Japan (including the territories of Korea, Taiwan, and Sakhalin), China, Manchukuo (which Japan has created as a puppet state after seizing Chinese territory in Manchuria), French Indochina, and the Dutch East Indies, this was, of course, not all of Asia. But 'the concept built on Pan-Asian notions of an "Asian community"' that had earlier developed in Japan on the presumption of a common identity as well as a common interest among the societies of East, South East, and South Asia.[9] Indeed, representatives from all over Asia were invited to the Greater East Asia Conference held in November 1943.[10]

Although the Greater East Asia Co-Prosperity Sphere was but one element of Japanese pan-Asianism, it had the most serious impact on the destinies of Asian states and the lives of their peoples. This was a concept of hegemonic region and regionalism. While it offered a platform for organizing the unity of those incorporated into it, it was not always on a voluntary basis but through coercive means. The Japanese imperialist region was marked by a high degree of trade interdependence, and it certainly inspired freedom struggles all over Asia. But in political terms, it degenerated into another form of foreign dominance, no less oppressive than that of the Western colonial powers. Myanmar's Aung San, who had earlier endorsed the Greater East Asia Co-Prosperity Sphere and even envisioned 'a common defence policy in East Asia as the best guarantee for the maintenance of the Greater East Asia Co-Prosperity Sphere',[11] eventually insisted that 'a new Asian order ... will not and must not be one like the Co-Prosperity Sphere of militarist Japan, nor should it be another Asiatic Monroe doctrine, nor imperial preference or currency bloc'.[12]

The legacy of Imperialist Asia would have a long-term effect, shaping regional perceptions of the superpower rivalry during the Cold War. SEATO, although not an outright imperial organization, was perceived as an attempt at neo-colonial domination by some sections in Asia, including India's Nehru and Indonesia's Sukarno. Though it did not last very long, it helped polarize Asia along the Cold War divide, probably disrupting the socialization of China.

## Universalist Asia

Even before Japanese imperialism swept through Asia, there had emerged another conception of Asia that may be termed 'Universalist Asia'. Its most eloquent proponent was Rabindranath Tagore, who combined a visceral distaste for nationalism with a passionate belief in the 'common bond of spiritualism' among Asia's peoples.[13] Although Tagore did not specifically advocate a political regionalism of states (this might have been premature given that Asia was still firmly under colonial rule), his recognition and intellectual promotion of the spiritual and civilizational affinities among Asia's peoples constituted an alternative conception of Asian regionalism in which societies rather than states take the centre stage and which thrives as much on ideational and cultural flows as on economic links or political purposes.

Tagore, however, was not alone in articulating a conception of Asia that was not premised on a narrow state-centric nationalism. Rebecca Karl, for example, has analysed an alternative form of regionalism, much more politically oriented than Tagore's, among Chinese intellectuals 'rooted in non-state-centered practices and non-national-chauvinist culturalism' that could be contrasted with Sun Yat-sen's 'state-based, anti-imperialist vision of Asia'.[14] This alternative regionalism that Karl speaks of was centred around the ideas and associates of Chinese intellectual Liang Qichao and the activities of a little-known organization called the Asian Solidarity Society set up in Tokyo in 1907 by Chinese intellectuals; Japanese socialists; and Indian, Vietnamese, and Filipino exiles. An interesting aspect of this regionalism was the recognition accorded to the 'first Filipino' José Rizal as 'the quintessential Asian patriot, from which China and other Asian[s] must learn'.[15] Although Rizal is better known as a champion of the unity of the Malay race, his message was appropriated by the non-state-centric variety of Asian regionalism.

## Nationalist Asia

Tagore's innate universalism put him at odds with the powerful currents of nationalism surging through Asia, including in the very places the poet visited in his voyages through Asia and which he imagined as being integral to his conception of Asia. This is not to say that the proponents of a third conception of Asia, which I call Nationalist Asia, were untouched by universalist values and instincts. Leaders such as Nehru, Aung San, and Sukarno saw little contradiction between nationalism and international cooperation. As Aung San put it, 'I recognise both the virtues and limitations of pure nationalism, I love its virtues, I don't allow myself to be blinded by its limitations, though I knew that it is not easy for the great majority of any nation to get over these limitations.'[16] Aung San's nationalism, like those of Nehru and Sukarno, could support both nationalism and internationalism—albeit these figures from Asia's new power elite did not empathize with Universalist Asia at the expense of nationalism.

This third vision of Asia, championed by its nationalist leaders such as China's Sun Yat-sen, India's Jawaharlal Nehru, Myanmar's Aung San, and Vietnam's Ho Chi Minh, was geared to harnessing Asia's rejuvenation to further the retreat of Western colonialism. Before the Second World War, especially around the time of the 1927 Congress of Oppressed Nationalities, a number of leaders within the Indian National Congress (a group that was believed to include M.K. Gandhi, C.R. Das, and later Nehru) had supported the idea of an 'Asian federation' to organize a joint struggle against Western colonialism.[17] Regionalism, in this sense, was not only compatible with, but also a bulwark for, Asia's nationalisms and hence to its restoration and rejuvenation.[18] Certainly, Ho Chi Minh was keen to use regional cooperation to further the cause of Vietnamese independence.[19]

In a speech to welcome Sarat Chandra Bose, the brother of Subhas Chandra Bose, at the City Hall of Rangoon (now Yangon) on 24 July 1946, Aung San stated that Myanmar would 'stand for an Asiatic Federation in a not very, very remote future; we stand for immediate mutual understanding and joint action, wherever and whenever possible, from now [on] for our mutual interests and for the freedom of India, Myanmar and indeed all Asia'.[20] In September 1945, Ho Chi Minh spoke of his interest in the creation of a 'pan-Asiatic community' comprising Vietnam, Cambodia, Laos, Thailand, Malaya, Myanmar, India, Indonesia, and the Philippines (China, Japan, and Korea were not included in Ho's vision of an Asiatic community).[21] His ostensible goal at this stage was to foster political and economic cooperation among these countries while maintaining good relations with the US, France, and Britain. This was a time when Ho still hoped that the colonial powers, exhausted by war, would voluntarily speed up the process of decolonization. But when this proved to be a false hope, Ho and other Southeast Asian nationalist leaders began considering the use of regional cooperation to oppose the return of European colonialism. This was clearly evident in Ho's letter to the Indonesian prime minister Sutan Sjahrir in November 1946 urging cooperation between the two countries to advance their common struggle for freedom. In this letter, Ho asked Indonesia to join him in getting India, Myanmar, and Malaya to develop initiatives towards a 'Federation of Free Peoples of Southern Asia'. But Indonesian leaders responded coolly to this idea, apparently worried that cooperating with the Vietnamese communists would give the Dutch an opportunity to use the fear of communism to delay Indonesia's own independence.

Advancing decolonization was a principal theme at the 1947 ARC in New Delhi, the first conference of Asian nations in the post-war period. It was even more central to the second ARC, also known as the Conference on Indonesia, which was directly and specifically aimed at supporting Indonesian freedom fighters after the second Dutch Police Action in 1948. Yet despite all the talk about pan-Asian unity, its proponents were willing to offer only political rather than material support for the region's independence movements. For example, India's aid to Indonesian freedom fighters (an exception) was not extended to Ho Chi Minh, much to the disappointment of his supporters.

And these early stirrings of pan-Asianism did not translate into concrete and durable forms of cooperation or a pan-Asian institution. There was an uncomfortable sense among the smaller nations of Asia that the pan-Asianists of India, Japan, and China 'were primarily concerned with their own countries', and their 'exhortations ... largely as an extension of their own distinctive cultures'.[22] Moreover, Southeast Asians saw in a pan-Asian community the potential for Chinese or Indian domination. As one delegate from Myanmar to the 1947 ARC put it, 'It was terrible to be ruled by a Western power, but it was even more so to be ruled by an Asian power.'[23] And the pan-Asian sentiments of India's leaders were stymied by their limited contacts with nationalist leaders in other parts of Asia, their misgivings about the nationalist government in China, and the rise of anti-Indian sentiments in Myanmar and other parts of Asia.[24]

## Regionalist Asia

While Nationalist Asia sought to channel regionalism as an instrument of anti-colonialism and national liberation, the fourth vision, Regionalist Asia, inspired those who wished to use the combined platform of the region's newly independent nation states to seek a collective voice at the world stage. There was considerable overlap between Nationalist Asia and Regionalist Asia, with Nehru, Aung San, and Ho Chi Minh belonging to both. But the regionalists went a step beyond merely securing independence from colonial rule. The logical next step to follow in the pursuit of Asianism was to seek a role in the management of regional and international affairs. As Aung San put it, 'Asia has been rejuvenated and is progressively coming into world politics. Asia can no longer be ignored in international councils. Its voice grows louder and louder. You can hear it in Indonesia, you can hear it in Indo-China, you can harken to it in Burma and India and elsewhere.'[25] One major example of this shift was the differences in the agendas of the ARCs of 1947 and 1949 and that of the Asian-African Conference in 1955, which, despite its hybrid name, was thoroughly dominated by Asians. While the ARCs fretted over support for decolonization, the 29 participants at Bandung, as its secretary general would put it, set out 'to determine ... the standards and procedures of present-day international relations', including 'the formulation and establishment of certain norms for the conduct of present-day international relations and the instruments for the practical application of these norms'.[26] In other words, while the ARCs were about independence (from colonial rule), Bandung was about intervention (security from great power or superpower intervention).

The regionalists also saw the possibility of restoring the historical linkages among Asian societies disrupted by European colonialism to forge a regional association. Nehru described the first ARC in New Delhi as an 'expression of the deeper urge of the mind and spirit of Asia which has persisted in spite of the isolationism which grew up during the years of European domination'.[27] (Ho Chi Minh's interest in a 'pan-Asiatic community' could be seen in the same light.) Immediately after the Second World War, Nehru himself would advocate a regional association, 'a closer union between India and South-East Asia on the one side, and Afghanistan, Iran, and the Arab world on the West'.[28]

But Southeast Asians were unnerved by the prospects of a larger Asian federation or even association. Even professing deep friendship with India, Aung San recognized that '[w]hile India should be one entity and China another, Southeast Asia as a whole should form an entity—then, finally, we should come together in a bigger union with the participation of other parts of Asia as well'.[29] Southeast Asians would find subregional unity more practical and palatable. Bear in mind that José Rizal had advocated the unity of the Malay race, although he was appropriated by pan-Asianists. Frustrated by the failure of his efforts to secure material aid from fellow Asian countries for his struggle against the French, Ho Chi Minh would turn to the idea of an Indochinese federation. As Ho argued, 'Because of the close geography and extricable relationship in military and politics between Vietnam, Laos and Cambodia, the success or failure of revolutionary liberation of one country will have a direct impact on that of the others. Our task is to help the revolutionary movements in Cambodia and Laos.'[30]

This Southeast Asian concern was evident at the 1947 ARC. Abu Hanifa, one of the Indonesian representatives to the conference, would write later that the idea of a wholly Southeast Asian grouping was conceived at the conference in response to the belief among the Southeast Asian delegates that the larger states, India and China, could not be expected to support their nationalist cause. At the meeting, delegates from Indonesia, Myanmar, Thailand, Vietnam, the Philippines, and Malaya 'debated, talked, [and] planned a Southeast Asian Association closely cooperating first in cultural and economic matters'. They envisioned that '[l]ater, there could perhaps be a more closely knit political cooperation. Some of us even dreamt of a Greater Southeast Asia, a federation.'[31]

But the legacy of Nationalist Asia was too strong and enduring to permit any quick and easy fulfilment of these early efforts at Regionalist Asia even at the subregional level. These efforts were at best intended to strengthen, not weaken, the autonomy of the nation state. Hence the creation of ASEAN was intended to serve and strengthen the national interests of its members, not to dilute or compromise them.

## Asia between Universalism and Exceptionalism

We have seen that the different conceptions of Asia gave rise to different regionalisms in the early post-war period. As Regionalist Asia continued to compete with Nationalist Asia for the support of Asia's new political elite, there would emerge a fifth conception of Asia, which might be termed 'Exceptionalist Asia', discussed ahead.

In the 1960s, post-Bandung, Southeast Asia took the lead in developing regionalism. The leadership of India and China had ended—India's because of internal distractions and rivalry with Pakistan (ironically, a member of the Colombo Powers fraternity that had collectively sponsored the Bandung gathering) and China's because of its violation of its own pledge of non-interference given at the Bandung Conference (one of the 10 principles of the Bandung Declaration). Most importantly, the Sino-Indian War undermined the claims of both to jointly lead Asia. In the meantime, Japan remained mired in the legacy of its imperial record, hesitant to launch new regional initiatives, especially with a political and security purpose. Southeast Asia itself was divided and prone to conflict, both domestic and interstate (especially with Sukarno's *Konfrontasi* (confrontation) against the newly formed Malaysia). Its first attempt to create a regional body, the Association of Southeast Asia (ASA) founded in 1961, failed because it did not include Southeast Asia's biggest player, Indonesia. A second body, Maphilindo, (Malaysia, the Philippines, and Indonesia) premised on the notion of the unity of the Malay race and thus recalling José Rizal's identification of the Philippines as a Malay nation, also collapsed over escalating tensions between Indonesia and Malaysia, as Sukarno called into question (with military force) the legitimacy of the Malaysian federation.

Yet even the subregional efforts were held by an underlying conception of Asianness. Thus, despite being an association of Southeast Asia, ASA's proponents saw themselves as part of a larger Asian cultural, political, and economic context. For the Thai foreign minister and a key architect of ASA Thanat Khoman, ASA was rooted in 'Asian culture and traditions'. Describing ASA as an example of 'Asian mutual co-operation', he argued that, 'Asian solidarity must be and will be forged by Asian hands and the fact that our three countries: the Federation of Malaya, the Philippines, and Thailand, have joined hands in accomplishing this far-reaching task cannot be a mere coincidence'.[32]

After these false starts, one segment of Southeast Asia comprising Thailand, Malaysia, Indonesia, the Philippines and Singapore finally held together to create Asia's first viable multipurpose regional organization, ASEAN. But even by then a more powerful force of regionalization in the sense defined earlier was to emerge in parallel with Southeast Asia's search for unity and identity. This was the idea of a Pacific (later Asia-Pacific) community. Proposed by Japanese and Australian academics and driven by the high economic growth and interdependence among the industrial economies of the Pacific Rim, the idea of a Pacific community finally gave Japan a platform to enter the fray of Regionalist Asia, albeit at first through non-official and semi-official groupings like the Pacific Basin Economic Council (PBEC, 1967), the Pacific Trade and Development Conference (PAFTAD, 1968), and the Pacific Economic Cooperation Council (PECC, 1980). Initially though, this was an Asia-Pacific construct, not Asia. Key roles in developing it belonged to individuals, think tanks, and governments not just from Japan but also from outside Asia, especially from Australia and the US. But the Pacific community idea gradually morphed into the Asia-Pacific (or Asia Pacific) idea, largely due to the need to involve ASEAN members who were deeply suspicious of the project as a move to marginalize the developing nations, and with an eye to China's future incorporation. ASEAN's consent and endorsement was necessary to make it work.

The Asia-Pacific idea would in 1989 lead to the first region-wide intergovernmental institution (outside the United Nations Economic and Social Commission for Asia and the Pacific [ESCAP] and the Asian Development Bank [ADB])—APEC. Its purpose was not to develop an EU-like supranational body. But neither was it geared to anti-colonial or anti-Western objectives, à la Nationalist Asia. By now, those objectives had receded into the historical background. The new agenda of regionalism was interdependence, not independence. The driver was not anti-colonial sentiments but the quest for growth and dynamism. Although no direct evidence can be provided linking regionalism of the Pacific or Asia-Pacific variety with the region's economic growth (it would be the other way around), there was little question that the idea behind it reflected economic performance and optimism for the future. Moreover, what started as an effort defined mainly in Pacific terms became one in which the Asian element would grow to be the more prominent one.

## Exceptionalist Asia

While Regionalist Asia persisted, it was joined by a somewhat newer vision of Asia, a fifth vision that may be termed Exceptionalist Asia. It was the product of the phenomenal economic growth enjoyed by some of Asia's economies. Claims about Asia's distinctiveness were always around, but they were largely the product of Western orientalism that imagined Asia to be exotic, romantic, and subservient. A new form of exceptionalism constructed by Asia's own power elite came to the fore in the 1990s, grounded in claims and assertions about how Asian culture might underpin its economic success. Proponents of Exceptionalist Asia were of course not averse to globalization. They actually thrived on its economic benefits, although uncomfortable with its political aspects, especially the spread of human rights and democracy.

The term *Asian values* emerged in the 1990s in parallel with the high growth of East Asian economies such as Japan, South Korea, Hong Kong, Taiwan, and Singapore. This led some commentators such as Singapore's Prime Minister Lee Kuan Yew to associate economic performance with cultural traits and habits. While Lee initially spoke of *Confucian values*, the latter eventually morphed into Asian values. The list of Asian values varies but generally includes hard work, thrift (high savings rate), emphasis on education, consensus, rejection of extreme individualism, national teamwork, and respect for authority. The term acquired a political connotation when critics viewed some elements of it such as respect for authority as a justification for authoritarian rule.[33] Critics argued that what passed as Asian values was in no way special or unique to Asian societies, and that the sheer political and cultural diversity of Asia could permit no such generalization about a set of commonly-held values across the region. How can one speak of a coherent set of values that can be uniquely 'Asian' and ignore the differences between Confucian, Muslim, and Hindu cultural norms? The Asian Financial Crisis of 1997 dealt a blow to the concept of Asian values, when its proponents, Lee Kuan Yew included, admitted that there could be 'bad' Asian values such as corruption and lack of transparency and accountability.

Coinciding with the emergence of Exceptionalist Asia, and partly deriving from it, a new form of regionalism challenged the hitherto Asia-Pacific movement of 'open regionalism', setting up a contest of sorts between APEC and Malaysian Prime Minister Mahathir Mohamad's East Asian Economic Grouping (EAEG) later renamed as the East Asian Economic Caucus (EAEC).[34] Following the 1997 Asian Financial Crisis, the idea of an East Asian community gained momentum. Its advocates saw East Asia as a distinctive region in the world, economically more integrated and politically and culturally more coherent than unwieldy Asia-Pacific forums like the ARF and APEC that include the US, Canada, and Australia. At 54 per cent of the region's total trade, compared to 35 per cent in 1980, intra-East Asian trade was higher than that in the North American Free Trade Agreement (NAFTA) region (46 per cent), and 'very much comparable to intraregional trade in the European Union before the 1992 Maastricht treaty'.[35] It is thus East Asia that offered the best hopes for a 'bona fide regional community with shared challenges, common aspirations and a parallel destiny' and for the development of a 'strong sense of regional identity and ... consciousness'.[36]

So far, East Asian regionalism has turned out to be less exclusivist than initially anticipated—thanks partly to the persisting trans-Pacific trade with, and security dependence on, the US and concern about a rising China dominating such an East Asia-only construct. The EAS inaugural in 2005 took a functional rather than geographic view of East Asia by giving a seat at the table to India, Australia, and New Zealand as well as to the US and Russia who joined in 2011.[37] But whether the non-East Asians would really be assured of an equal status within the East Asian community or being part of the core group who could drive the community-building process remains to be seen. Should the 'purist'[38] view of East Asia prevail, these nations would have good reason to be unhappy over their 'second-class' status. And while the broadening of the EAS might have dispelled fears of Chinese dominance, this could engender Chinese disinterest in the summit process. The key continuing challenge for East Asian visionaries and leaders would be to find the balance between Chinese dominance and Chinese disinterest.

In the meantime, echoes of Exceptionalist Asia can be heard in the 'rise of Asia', 'Rising Asia', or 'Asia rising' discourse inspired by the massive economic growth, military build-up, and the attendant political clout of China and, to a lesser extent, India. While Nationalist Asia spoke of Asia's emancipation and re-emergence from Western dominance, often in spiritual and moral terms, 'Rising Asia' proponents speak of the possibility of Asia displacing the West from its perch of global leadership. How the Asian powers might cooperate to create a common Asian home, much less an Asian powerhouse, remains unclear in the Rising Asia discourse.[39]

The exceptionalists, realizing the region's sheer dependence on economic globalization, are likely to keep their regionalism relatively open. Moreover, the emerging transnational civil society in Asia seems more firmly wedded to the universalist values of human rights, democracy, and increasingly, the environment, which could keep under check the exceptionalists' urge to 'Asianize' or truncate these values. Hence, the Asia that we may see in the coming decades may well be shaped by the contestations and compromises between Universalist Asia and Exceptionalist Asia. In the meantime, some fear that before the contest is settled, Imperialist Asia, with support and sustenance from Exceptionalist Asia, especially from within China, might take over and fundamentally reshape the Asian order in the twenty-first century. This will happen if China continues with its relentless rise and imposes its version of a Monroe Doctrine-like sphere over its neighbours. The best hope against this would be the strengthening of Regionalist Asia. But as yet, limitations of Regionalist Asia abound. Asian regional institutions are still sovereignty-bound, unwilling and unable to undertake any major role in conflict resolution. The doctrine of non-interference still remains sacred. It will take time to change these underpinnings of Nationalist Asia for a truly Regionalist Asia to take over.

To conclude, a prominent place in the construction of Asia has to be given to regionalism and regionalization.[40] Without regionalism, there might not even be any idea of Asia for us to talk about. Speaking of the idea of Asia, Rebecca Karl shows that 'far from always meaning the same thing or even including the same configurations of peoples and states, it has been mobilized for very different purposes at different times'.[41] Similarly, regionalism in Asia has not been a singular or coherent set of beliefs. Nor has it been an unchanging phenomenon. It has incorporated and contributed to different conceptions of the region in different times, sustaining Asia's diversity and pointing to alternative futures.

## Asia Rising?

It is often said that Asian regional institutions that would otherwise help to legitimize the idea of Asia are themselves a reminder of Asia's diversity, especially among the subregions. But regional institutions also help blur subregional boundaries. There is no reason why subregional identities cannot coexist with a larger regional one. In fact, there is growing evidence that subregional boundaries are being blurred. Indeed, they have always been questionable somewhat. In 1954–5, South Asia and Southeast Asia were inseparable. Nobody complained when the Asian-African Conference in Bandung was sponsored by a group officially known as the Conference of South-East Asian Prime Ministers, or more informally as Colombo Powers. It included Ceylon (now Sri Lanka), Pakistan, India, Myanmar, and Indonesia. The rise of Chinese power has led some to question whether an independent 'region' of Southeast Asia is really relevant. Yet ASEAN today is unlikely to take China, India, and even Sri Lanka (which was invited in 1967 to join the grouping as its founding member) as full members but only as dialogue partners.

Perhaps one should not be too bothered by whether Asia is too diverse to merit a single name, or whether Asia's rivalries are a justification for dismissing the term's relevance. There was an idea of Europe at the height of Europe's internecine wars and prior to the European Union's constructed peace. What is more worrisome, however, is the conflation of Asia with its rising power. The early imaginings of Asia were partly a defensive reaction to Western dominance. They were ideational and spiritual in content. By contrast, the new imagining of Asia, both by westerners and Asians, seems to be inextricably linked to power politics (internationally) and in some cases to authoritarian politics (domestically). Take, for example, the notion of 'Asian values' that finds an integral place in some versions of the 'rise of Asia' discourse. The economic growth of Asia is said to be underpinned by a set of communitarian values, which in turn has laid the foundation of an Asian Century. But these metaphors of Asia distort history and risk delivering more damage than good to the idea of Asia.

By contrast, Asian leaders from an earlier post-war generation who spoke of Asian identity were referring to a restoration of Asia's dignity rather than its once and future global dominance.[42] One of the first Asian leaders to speak of Asian values was India's Nehru—nobody's idea of a tinpot dictator—and ironically, an early inspiration if not role model for Lee Kuan Yew. Nehru spoke of democracy and what he hoped would be India's and Asia's democratic politics. Moreover, early Asian leaders from India, Myanmar, and China spoke of Asian values in normative and emancipatory rather than simply material terms, with their focus being liberation from Western dominance. As Mahatma Gandhi, who addressed the ARC in New Delhi in 1947 (the very first gathering of liberated Asian nations), put it, 'The message of Asia is not to be learnt through European spectacles, not by imitating the vices of the West, its gunpowder and atom bomb. If you want to give a message of importance to the West, it must be a message of love, it must be a message of truth.'[43] China's Sun Yat-sen spoke of Asian virtues, albeit in juxtaposition to both European and Japanese colonialism. He urged Japan to develop pan-Asianism not through empire but through Asian virtues such as ethics, righteousness, and benevolence. He also contrasted European materialism and militarism (the ways of a hegemon) with these Asian virtues. By contrast, today's 'rise of Asia' discourse is distinguished by its very material and instrumental nature.

To say that Asia had been constructed from within does not mean that this inside construction was/is unproblematic. It has not been devoid of nation-centrism and dominance.

Japan's Okakura Kakuzo saw his country as the best of Asian civilization that 'mirror[ed] the whole of Asian consciousness'.[44] Asia was equated with Japan's rise. Some versions of Japan's pan-Asianism were blatantly hegemonic. Japan espoused pan-Asianism to counter Western dominance, but in that process staked a claim to its own centrality and empire. China's new Asianism also smacked of Sinocentrism. The opening issue of the journal *Xinyaxiya* (New Asia) launched in China in 1930 to advance Sun Yat-sen's nationalist cause argued that 'the regeneration of China is the starting point of the regeneration of the Asian peoples'.[45] The magazine claimed that Sun was the only leader who can come to the rescue of the peoples. And Sun did favour the Asian order as a revival of the Sinocentric tributary system. Not to be outdone, Nehru saw India as the 'natural centre and focal point of many of the forces at work in Asia' including geography.[46] He stressed geography and civilizational flows into and out of India. In convening the ARC in 1947,[47] India organized an 'Inter-Asian Art Exhibition' for the visiting delegates. Despite its name, the exhibition was essentially a portrayal of India's historical links with its neighbours encompassing Iran, Indonesia, China, and Central Asia. The official script of the exhibition prepared by the Indian hosts spoke of an Indian 'cultural empire' that 'once embraced these distant lands for several centuries' over an area encompassing Myanmar, Malaya, Siam, Cambodia, Champa, and Indonesia (Java, Bali, Sumatra).[48] Whatever their intentions, the exhibition was too Indo-centric not to have had a sobering impact on foreign participants, already wary of India's political dominance of Asian regionalism. Indeed, the fear of Indian dominance (as well as dominance by China whose then nationalist government had asked for and received the right to host the next ARC) led a group of Southeast Asian delegates attending the Delhi conference to imagine a regional association of their own—meaning the

Southeast Asian countries minus India and China. This was in a way a stepping stone to ASEAN that has a better record of longevity than the short-lived Asian Relations Organization that came out of the 1947 ARC.

Thus, those who spoke of Asia's emergence then were to some extent imagining the dominance of their own countries and cultures over Asia. Just as Japanese ideas about Asia (Greater East Asia Co-Prosperity Sphere) masked its quest for regional hegemony, today's 'Asia rising' discourse carries the risk of turning it into a cover for dominance within and between states. Thus, it behooves the audience to be wary, especially now that we are hearing so much talk again of Asia's emergence. The protagonists of Asia's rise should themselves be wary as well because past such projects have often ended in disillusionment and humiliation.

This is so because there are serious questions about to what extent the 'rise of Asia' is real or hype. Some of it is undoubtedly real. Poverty reduction is Asia's singular achievement. But as Minxin Pei pointed out in 2009, the per capita GDP of the United States was nine times larger than that of China, and at the current growth rates, it would take an average Asian country 77 years to match the per capita GDP of the US.[49] As the Nobel Prize winners for Physics and Chemistry for 2009 suggested, Indian and Chinese scientists need to leave home for the West before they can achieve excellence in innovation. While countries like China and Singapore have invested massively in education, political authoritarianism and regulation continues to stifle creativity and innovation. The pan-Asian discourse of the pre- and early-post-war period was not followed by economic or technological progress. The 'rise of Asia' is neither linear nor irreversible. There is a need for a critical perspective. The idea of Asia should be based on an understanding of Asia's strengths and limitations.

Moreover, to conflate Asia with the 'rise of Asia' simply imposes an essentially Western discourse of power politics (the rise and fall of nations, of powers, and of regions) on what had earlier been, to a large extent, Japanese, Chinese, and Indian ethnocentrism notwithstanding an emancipatory and civilizational idea. Are we to assume that nations that are not part of the economic rise of Asia are excluded from it—like India before the 1990s, or North Korea and Myanmar now? What if Asia suffers a terminal economic breakdown? Will the term disappear? Most certainly, it will not.

Hence, neither geography nor geopolitics, nor power, nor prosperity is a sufficient basis for claiming the relevance of Asia as a region. Asia is, and will remain, a contested notion. But three things about the present and future of the idea of Asia stand out. First, the idea of Asia is not just about the rising power of Asia. It is as much an ideational as a material construct. Second, Asia is not merely the sum of its parts. The woods are indeed different from the trees. National and subregional differences do not obscure or prevent the construction of an Asian identity. Third, Asia will be increasingly constructed from inside rather than from the outside.

But the local imagining and construction of Asia must not and need not be monopolized by a narrow regional elite clinging to a 'rising Asia' discourse. It needs to be more broad-based and people-centric and reflect a genuine sense of Asian universalism. Small states and vulnerable populations of Asia living under authoritarian rule have much to fear from the rise of Asia, especially from the idea of a rich, powerful, and authoritarian Asia displacing the West from its perch of global supremacy.

Those who speak of 'the West and the East' in binary terms are easily contradicted by Asia's recent historical trajectory. In the early aftermath of the Second World War, Asia's regional architecture was shaped by economic nationalism, security bilateralism, and political authoritarianism. Over the decades, these have gradually given way to economic openness and interdependence, security multilateralism (though still in competition with bilateralism), and democratic transitions (largely peaceful—contrary to a popular myth—and certainly relative to the murderous record of enduring dictatorships in the region). Asia has moved on, slowly bridging the gap between Kautilyan power politics, Confucian communitarianism, Nehruvian idealism, and Kantian liberalism. Hence the true basis for an Asian identity need not be a culturally exceptionalist, politically backward, strategically competitive (West denouncing), and psychologically self-gratifying discourse of 'Asia rising', but the local construction and manifestation of enduring universal principles, including human security, multilateralism, and democracy.[50]

## Notes and References

1. François Godement, *The New Asian Renaissance: From Colonialism to the Post-Cold War* (London: Routledge, 1997), p. 4.
2. 'In the Shade of the Banyan Tree', *The Economist*, 11 April 2009, p. 43, available at http://www.economist.com/node/13446191 (accessed on 2 October 2016).
3. Bill Emmott, *Rivals: How the Power Struggle Between China, India and Japan Will Shape Our Next Decade* (Orlando: Houghton Mifflin Harcourt, 2008).
4. Brij Tankha and Madhavi Thampi, 'Preface', in *Narratives of Asia: From India, Japan and China* (Kolkata and New Delhi: Sampark, 2005), p. 7.
5. Prasenjit Duara distinguishes between 'region' and 'regionalization', taking the former to mean 'the relatively unplanned or evolutionary emergence of an area of inter-action and inter-dependence', and the latter as 'the more active, often ideologically-driven political process of creating a region'. See Prasenjit Duara, 2010, 'Asia Redux: Conceptualizing a Region for Our Times', *The Journal of Asian Studies*, 69(4): 963–83.

   While this is a valid distinction, it risks obscuring (although it is subsumed under 'regionalization') the concept and practice of regionalism. Indeed, regionalization and regionalism can be analytically separated. The former is normally understood in the political economy literature as market-driven, as opposed to state-led, advance of transnational economic linkages, including trade, investment, and production. Hence, a relevant term here is the 'regionalization of production' in East Asia, which was spurred by the southward movement of Japanese companies and capital following the re-evaluation of the yen after the Plaza Accord of 1985, thereby bringing South Korea, Taiwan, Hong Kong, Singapore, and other Southeast Asian countries under its ambit and creating a de facto economic region of East Asia. See Mitchell Bernard and John Ravenhill, 1995, 'Beyond Product Cycles and Flying Geese: Regionalization, Hierarchy, and the Industrialization of East Asia', *World Politics*, 47(2): 171–209.

The latter, as understood in political science/international relations literature, implies the deliberate act of forging a common platform, including new intergovernmental organizations and transnational civil society networks, to deal with common challenges, realize common objectives, and articulate/advance a common identity. While much of this can be subsumed under regionalization in the sense that Duara speaks of, regionalization can proceed in the absence of 'the more active, often ideologically-driven political process of creating a region', especially when the latter entails formal regional institutions. Asia was far into the process of economic interdependence and transnational production networks before the first formal intergovernmental regional economic grouping—APEC—was created in 1989. But it is regionalism that brings the notion of Asia alive.

6. I have argued elsewhere that regions should be understood in terms of (a) material and ideational—regionalist ideas and regional identity that move the study of regions beyond purely materialist understandings; (b) whole and parts—regional (as opposed to mainly country-specific) perspective based on a marriage between disciplinary and area-studies approaches; (c) past and present—historical understanding of regions, going beyond contemporary policy issues; (d) inside and outside—internal construction of regions, stressing the role of local

agency, as opposed to external stimuli or the naming of regions by external powers; and (e) permanence and transience—the fluidity, 'porosity', and transience of regions. See Amitav Acharya, *The Making of Southeast Asia: International Relations of a Region* (new edition of *The Quest for Identity: International Relations of a Region*) (Singapore: Institute of Southeast Asian Studies, and Ithaca: Cornell University Press, 2011).

7.  Okakura Kakuzo, 1904, *The Ideals of the East: With Special Reference to the Art of Japan*, available at http://www.sacred-texts.com/shi/ioe/ioe08.htm (accessed on 1 July 2010).

8.  John M. Steadman, *The Myth of Asia* (London: Macmillan, 1969), pp. 32–3.

9.  Peter Duus, 2008, 'The Greater East Asian Co-Prosperity Sphere: Dream and Reality', *The Journal of Northeast Asian History*, 5(1): 146.

10. Duus, 'The Greater East Asian Co-Prosperity Sphere', pp. 151–2.

11. Josef Silverstein, *The Political Legacy of Aung San* (New York: Department of Asian Studies, Southeast Asian Program, Cornell University [Data paper 86], 1972), p. 21.

12. Silverstein, *The Political Legacy of Aung San*, p. 101.

13. Rabindranath Tagore, *Nationalism* (London: Macmillan, 1918).

14. Rebecca Karl, 1998, 'Creating Asia: China in the World at the Beginning of Twentieth Century', *The American Historical Review*, 103(4): 1096–7.

15. Karl, 'Creating Asia', p. 1106.

16. Aung San, *Burma's Challenge* (South Okkalapa: U Aung Gyi, 1974), p. 193.

17. T.A. Keenleyside, 1982, 'Nationalist Indian Attitude towards Asia: A Troublesome Legacy', *Pacific Affairs*, 55(2): 216.

18. Amitav Acharya, *The Quest for Identity: International Relations of Southeast Asia* (Singapore: Oxford University Press, 2000).

19. Christopher E. Goscha, *Thailand and the Southeast Asian Networks of the Vietnamese Revolution, 1885–1954* (Surrey: Curzon Press, 1999), p. 244.

20. Aung San, *Bogyoke Aung San Maint-Khun-Myar (1945–1947)* [General Aung San's Speeches] (Yangon: Sarpay Bait Man Press, 1971), p. 86.

21. Goscha, *Thailand and the Southeast'*, p. 244.

22. Steadman, *The Myth of Asia*, p. 33.

23. Cited in William Henderson, 1955, 'The Development of Regionalism in Southeast Asia', *International Organization*, 9(4): 462–76.

24. Keenleyside, 'Nationalist Indian Attitude towards Asia'.

25. Silverstein, *The Political Legacy of Aung San*, p. 101.

26. Roselan Abdulghani, *The Bandung Spirit* (Jakarta: Prapantja, 1964), pp. 72, 103.

27. Jawaharlal Nehru, 'Inaugural Address', in *Asian Relations: Report of the Proceedings and Documentation of the First Asian Relations Conference*, March–April 1947 (New Delhi: Asian Relations Organization, 1948), p. 23.

28. Cited in Keenleyside, 'Nationalist Indian Attitude towards Asia', pp. 216–17.

29. Cited in Amy Vandenbosch and Richard Butwell, *The Changing Face of Southeast Asia* (Lexington: University of Kentucky Press, 1966), p. 341.

30. Ho Chi Minh, *Ho Chi Minh Talks about History,* translated by Houng Nguyen (Hanoi: NhàXuấtBảnĐạiHọcSưPhạm, 1995), p. 82.

31. Goscha, *Thailand and the Southeast'*, p. 255.

32. Association of Southeast Asia, *Report of the Special Session of Foreign Ministers of ASA* (Kuala Lumpur/Cameron Highlands: Federation of Malaya, 1962), p. 33.

33. Amartya Sen, 1997, 'Human Rights and Asian Values: What Kee Kuan Yew and Le Peng Don't Understand about Asia', *The New Republic*, 217: 33–41.

34. Richard Higgott and Richard Stubbs, 1995, 'Competing Conceptions of Economic Regionalism: APEC versus EAEC in the Asia Pacific', *Review of International Political Economy*, 2: 516–35.

35. 'Towards a Borderless Asia: A Perspective on Asian Economic Integration', speech by Haruhiko Kuroda, the president of the ADB, Emerging Markets Forum, 10 December 2005, Oxford, UK cited in Jiangyu Wang, 'China, India, and Regional Economic Integration in Asia: The Policy and Legal Dimensions',

*Singapore Year Book of International Law*, Vol. 10 (Bukit Timah: Faculty of Law, National University of Singapore, 2006), p. 279.

36. East Asia Vision Group, 2001, *Towards an East Asian Community: Region of Peace, Prosperity and Progress*, East Asia Vision Group Report, pp. 2, 6, 24, available at http://asean.org/wp-content/uploads/images/archive/pdf/east_asia_vision.pdf (accessed on 10 October 2016).

37. The chairman's statement of the 6th EAS in Bali, Indonesia, 19 November 2011, reads, 'We welcomed the participation of the United States of America and the Russian Federation in the EAS which will strengthen EAS efforts to advance its common endeavours.' See 'ASEAN Community in the Global Community of Nations', available at http://www.asean.org/images/2013/external_relations/11_chairmans%20statement%20of%20the%206th%20eas.pdf (accessed on 31 July 2015).

38. Sung-Joo Han, 2005, 'Roadmap for an East Asian Community', *IRI Review* (Seoul), 10(2): 131–51.

39. Amitav Acharya, 2010, 'The Idea of Asia', *Asia Policy*, 69(4): 32–9.

40. For the distinction between regionalism and regionalization, see footnote 5.

41. Karl, 'Creating Asia', p. 1118.

42. Amitav Acharya, *Whose Ideas Matter?: Agency and Power in Asian Regionalism* (Ithaca, NY: Cornell University Press, 2011).

43. See http://icwadelhi.info/asianrelationsconference/images/stories/mahatmagandhi.pdf (last accessed on 2 October 2016).

44. Tankha and Thampi, *Narratives of Asia*.

45. Tankha and Thampi, *Narratives of Asia*, p. 108.

46. Tankha and Thampi, *Narratives of Asia*, p. 31.

47. At the time of the conference, India was still under British rule but prime minister-in-waiting Nehru was allowed a free hand by the British in hosting the event through the non-official Indian Council of World Affairs. For details, see *Asian Relations: Being Report of the Proceedings and Documentation of the First Asian Relations Conference, New Delhi, March–April 1947* (New Delhi: Asian Relations Organization, 1948).

48. *Asian Relations*, p. 302.

49. Minxin Pei, 'Bamboozled: Don't Believe the Asia Hype', *Foreign Policy*, 21 June 2009, available on http://foreignpolicy.com/2009/06/21/think-again-asias-rise/ (accessed on 7 November 2016).

50. Amitav Acharya, *Asia Rising: Who is Leading?* (Singapore: World Scientific, 2007).

# 2.

# From 'Indianization' to 'Look East'

*I*ndia's relations with the countries of what is known as 'Southeast Asia' today dates back to antiquity. Early Indian texts referred to Southeast Asia as *Suvarnabhumi* (literally, the Land of Gold). Trade and transmission of Hindu and Buddhist religions were key elements of India's early interaction with Southeast Asian lands, including Myanmar, Thailand, the Indochinese Peninsula, Malay, and Indonesia. However, this was not a one-way traffic, for Southeast Asians, particularly traders of the Malay world across the Bay of Bengal, constituted part of this interaction. The flow of Indian priests, traders, and adventurers carried with it a wealth of culture and political ideas which, along with intermarriages and cultural assimilation, left a deep and lasting impact on the cultural landscape of Southeast Asia. Indian ideas played an important role in the political and institutional development of Southeast Asia. By the eleventh century, there existed a number of strongly 'Indianized' kingdoms such as Funan and Champa in the Indochinese Peninsula, and Nakhon Si Thammarat in the Malay Peninsula.

## The 'Indianization' of Southeast Asia

Paul Wheatley notes that 'the process by which the peoples of western Southeast Asia came to think of themselves as part of *Bharatavarsa* (even though they had no conception of "India" as we know it) represents one of the most impressive instances of large-scale acculturation in the history of the world'.[1] The distinguished historian of Southeast Asia, George Cœdès describes 'Indianization' as 'the expansion of an organized culture that was founded upon the Indian conception of royalty, was characterized by Hinduist or Buddhist cults, the mythology of the *Puranas*, and the observance of the *Dharmasastras*, and expressed itself in the Sanskrit language'.[2] Other features of Indianization included the use of alphabets of Indian origin; the pattern of Indian law and administration; and monuments, architecture, and sculpture influenced by the Indian arts. But the subject of 'Indianization' or 'Hinduization' of Southeast Asia has been controversial. Indian nationalist views of Southeast Asia as 'greater India' or 'further India', popularized by groups like the nationalist Greater India Society of Kolkata and historians like Ramesh Chandra Majumdar and K.A. Nilakanta Sastri, have been rejected in contemporary Southeast Asian historiography.

Majumdar provides a particularly blunt expression of the Indian 'colonization' theory:

> [Indian] intercourse in the region first began by way of trade, both by land and sea. But soon it developed into regular colonization, and Indians established political authority in various parts of the vast Asiatic continent that lay to the south of China and to the east and southeast of India. The Hindu colonists brought with them the whole framework of their culture and civilization and this was transplanted in its entirety among the people who had not yet emerged from their primitive barbarism.[3]

In so far as the process through which Indian influence in Southeast Asia spread, there have been three explanations. The first is the *ksatriya* (Sanskrit for warrior) theory, which sees the transmission of Indian ideas as the result of direct Indian conquest and colonization of large parts of Southeast Asia. And the second is the *vaisya* (merchant) theory, which emphasizes the role of Indian traders with their extensive commercial interactions with Southeast Asia, who brought with them not just goods but also Indian cultural artefacts and political ideas.[4] But these first two theories were rejected in 1934 by Jacob Cornelis van Leur, a Dutch economic historian and colonial official in Indonesia.[5] He saw no evidence that the Indian approach to Southeast Asia amounted to conquest; on the contrary, it was through peaceful means. Nor could the transmission of Indian ideas have been the handiwork of Indian traders despite substantial commercial linkages between India and Southeast Asia. The Indian trading class, primarily consisting of peddlers (Southeast Asian trade was mostly of the pre-capitalist, peddling type), could not be expected to have mastered the complexities of Hindu ideas and political organization to appear credible before their Southeast Asian recipients. Instead van Leur offered a third explanation: the Brahmana (the Indian priest) theory. Since Indian influence was most directly evident in Southeast Asian royal courts, and involved matters of high culture such as 'art, literature, ideas of power, sovereignty and kingship',[6] it must have been the work of the Brahmanas who alone possessed the mastery of 'sacral magical power and sacral religion'.[7] The Brahmanas were actively solicited by Southeast Asian rulers who wanted to learn from Indian ideas about political organization that—thanks to their relatively organized form and their heavy emphasis on magic and mystery—offered an attractive way of enhancing the ruler's legitimacy and authority. In short, Brahmanas were the classical equivalent of modern-day 'entrepreneurs' of Indian ideas to Southeast Asian courts. And Indian ideational influence in Southeast Asia was largely a matter of 'deliberate Southeast Asian borrowing of ideas, artistic styles and modes of political organization' that helped the emergence, consolidation, and enlargement of local polities.[8] To cite van Leur:

> The initiative for the coming of Indian civilization [to Southeast Asia] emanated from the Indonesian ruling groups, or was at least an affair of both the Indonesian dynasties and the Indian hierocracy. That cultural influence had nothing to do with trade. The course of events amounted essentially to a summoning to Indonesia of Brahman priests, and perhaps alongside them of Indian *condottieri* and Indian court artificers ... Indian priesthood was called eastwards—certainly because of its wide renown—for the magical, sacral legitimation of dynastic interests and the domestication of subjects, and probably for the organization of the ruler's territory into a state.[9]

Van Leur's thesis, representing another extreme to Majumdar's 'colonization' thesis, has been challenged by 'more recent writers [who] have stressed the interaction between the local and imported cultures'.[10] But the 'idea of the local initiative', or the belief that Southeast Asians were not passive recipients but active borrowers of foreign ideas, including Indian ones, has found general acceptance among Southeast Asian historians. F.D.K. Bosch observes that Indian influence was stronger in inland kingdoms than coastal regions (suggesting a lesser role of traders as transmitter of ideas) and there is a lack of references to Indian conquests in Southeast Asian inscriptions.[11] This offers support for van Leur's thesis about the role of the Brahmanas in the borrowing of Indian culture by Southeast Asian rulers. Cœdès argued that an initial process of transmission of Indian ideas by traders could have laid the foundation for Southeast Asian polities and prepared them to receive, on their own initiative, Indian concepts of kingship and power.[12] SarDesai believes that the initiative for the Indianizing process in Southeast Asia 'most certainly came from the region's ruling classes who invited Brahmans to serve at their courts as priests, astrologers and advisers'.[13] Paul Wheatley maintains that while local rulers used Indian ideas to enhance their status, this was a dynamic social process in which Indian ideas and culture played a vital role.[14] Some scholars have argued that there was 'an approximate equality between giving and receiving cultures'.[15]

It is important to note that while scholars involved in the 'Indianization' debate were speaking of the transmission of Indian cultural ideas, the latter itself was of a broad range, including religion, art, architecture, statecraft, concepts of power, authority, and legitimacy as well as ideas about political stratification, territorial organization, political institutionalization, diplomatic practice, and law. Moreover, these aspects were closely interrelated. As Wolters put it, 'art, religion and government are inseparable phenomena in earlier Southeast Asia'.[16] But it was not just religious ideas such as divine kingship which dominated the flow; there were also a number of secular Indian legal, political, and diplomatic texts that made their way into the ancient Southeast Asian political landscape. These included the *Manusmriti* (Code of

Manu), the *Dharamashastra*s (legal treatises), and above all, the purely secular *Arthasastra*, the most famous Indian classic text on statecraft—all of which were 'widely revered' in classical Southeast Asia.[17]

Support for the local initiative or deliberate-borrowing thesis also comes from the fact that Southeast Asians were not undiscriminating in their borrowing of Indian ideas and practices. Only those that conformed to indigenous patterns (as well as the need, especially for power and legitimacy, which we have already seen in the case of van Leur's thesis concerning local initiative) were acquired or when they were presented before Southeast Asians, accepted. Some were summarily rejected or significantly modified so that they scarcely resembled the original Indian idea. Among the foremost examples of this is the Indian caste system that found little acceptance in Southeast Asia, despite superficial similarities. Mabbett offers an important example of how Indian ideas were modified when they arrived in Southeast Asia in the Indian caste system, or varna, which in Angkor was institutionalized and practised differently than in India.[18] In the latter, caste was a general division of the population, while in Angkor it applied to divisions of elite groups at the royal court. Brahman status was less important and exalted in Angkor.[19] Myanmar rejected aspects of Manu's law concerning marriage. Christiaan Hooykaas has identified several features of Balinese Hinduism which are different from the Indian brand. These include the Balinese belief that one is reborn within one's groups of blood relatives, that gods normally live in mountains and lakes and not in temples, and that cremation should be performed only depending on one's social position.[20]

Furthermore, some Indian ideas were modified to conform to indigenous or pre-existing beliefs, practices, and institutions. This leads to a related issue in the Indianization process: its effects on local culture and civilization. Wolters shows how Myanmar adjusted the Indian legal code of Manu, rejecting the latter's notion of marriage, while in Champa and Cambodia local practice reflected in similar deviations from Indian legal texts with respect to property and land.[21] Another example of such localization could be found in how Indian law texts were adapted in Indonesia. As Hooker shows, one of the Indian legal practices adopted by the Javanese was that of *Jayapatra* or 'note of victory'. It was a document stating the fact that a case had been settled. It contained a statement by both parties to the litigation—the evidence considered, the particular text of law or *smrti* applied, and the judgement itself with the seal. The earliest Jayapatras in Java date from AD 907. But some of the Jayapatras found in Java do not make any reference to Indian law texts. Moreover, while in India the trial was usually conducted by a judge (*pradivaka*), in Java it was conducted by a judge-arbitrator (*samget*), who was 'assisted by a council of notables whose decisions were of a collegiate nature'. The proceedings of the trial in Java 'seem to have been in the nature of searching for a compromise, thus negating the need for the citation of *smrti*, a reference to which need not necessarily be basic to a decision'.[22] Thus, the Javanese practice appears to have been an important adaptation of the Indian system, in which the Jayapatra served as a 'form for recording a decision based upon an Indian model but did not require the application of principles of Indian law'.[23]

Other examples of modification and adaptation of Indian ideas by Southeast Asian rulers so as to make them conform to local tradition can be found in the Balinese conceptions of the Hindu gods, Shiva and Visnu. In Indian mythology, Visnu is the Protector who reincarnates periodically to save the world from calamity. In Bali, Visnu is localized to become a 'rising prince', who emerges from the periphery to infuse the community with new spiritual energy and status. This localization of Visnu can be understood in the context of 'the Balinese cultural background' that is one in which new men appear from time to time from the fringes of extensive and ascendant ancestor-groups, build up networks of alliances by demonstrating their capacity for leadership, and eventually become Ancestors in a particular generation by virtue of their achievements during their lifetime on behalf of their kindred. Localization in Bali means that Visnu's periodic reappearances fit into a Balinese statement constrained by local mechanisms for social mobilization.[24]

Wolters terms the process by which the foreign ideas were modified to suit Southeast Asian local need as 'localization' and 're-localization'.[25] He advances this concept to explain how different parts of Southeast Asia reflected different degrees of congruence with Indian law. Cultural adaptation is not just about how non-Southeast Asian ideas were adjusted and altered leading to variations between India and Southeast Asia, but also about how different parts of Southeast Asia developed variations of the same outside influence. Differences in the practice of Theravada Buddhism between Thailand and Myanmar are a case in point: there is a greater emphasis on metaphysics in Myanmar than in Thailand, while monastic discipline is more emphasized in Thailand than in Myanmar. Buddhists in Myanmar place more emphasis on the institution of the noviciate, while Thais emphasize monkhood.[26] Varying uses of Sanskrit in the region offer another example of re-localization. In Champa, for example, Sanskrit continued until the fifteenth century, while in Cambodia it remained dominant until the fourteenth century and in Java, the tenth century.[27] Wolters also draws attention to the process through which Indian literary materials were 'fractured and restated' in different parts of Southeast Asia. 'Not only did Indian materials have to be localized everywhere but those which had been originally localized in one part of the region would have to be re-localized before they could belong elsewhere in the same sub-region.'[28] He adds:

The materials, be they words, sound of words, books, or artifacts, had to be localized in different ways before they could fit into various local complexes of religious, social, and political systems and belong to new cultural 'wholes'. Only when this had happened would the fragments make sense in their new ambiences, the same ambiences which allowed the rulers and their subjects to believe that their centers were unique.[29]

Thus, to study how Indian ideas impacted Southeast Asia was to study the 'processes behind the endless elaboration of new local-foreign cultural "wholes"' in which local people and norms acted as a prism through which Indian ideas were adapted. As Wolters put it, 'local beliefs, operating under cultural constraint, were always responsible for the initial form the new "wholes" took'.[30]

Wolters argues that Hindu ideas did not supplant Southeast Asian political organization but enhanced the authority of the ruler. Hindu ideas and practices 'brought ancient and persisting indigenous beliefs into sharper focus'.[31] Even after Hindu ideas amplified their status and authority, indigenous pre-Hindu beliefs in the individual physical and magical powers of the ruler remained important.[32] This is so because '[t]he "Hinduized" polities were elaborations or amplifications of the pre-"Hindu" ones'.[33] In other words, adaptation did not lead to the disappearance of the existing beliefs and practices. Instead the latter were amplified. Foreign ideas were used to enhance the status and legitimacy of local rulers, but they were rarely accepted in their pure form. They were used to express local ideas and pursue local interests. Southeast Asian rulers constructed Indian notions of devotionalism to enhance their legitimacy. The local beliefs and practices continued, albeit finding new modes of expression, and were sometimes amplified. Thus, the institution of monarchy was amplified; soul stuff, already denoting innate spiritual energy, was amplified with Indian divine mysticism; and prowess was amplified when

Southeast Asian rulers used Indian deities such as Siva to claim legitimacy. Two examples are in order. The first shows how local rulers used a Hindu concept to amplify their authority. In seventh-century Cambodia, King Jayavarman I was said to be a 'portion' Siva, while Bhavavarman was said to have used Siva's *sakti* or divine energy to 'seize the kingship'.[34] Vietnamese ruler Trần Thái Tông in 1258 sought to protect his kingdom from Mongol invasion by assuming the name of the Chinese ruler and sage Yao. He also nominated an heir even while he was still in his prime. This mimicked a similar move by Yao, which had attracted the praise of the Chinese sage Mencius. This way the king could establish a parallel with the Chinese rulers.[35] The second is an example of how Southeast Asian rulers used Indian concepts to legitimize themselves: in Cambodia, in fifth century AD, it was said that 'it was because the grace of Siva was all pervasive that the populace submitted willingly to authority'.[36] Analysing Vietnamese poetry, Cambodian inscriptions, and Khmer art (bass reliefs in Angkor Wat), Wolters argues that Indian symbols had a 'decorative' role, that they were used to highlight the power and authority and the exalted position of the king and the golden age of his rule, and they were 'signifiers' which 'were being employed in this [Cambodian] society to express important local ideas'.[37] Indian art was used to send the message that 'the king was the source of creative and life-sustaining authority in Cambodia'.[38]

The quest for legitimation through Indian religious and political ideas emerges as a key factor in the state-formation process in classical Southeast Asia. Until the advent of Indian ideas, the numerous small territorial units that dotted the landscape of the region could only be occasionally centralized through the personal efforts of what Wolters calls a 'man of prowess'—a 'big man' who was thought to possess a lot of 'soul stuff' (an abundance of magical and spiritual power). Hindu devotional ideas filled an important gap in a ruler's search for authority and legitimacy. A Southeast Asian ruler could now identify himself with Indian divine figures to augment his innate 'soul stuff' and develop a more enduring basis of power. Indian religious ideas thus helped the 'legitimation of dynastic interests and the domestication of subjects, and ... the organization of the ruler's territory into a state'.[39] But in this process, the influence of Indian ideas was heavily mediated by indigenous beliefs and practices already prevailing in the region. Ideas that fitted indigenous traditions or that could be adapted to enhance local interests and practices were better received than those that did not. For example, the Indian practice of according lower status to women was not popular in the societies of Southeast Asia, where women traditionally enjoyed a better status.

To sum up, recent Southeast Asian historiography places less emphasis on how Southeast Asians adopted Indic art, religion, political concepts, and practices, and more on how they 'adapted these foreign ideas to suit their own needs and values'.[40] The region's 'symbolic and organizational patterns' that were once regarded as being of Indian origin were now seen to be 'merely redefinitions of indigenous institutions'.[41] While not dismissing the significance of Indian influence, scholars have pointed to important variations between Indian and Chinese ideas and practices and those found in Southeast Asia. Among the examples of adaptation and localization cited most frequently were: Southeast Asia's rejection of the Indian caste system; the 'own individual character' of temple art of Hindu–Buddhist kingdoms of Pagan, Angkor, and Java that differed from those of India; and the nature of Buddha images in Thailand that were 'quite different from the images to be found in India'.[42]

The decline of Buddhism by the end of the twelfth century, the erosion of Hindu political power due to the advent of Muslim rule, as well as internal reasons such as the rigidities of the caste system contributed to the decline of Indian influence in Southeast Asia. Ironically, Islam came to Southeast Asia by way of India. The conversion of Malacca in the fifteenth century saw Islam supplanting Hinduism and Buddhism. Indian Muslim merchants took along with them mullahs, Sufi mystics, and Arab preachers. Indians played a major role in the rise of Malacca. While Hindu merchants remained, Muslim traders, and Tamil and Gujarati merchants influenced its commercial and foreign policy through intermarriage and other means. They became kingmakers and a major force in the royal court intrigues of Malacca. Many Indian influences can still be found in the country. The fall of Malacca to the Portuguese encouraged the further spread of Islam.

The European intrusion into Asia and the restrictive trade policies of the Dutch and the British severely undermined India's commercial links with Southeast Asia. The Europeans took control of the trade in spice and textile, the staple of India–Southeast Asia trade. Under the British Raj, the Indian economy transformed from being an exporter of manufactured goods to a supplier of raw materials for Britain. The British also actively curbed Indian shipbuilding and shipping—a further blow. But British rule started a new type of migration from India to Southeast Asia, especially to Malaya. Thus migration, which dates from the foundation of Penang in 1786, was more regulated and more large-scale, and consisted chiefly of indentured and illiterate labourers. This contrasted with the early Indian migrant, drawn from traders and financiers, or priests and pandits. The imposition of colonial rule in Asia saw India as the centre of the British empire in Southeast Asia. But colonialism also disrupted the traditional patterns of Indo-Southeast Asian trade and the trade network from China to the Middle East in general. This fundamentally changed India's relations with Southeast Asia.

# The Postcolonial Period[43]

## Romancing Asia

As modern India began to construct its identity at the turn of the twentieth century, an emphasis on the cultural affinity with Asia became an important component of the national movement. The common struggle for independence against Western imperialism was only one of the sources of defining India's Asian identity. The rediscovery of shared civilizational history and the new awareness of ancient India's contributions to the evolution of Asia deepened India's sense of being the prime mover of the great continent. India's new Asian romanticism, however, ran into the real world of competing Asian perceptions. Rabindranath Tagore's critique of nationalism and materialism was received with scepticism in Japan and China. The Indian national movement also found itself divided in dealing with the inter-imperialist rivalries between Japan and the West. Despite the Indian national movement's strong expression of solidarity with their Chinese brethren, the former was focused on fighting the British and latter on Japanese imperialism. Worse still, if India saw itself as the natural leader of Asia, many in China and Japan looked down upon colonial India as a defeated and pacifist nation. Even as they admired Indian leaders, many smaller Asian nations were also afraid of India emerging as a dominant power. These contradictions between India's self-perception of its role in Asia and its image in other Asian countries would prove to be enduring during the rest of the twentieth century.

During the Japanese occupation of the region, Southeast Asia became a launching point of the military campaign led by Netaji Subhas Chandra Bose and his Indian National Army drawn mainly from Indians in Southeast Asia to oust the British from India. In the early post-war period, Indian interests in Southeast

Asia comprised strategic, political, and economic dimensions. The Japanese conquest of Southeast Asia and the advance of the Japanese army to the border region between Myanmar and British India underscored India's strategic vulnerability to attacks through Southeast Asia. The Indian diplomat and strategic thinker K.M. Panikkar, who is credited with being among the first to use the term 'Southeast Asia', suggested the creation of an 'Indian security sphere' extending from the Persian Gulf to Myanmar, Siam, the Indochinese Peninsula, Malay, and Singapore. Economically, Southeast Asia was a major market for Indian textiles (Myanmar was an almost exclusive Indian market), while India was heavily dependent on Myanmar, Indonesia, Malay, Thailand, and Indochina for oil, rubber, tin, rice, and timber. Politically, India shared a common interest with the political elite in Southeast Asia in fostering decolonization and promoting Asian unity. Mohammed Ayoob suggests three key reasons for India's interest in Southeast Asia:[44] first, the Indian nationalist leadership viewed the anticolonial struggles in Southeast Asia as being indivisible from their own struggle. Second, India saw Southeast Asia as a region of geostrategic significance, especially from the viewpoint of maritime strategy. Third, the emergence of China as a major Asian power introduced an important new dimension to India's interest in Southeast Asia. Last but not the least, an estimated 1.3 to 1.8 million Indian immigrants in Southeast Asia provided another crucial link between India and this region. The treatment of Indian migrants in Myanmar did become an issue in Indian relations with that country. Strategically, Indian leaders such as the former deputy prime minister Sardar Vallabhbhai Patel were concerned about instability and communist insurgency in the region (both India and its Southeast Asian neighbours), especially after the communist-organized Southeast Asian Youth Congress held in Calcutta (now Kolkata) in February 1948.

## Leading Southeast Asia

If the precolonial interactions between India and Southeast Asia were mediated by culture and commerce, those following the end of the Second World War were dominated by nationalism and a common quest for decolonization. India's struggle for independence from British rule was viewed in Southeast Asia with great interest. Once India became the second Asian country after the Philippines to achieve its independence in 1947, it played an important role in the campaign for self-determination in Southeast Asia.

If Tagore articulated the vision of an Asian spiritual civilization, it was Nehru who forged it into an ambitious political agenda aimed at building a new Asian century through regional solidarity and unity. However, as discussed in Chapter 1, Indian support was mainly political and diplomatic rather than military. Nehru refused Ho Chi Minh's request for material support against the French, which had been specifically asked for by the DRV (Democratic Republic of Vietnam, controlled by Minh) delegation in the ARC in New Delhi in March–April 1947. He took a more active role in supporting Indonesia's struggle against the Dutch but without providing material support. This would cost him some legitimacy as a champion of Asian unity.

Nehru was an early advocate of Asian unity. He took the lead in organizing Asian cooperation by hosting the ARC in 1947. The unofficial ARC organized in New Delhi under Nehru's chairmanship attracted delegations from all Southeast Asian countries. Here, India sought the creation of a regional organization, although the resulting Asian Relations Organization was moribund and short-lived. The conference revealed the deep differences on contemporary economic and political issues among the Asian nations. India, despite its early start as an independent Asian nation and an international actor, was resented and feared in Asia because of its diplomatic style and domineering attitude. In fact, ironically, the ARC planted the seeds of a Southeast Asian regional consciousness that sought to distance itself from pan-Asian frameworks that could have been dominated by larger powers like India and China. India took the lead in convening the 1949 Conference on Indonesia to show support for Indonesian nationalists after the Second Dutch police action. India sought to mediate the conflict between the French and North Vietnamese following the Geneva Accords in 1954.

Most importantly, Nehru would be a key player in the Bandung Conference of Asian and African countries in 1955. At this time, the regional identity of Southeast Asia remained closely tied to that of India. Exemplifying this is the fact that the Bandung Conference was convened by the Conference of Southeast Asian Prime Ministers (also known as the Colombo Powers), a regional grouping that included the leaders of Pakistan, India, and Sri Lanka, as well as Indonesia and Myanmar. The Bandung Conference, though successful in articulating a sense of solidarity among the newly independent countries, revealed serious differences between India and the pro-US Southeast Asian nations, that is, Thailand and the Philippines. This will be discussed in chapters 3 and 4.

A key aspect of Indian diplomacy during this period was its policy towards China. Nehru originated the 'engaging China' formula and shared Mao's contempt for the US secretary of state John Foster Dulles. Nehru insisted on inviting China to the Bandung Conference despite opposition from the West and without securing from Chou En-Lai an understanding that non-interference had to include cessation of Chinese support for the spread of communist ideology. Although Chou (but not necessarily other Chinese leaders) respected Nehru and the talk of a Nehru–Chou rivalry at the Bandung Conference was somewhat played up by the pro-Western media, Nehru's China policy ran into trouble because of his misreading of Chinese intentions and his disagreement with Chou on setting up a permanent regional organization. As India drifted into a war with China, the idea of Asian solidarity under Indian leadership could no longer be sustained.

At Bandung, Nehru bitterly condemned military alliances between Asian nations and the superpowers, targeting SEATO specifically. This did not go down well with the leaders of pro-Western countries such as the Philippines, who sought security from communist threat through an alliance with the US. Even ideologically like-minded nations like India and Indonesia, despite being co-sponsors of the Afro-Asian solidarity movement and the Non-Aligned Movement (NAM), harboured mutual misgivings. Indian leaders took a sceptical view of Indonesian leadership in regional affairs, while Indonesian officials resented their Indian counterparts, who they saw as heavy-handed and arrogant in contrast with the quiet and subtle style of diplomacy preferred by the Indonesians.

India also stepped up its diplomacy in the escalating Indo-China conflict, which included Nehru's call for an immediate ceasefire in February 1954. He used the Colombo Powers Conference in April to discuss a six-point proposal for a settlement. Nehru sought to prevent Chinese military intervention in support of Ho Chi Minh and also prevent large-scale US intervention that might have included nuclear weapons. India's role led to its appointment as the chairman of the International Control Commission (ICC) on Indochina whose role was to control the flow of armaments into Laos, Cambodia, and Vietnam. But ultimately, this effort failed: Laos moved closer to the West, Cambodia to China. But Indian diplomacy also suffered failures. The ICC suffered from a weak mandate and shortage of manpower as well as a lack of enforcement authority. It, however, achieved the separation of the opposing forces in Vietnam, the transfer of power to the

Viet Minh in Hanoi, the withdrawal of the Viet Minh from Cambodia, and the conclusion of an agreement in Laos between the royal government and the communist Pathet Lao. But the decline of the Geneva spirit of accommodation among the major powers made the ICC's work difficult. India found it difficult to maintain and pursue its non-aligned policy in Southeast Asia, and while Nehru seemed more preoccupied with domestic issues, China made diplomatic and commercial gains in Southeast Asia at India's expense.

## Leaving Asia

After Bandung, India shifted its attention away from Asian neutralism towards global non-alignment, considering Asia to be too small a stage for its diplomacy. This was a strategic mistake, as it would cost India the membership of ASEAN, which was set up in 1967 as Asia's first multipurpose regional organization. In the 1960s and 1970s, India's political and economic relations with Southeast Asia eroded substantially, resulting in the near-total disengagement of India from Southeast Asian affairs. The 1962 war between India and China dashed any remaining hopes of Indian interaction with Southeast Asia within a pan-Asian framework. This was accompanied by a growing divergence of their national economic policies and development strategies. India pursued a socialist, centrally planned economy with heavy emphasis on the public sector, while the non-communist Southeast Asian countries with the exception of Myanmar adopted market-oriented development strategies that relied heavily on openness to foreign investments and multinational enterprise. The divergence in strategic outlook was equally pronounced. India's non-aligned outlook, albeit with a tilt towards Moscow over Cold War issues, conflicted with ASEAN's pro-US stance camouflaged in its doctrine of a Zone of Peace, Freedom and

Neutrality (ZOPFAN) in Southeast Asia, despite India's official endorsement of ZOPFAN. Moreover, India remained preoccupied with its domestic problems and the conflict with Pakistan over Kashmir, while ASEAN remained concerned with the threat of communist insurgency and potential Chinese and Vietnamese expansionism. ASEAN developed a separate regional identity excluding India. India showed little interest in joining ASEAN. India had snubbed ASEAN by failing to send its foreign minister to an ASEAN ministerial meeting in 1980. Such actions delayed any ASEAN interest in granting India the status of its dialogue partner.

The Indian intervention in East Pakistan in 1971 that led to the creation of Bangladesh might have helped its military credibility in the eyes of Southeast Asian states. But this was offset by two developments. The first was the Nixon visit to China and the Sino-US rapprochement. This was of greater importance to Southeast Asia than the Indian victory over Pakistan. The second was the signing of the Indo-Soviet Treaty of Peace, Friendship, and Cooperation in August 1971. Though intended to deter any Chinese or American intervention in support of Pakistan in a war with India, this treaty was seen in Southeast Asia as compromising India's non-alignment and made India seem pro-Soviet. Given ASEAN's suspicions of the Soviet Union, this meant a suspicion of Indian intentions in Southeast Asia as well. Finally, India remained more interested in the Gulf and the Middle East, especially after the 1973 oil crisis.

While ASEAN saw a link between the Soviet invasion of Afghanistan and the Vietnamese invasion of Cambodia, India did not see it that way. India could not support any regional-defence arrangements in Southeast Asia against China because it had enough problems of its own, and its security forces were fully stretched out. India also favoured wider regional groupings like the Colombo Plan, the ADB, and the Economic

Commission for Asia and the Far East (ECAFE). ASEAN saw India's role in the region constrained by its problems with Pakistan. Rejecting any suggestion that India should be part of ASEAN, Adam Malik, the foreign minister of Indonesia, argued that India was seen as not 'geographically included in Southeast Asia'. India also took a more positive attitude towards the Soviet proposal for a system of collective security in Asia.

The late 1970s was a major turning point in India's relations with Southeast Asia. The Vietnamese invasion of Cambodia in late December 1978 saw India, a treaty ally of the Soviet Union, express support for Vietnam and recognize the Vietnamese-installed Heng-Samrin regime in Cambodia. This was at serious odds with ASEAN's effort to condemn and isolate Hanoi. Moreover, in the 1980s, India's naval modernization programme caused some apprehension in Southeast Asia. Strategic commentators in Southeast Asia and Australia expressed alarm that India's move to develop a blue-water navy could upset the regional balance of power and usher in an effort at regional dominance. But with the end of the Cold War and the rise of China, India's naval programme was seen by the ASEAN countries in a more favourable light.

Economically, during the 1970s and 1980s the ASEAN countries experienced robust economic growth, while India could only muster what was derisively called the 'Hindu' rate of growth of around 5 per cent. Overall, ASEAN and India pursued divergent trajectories both strategically and economically. India's democratic system invited unfavourable comments from Singapore's Lee Kuan Yew, who favoured 'discipline over democracy' and credited East Asia's economic miracle to 'Confucian values'.

## Returning to Southeast Asia

The coolness and mutual neglect in India–ASEAN relations persisted until the early 1990s. Then a major shift occurred when the then Indian prime minister Narasimha Rao outlined a vision of an Indian 'Look East' policy whose main thrust was 'to draw, as much as possible, investment and cooperation from the Asia-Pacific countries, in consonance with our common concept and solidarity and my faith in our common destiny'.[45] The 'Look East' policy was a logical and necessary extension of India's domestic economic liberalization drive, which was forced upon the Rao government by harsh domestic, economic, and political realities. ASEAN was a key part of the 'Look East' policy.

The initial focus of India's 'Look East' policy and India–ASEAN ties was on the economic arena. Their economic cooperation, however, if viewed from trade and investment flows, fares relatively weak compared to ASEAN's other dialogue partners. (Further discussion of ASEAN–India economic ties can be found in Chapter 5.)

Since economic cooperation remained on the driver's seat of ASEAN–India relations, both sides sought to optimize the economic potential of their linkages. Agreeing to deepen trade and investments and to establish an ASEAN–India Free Trade Area (FTA) was geared towards this common goal.[46]

While India began the re-engagement of Southeast Asia in the early 1990s, this was different from the manner of China's changing relationship with its Southeast Asian neighbours. China was 'engaged' by its neighbours because of its rising economic and military power, under terms strikingly similar to those pursued by Nehru a generation ago. But Southeast Asian countries, unlike Nehru, also hedged against Chinese expansionism by keeping close security ties with the US. While China was courted by ASEAN, it was India that initiated its re-engagement with Southeast Asia due to pressing economic and, to a lesser extent, strategic reasons. ASEAN, of course, has reciprocated India's 'Look East' policy, but slowly and warily, in contrast to its enthusiastic engagement of China. After being excluded from its founding, India was accepted as a member of the ARF, but in contrast to the

1940s and 1950s, India has now tended to be a junior and passive partner in contemporary Asian regional institutions.

After a slow start, it was the turn of India's eastern neighbours to rediscover and engage India. This was due to a growing recognition of India's economic potential and rising power. The changing strategic climate in the Asia–Pacific region appeared to favour the development of closer political and security ties between India and Southeast Asian countries. India has no border or land disputes in Southeast Asia and has already marked out her maritime boundary with Indonesia and Thailand. Currently, no Southeast Asian nation considers India to be a threat; India does not expect any threats to its security from any of the ASEAN countries. Some Asian strategic analysts have cast India and China as 'natural rivals' for influence in Southeast Asia. Indian officials have been, at least until now, wary of any move to 'contain' China. India prefers a policy of 'engagement' with China to bring it into a system of regional order. The growing military ties between Myanmar and China, which had been a source of concern to Indian strategists, became less relevant with the political opening of Myanmar in 2011. The Sino-Myanmar relationship was a security concern shared by India and the ASEAN states. ASEAN's decision to grant full membership to Myanmar in 1997 in the face of widespread international condemnation of the move was partly an effort to reduce Myanmar's dependence on China. India, too, opposed the isolation of Myanmar and welcomed its entry into ASEAN, despite pressure from human rights groups in India.

The 1990s saw increased defence contacts between India and ASEAN countries. The Indian navy conducted a number of 'friendship exercises' with ASEAN navies, including those of Singapore, Indonesia, Thailand, and Malaysia. These were mainly 'passing' exercises with little, if any, military significance. India and Malaysia cooperated in a programme (since terminated) to provide familiarization and maintenance training for Russian-supplied MiG aircraft (not flying training, as some have erroneously reported) to the Malaysian air-force personnel in India. Modest defence contacts have also been established with Northeast Asian countries. Also, there have been joint patrols by Indian and US navies in the Straits of Malacca. Overall, ASEAN has been less alarmed by the Indian naval power.

While Indian strategic planners recognized the importance of global trade routes through Southeast Asia and share a concern about the rise of the Chinese military power, there is little indication that India has any grand plans for assuming a major security role in the Asia–Pacific region. Until now, the Indian navy remained the only one in Asia with medium-sized aircraft carriers (Thailand has become the second Asian nation to have a carrier). India also has a relatively modern submarine force and active programmes to build principle combatants. But India, rather than Southeast Asia, appeared to be more concerned with developing a naval presence in the Indian Ocean. There were suggestions by some Indian analysts that India might be involved in a future war in East Asia. This appears rather far-fetched. A more likely scenario is Indian participation in the UN peacekeeping operations in the region, as it had done in Cambodia.

India's 'Look East' policy in the 1990s offered it a chance to put its relationship with Southeast Asia on a new footing and return to the region where it was once seen as a leader. Although the policy is directed at the entire Asia–Pacific region, Southeast Asia was and remains a key theatre.

Culture and identity play an important part in India's understanding of, and interaction with, Southeast Asia. But as India pursues this policy, it should be mindful of not repeating the past mistakes, including its sense of cultural superiority and arrogance, and acknowledge the main lesson of the 'Indianization' debate, that is, the distinctive culture and agency of Southeast Asians. It is important to be careful about bringing history to the table in forging good neighbourly relations. History can be a double-edged sword. It is far better for Southeast Asians to make the point about India's civilizational influence in Southeast Asia, than for Indian scholars, not to mention Indian officials, to belabour the point in diplomatic gatherings in Southeast Asia. India's 'Look East/Act East' policy of reconnecting with its eastern neighbours, which will be further discussed in Chapter 5, is widely noted in Asia and much celebrated in New Delhi. Yet there is no room for a return to cultural or diplomatic arrogance as was evident during the early post-war period.

## Notes and References

1. Paul Wheatley, 1982, 'Presidential Address: India beyond the Ganges—Desultory Reflections on the Origins of Civilization in Southeast Asia', *The Journal of Asian Studies*, xlii: 27–8.
2. George Cœdès, *The Indianized States of Southeast Asia,* Walter F. Vella (ed.), translated by Sue Brown Cowing (Honolulu: University of Hawaii Press, 1968), pp. 16–17.
3. Ramesh Chandra Majumdar, *India and South East Asia*, K.S. Ramachandran and S.P. Gupta (eds), (Delhi: B.R. Publishing, 1940), p. 21; see also Majumdar, *Greater India*, second edition (Mumbai: National Information and Publications, 1948).
4. I.W. Mabbett, 1976, 'The "Indianization" of Southeast Asia: Reflections on the Historical Sources', *Journal of Southeast Asian Studies*, 8(1): 143–4.
5. J.C. van Leur, *Indonesian Trade and Society: Essays in Asian Social and Economic History* (The Hague: W. van Hoeve, 1955).
6. John Legge, 'The Writing of Southeast Asian History', in Nicholas Tarling (ed.), *The Cambridge History of Southeast Asia* (Cambridge: Cambridge University Press, 1992), p. 8.
7. van Leur, *Indonesian Trade and Society,* p. 357.
8. Legge, 'The Writing of Southeast Asian History', p. 8
9. van Leur, *Indonesian Trade and Society,* pp. 103–4.
10. Mabbett, 'The "Indianization" of Southeast Asia', p. 144.

11. F.D.K. Bosch, *Selected Studies in Indonesian Archaeology* (The Hague: Martinus Nijhoff, 1961).

12. Cœdès, *The Indianized States of Southeast Asia.*

13. D.R. SarDesai, *Southeast Asia: Past and Present*, third edition (Boulder: Westview Press, 1994), p. 17.

14. Paul Wheatley, 'Desultory Remarks on the Ancient History of the Malay Peninsula', in J. Bastin and R. Roolvink (eds), *Malayan and Indonesian Studies: Essays Presented to Sir Richard Winstedt on His Eighty-Fifth Birthday* (Oxford: Clarendon Press, 1964), pp. 33–75; Wheatley, 'Comments on the Dynamics of the Process of Indianization', in K.S. Sandhu (ed.), *Early Malaysia: Some Observations on the Nature of Indian Contacts with Pre-British Malaya* (Singapore: University Education Press, 1973), pp. 37–49.

15. Mabbett, 'The "Indianization" of Southeast Asia', p. 144; B.P. Groslier, 1960, 'Our Knowledge of Khmer Civilization: A Reappraisal', *Journal of Siam Society*, 48(1): 1–28.

16. O.W. Wolters, *History, Culture and Region in Southeast Asian Perspectives* (Singapore: Institute of Southeast Asian Studies, 1982), p. 43.

17. The *Arthasastra*, according to D.G.E. Hall, 'for centuries was almost the nature of a prescribed textbook at South-East Asian courts'. The text prescribed ideas and norms for both domestic governance and interstate relations, covering areas such as the pacification of newly acquired territories, prescriptions regarding maintenance of good customs and abrogation of bad ones, procedures for settling lawsuits, the uses of spies, and principles for the levying and collection of revenues. See D.G.E. Hall, *A History of Southeast Asia* (New York: St. Martin's, 1981), p. 250.

   Other Indian influences included writing systems in Southeast Asia, which with the exception of those of Muslim Malays and the Vietnamese, were based on the Indian alphabet, the terminologies for law and administration. 'Even where the Indian governmental system was not fully introduced, as among the Bugenese and the eastern Indonesian islanders, Hindu influences were reflected at the higher levels of social stratification.'

See John F. Cady, *Southeast Asia: Its Historical Development* (New York: McGraw-Hill, 1964), p. 45.

18. I.W. Mabbett, 1976, 'The "Indianization" of Southeast Asia: Reflections on the Prehistoric Sources', *Journal of Southeast Asian Studies*, 8(1): 1–14.

19. Wheatley, 'Presidential Address', p. 27.

20. Hooykaas cited in Wolters, *History, Culture and Region*, p. 59.

21. M.B. Hooker, *A Concise Legal History of South-East Asia* (Oxford: Clarendon Press, 1978), pp. 35–6.

22. Hooker, *A Concise Legal History*, pp. 35–6.

23. Hooker, *A Concise Legal History*. Another example of such adaptation may be noted. The Hindu manual of Manu's laws identified 18 points of litigation. This was used in Java where some of the laws were modified to accommodate Javanese customary law without altering the number 18. See Wolters, *History, Culture and Region*, p. 42. Beginning in the thirteenth century, Vietnamese historians used Chinese formats for writing imperial history as a model for writing Vietnamese history. But the important thing is that it was a Chinese format, while the substance was Vietnamese. See Wolters, *History, Culture and Region*, pp. 42–3.

24. Wolters, *History, Culture and Region*, p. 59.

25. Wolters's concept of localization is similar to 'adaptation', 'synthesis', or 'syncretism'. But he prefers 'localization' because the other terms 'seem to shirk the crucial question of where and how foreign elements began to fit into a local culture. "Adaptation" and "synthesis" give an impression of the outcome of the process, while "syncretism" does likewise and also begs the question by conveying a dictionary sense of reconciliation of originally contradictory differences. The three terms smother the initiative of the local elements responsible for the process and the end product.' See Wolters, *History, Culture and Region*, p. 53.

26. Wolters, *History, Culture and Region*, p. 48.

27. Wolters, *History, Culture and Region*, p. 47.

28. Wolters, *History, Culture and Region*, pp. 53–4.

29. Wolters, *History, Culture and Region*, p. 52.

30. Wolters, *History, Culture and Region*, p. 53.
31. Wolters, *History, Culture and Region*, p. 9.
32. Wolters, *History, Culture and Region*, p. 102.
33. Wolters, *History, Culture and Region*, p. 103.
34. Wolters, *History, Culture and Region*, p. 10.
35. Wolters, *History, Culture and Region*, p. 64.
36. Wheatley, 'Presidential Address', p. 20.
37. Wolters, *History, Culture and Region*, p. 89.
38. Wolters, *History, Culture and Region*, p. 89.
39. van Leur, *Indonesian Trade and Society*.
40. Milton Osborne, *Southeast Asia: An Introductory History* (Sydney: Allen and Unwin, 1979), pp. 5–6.
41. Wheatley, 'Presidential Address', p. 27.
42. Osborne, *Southeast Asia*, p. 13.
43. Some of the discussion in this section repeats that in the other chapters, but is useful here in illustrating the evolution of India's relations with Southeast Asia.
44. Mohammed Ayoob, *India and Southeast Asia: Indian Perceptions and Policies* (London: Routledge, 1990), p. 3.
45. Prakash Nanda, *Rediscovering Asia: Evolution of India's Look-East Policy* (New Delhi: Lancer Publishers, 2003), p. 320.
46. 'Overview of ASEAN–India Dialogue Relations', January 2015, available at http://www.asean.org/news/item/overview-of-asean-india-dialogue-relations (accessed on 31 July 2015).

# 3.

# Jawaharlal Nehru at Bandung: East versus West?

'{T}here is no friendship when nations are not equal, when one has to
obey another and when one only dominates another.'
—Jawaharlal Nehru[1]

On the eve of the fiftieth anniversary of the Asian-African
Conference in Bandung, the Chinese government released a

documentary film entitled *Zhou Enlai in Bandung*. The film painted Chou as a hero of the conference, the man who not only represented communist China splendidly—attending its first international conference without the Soviet Union being present—but also salvaged the conference from disarray and failure through his moderation, compromise, and, above all, personal charm. Indeed this was the *original* Chinese charm offensive well before the term came into vogue in the 1990s.

What about India's Nehru? Many historians paint Nehru as having flopped at Bandung. In contrast to Chou's star power and charm, Nehru performed below expectations. He was often seen as arrogant, sullen, and overbearing. Nehru, of course, had a special role at Bandung. Although the idea of the Bandung Conference was Indonesia's, Nehru's consent was crucial to Indonesia's ability to get agreement to hold the conference. Ali Sastroamidjojo, the then prime minister of the host nation Indonesia, wrote: 'For me, Nehru's opinion was the most important, because his influence on the policies of India's neighbours at the time was indeed great. So, it more or less depended on Nehru's attitude whether the other Asian nations would support our government's plans.'[2] This Indonesian deference owed much to India's prime minister's normative authority for being a forerunner of Asian—and later Asian-African—regionalism.

Nehru was at this time the undisputed champion of Asian unity. He was highly regarded for his intellect, even by his detractors (there were quite a few). This was the era of *Hindi–Chini Bhai-Bhai* (Indians and Chinese are brothers) and Nehru went out of his way to be friendly to Chou. The film *Zhou Enlai in Bandung* makes much of the fact that Chou insisted on taking an Air India plane to Bandung after the original Air India plane named the *Kashmir Princess*, which he was supposed to take, but had luckily missed, had been bombed and destroyed in the South China Sea as the result of an alleged Kuomintang plot. Chou's trust in Nehru was underscored in a secret British report, which noted: 'Chou had at one stage said that any English phrase which was acceptable to Nehru would be acceptable to him.'[3] Nehru sought to wean China away from the Soviet Union by giving it a chance to engage with Asia.

I will return later to the Nehru–Chou relationship, which was painted by many Western observers with considerable exaggeration as Nehru–Chou rivalry. In that narrative, Chou was a winner and Nehru a loser. But in this chapter, let me highlight how Nehru shaped Bandung in challenging American geopolitics in Asia. Contrary to a popular perception, Nehru did not lose in Bandung any more than Chou 'won' there. But he ensured that the US 'lost' India and much of the Third World. Due to a stubborn, ideologically charged policy by the US and the UK to subvert Bandung, the US would lose influence over India and Indonesia, two of the most populous nations of the world.

The role the Bandung Conference played in India's strategic and normative approach to Asian security and world order was a key element in the evolution of Nehru's non-alignment policy, especially its rejection of the Cold War military alliances. In this respect, it marked a turning point in Nehru's break with the West led by the US. Whether this was a gain or loss for India is debatable, but Indian foreign policy would never be the same after Bandung. At the same time, Nehru was not able to use the Bandung Conference to bring about a long-term engagement of communist China, which was one of the key objectives of his foreign policy. Bandung thus proved to be a crucial stage for the encounters between India, China, and Southeast Asia and also for the evolution of the overall post-war regional and international order.

## American Power Politics

In coming to Bandung, Nehru's primary objective was not to foster Asian unity, but to frustrate American power politics. The lynchpin of the US strategy was the creation of regional collective defence arrangements in Asia and the Middle East (the Manila Pact/ SEATO and the Baghdad Pact/Central Treaty Organization [CENTO]). The US approach intensified as the Cold War progressed.

The Truman administration was presented with the idea of a collective defence system for the Pacific, proposed by Elpidio Quirino of the Philippines and backed by its other Cold War Asian allies such as Syngman Rhee of South Korea and Chiang Kai-shek of the Republic of China. But it rejected this idea—a wise move perhaps, given the controversial standing of these Asian leaders both within their own countries and regionally. The Harry S. Truman administration subsequently did consider a multilateral security arrangement to accompany the US–Japan defence treaty. This idea, though, was opposed by John Foster Dulles (who was appointed by Truman to oversee the negotiations regarding the US–Japan treaty) and abandoned once the treaty was successfully concluded. But Dulles appear to have shifted his position[4] following the Korean War and certainly by the time of the 1954 Geneva talks on Indo-China (by then, he had been installed as the secretary of state). He had been calling for a Southeast Asian collective defence pact, believing that the Geneva Agreement would be a sell-out to the communists. He saw a Southeast Asia defence treaty as a means of preventing communist gains in Indochina, including a possible Chinese takeover of the region. In a discussion with Congressional leaders in May 1954, he had taken the position that 'if the communists gained Indochina and nothing was done about it, it was only a question of time until all of Southeast Asia falls along with Indonesia, thus imperilling our Western island of defence'.[5] A month-and-a-half later, he was even more apocalyptic in discussing Indochina with Eisenhower:

> I expressed the thought that it might well be that the situation in Indochina itself would soon have deteriorated to a point where nothing effectual can be done to stop the tide of Chinese communists over-running Southeast Asia except perhaps diversionary activities along the China coast, which would be conducted primarily by the Nationalist forces, but would require sea and air support from the United States.[6]

This perspective is important for two reasons. First, it suggests that the rationale for collective defence was based on a calculation of the PRC challenge. It shows how seriously Dulles viewed the threat of Chinese expansion. The reference to 'the tide of Chinese Communists over-running Southeast Asia' would challenge those who believed that sections in the US did not take the threat of communism seriously enough to propose an Asian NATO (North Atlantic Treaty Organization). The Dullesian formulation blurred the distinction between gains by local communist parties backed by the PRC and direct communist Chinese expansion. Second, the thought of using the Nationalist Chinese government in Taiwan for a 'diversionary' move is significant. It suggests that the threat of a US–PRC conflict at this time was as much, if not more, due to US actions resulting from concerns about PRC Chinese manoeuvrings in Southeast Asia, rather than a takeover of Taiwan itself. At the Bandung Conference, Chou En-Lai would take a moderate stance on Taiwan, offering to negotiate with the US, while the latter would not only be dismissive of the overture but was also prepared (although Dulles's view would have been countered by other sections of the US national security establishment) to initiate hostilities with the PRC that would have surely resulted from any 'diversionary' action involving Taiwanese forces backed by the US.

## Nehru's Ideas

As discussed in the previous chapters, Nehru was the leading figure behind early post-war Asian regionalism. He played a central role in five post-war pan-Asian regional conferences: the 1947 ARC and the 1949 Conference on Indonesia (both of which he organized) as well as the Conference of Southeast Asian Prime Ministers, Colombo, 1954; the Conference of Southeast Asian Prime Ministers, Bogor, 1954; and the Asian-African Conference, Bandung, 1955.[7]

An important statement of Nehru's approach to international relations can be found in *The Discovery of India*, which he wrote in prison in 1944. There, under the heading 'Realism and Geopolitics: World Conquest or World Association?', Nehru forcefully rejected regional security systems under great power 'orbits', as proposed by Walter Lippmann, characterizing them as 'a continuation of power politics on a vaster scale' and arguing that 'it is difficult to see how he can see world peace or co-operation emerging out of it'. Apart from rejecting power politics, it also signalled his desire and hope for greater international cooperation, not in the form of military alliances that would reflect power politics, but by way of a 'commonwealth of states', or a 'world association'.[8] Two years later, in a speech delivered on 7 September 1946, he offered a further elaboration of his normative beliefs:

> We propose, as far as possible, to keep away from the power politics of groups, aligned against one another, which have led in the past to world wars and which may again lead to disaster of an even vaster scale. We believe that peace and freedom are indivisible and that denial of freedom anywhere must endanger freedom elsewhere and lead to conflict and war.

We are particularly interested in the emancipation of colonial and dependent territories and peoples and in the recognition in theory and practice of equal opportunities for all peoples.... We seek no domination over others and we claim no privileged position over other peoples.... The world, in spite of its rivalries and hatreds and inner conflicts, moves inevitably towards closer cooperation and the building up of a world of commonwealth. It is for this one world free India will work, a world in which there is free co-operation of free peoples and no class or group exploits another.[9]

These words defined a framework of 'moral sovereignty' proposed by Nehru. While 'the emancipation of colonial and dependent territories and peoples' was its key element, the foreign policy of a sovereign nation would also involve abstaining from 'the power politics of groups, aligned against one another' and exercising 'domination over others'. Nehru's early efforts at international cooperation based on this framework focused on India's neighbourhood. A key aim of his championing of Asian unity was equality; the 'Asian countries needed to find a way of relating as equals to the richer powers of the Western world'.[10] Nehru would also assure his Asian neighbours that they 'should not fear any intervention or dominance by India, whether in the political or in the economic sphere'.[11] His advocacy of 'non-involvement' (later non-alignment) has been described as essentially a political 'means of minimizing, if not totally excluding, political and military intervention by the great powers in regional affairs'.[12] And at the centre of this approach was his opposition to the pressures exerted by the superpowers on the newly independent countries to join their respective military alliances.

Against the backdrop of his prior beliefs on international order, it is hardly surprising that Nehru would oppose a US-led collective defence system in Southeast Asia when the idea gathered momentum in 1954. He believed that the proliferation of such regional pacts would reduce the 'area of peace' and encourage great-power interference and intervention in the internal affairs of the new states. Acceptance of offers of 'protection' by the superpowers could hardly be distinguished from 'a condition of colonialism or dependency'.[13] His chief (but controversial) foreign-policy lieutenant, V.K. Krishna Menon, likened collective defence pacts to 'a roving commission to protect people who did not want to be protected, affecting the sovereignty of the nations of the area'.[14] Nehru's opposition to collective defence pacts also invoked the principles of representation and participation. 'When decisions of vital significance are made for an area excluding the views of the vital part of that very area,' he argued, 'then there is something wrong.'[15] Hence the 'whole [SEATO] approach was wrong from the point of view of any Asian country'.[16]

There can be alternative *realpolitik* explanations of Nehru's resistance to collective defence. He saw in SEATO and CENTO, especially with Pakistan's involvement in both, a threat to India's security. These alliances brought the Cold War to India's doorstep. Moreover, some Indian scholars have argued that his rejection of SEATO reflected India's own aspiration for regional dominance.[17] But such self-interested behaviour need not be incompatible with normative approaches to international relations.[18] More importantly, they do not invalidate the normative basis of Nehru's opposition to defence pacts within great power orbits, which, as noted, was evident *before* the creation of Pakistan and *before* the Cold War alliances came into existence. Hence the realpolitik underpinnings of Nehru's foreign policy approach could be overstated.[19] Moreover, Nehru's belief that despite the ongoing international conflicts, a cooperative international order leading to a 'world of commonwealth' was dawning was clearly not a realpolitik view of international relations. His rejection of Cold War collective defence pacts was not simply a response to India's changing strategic circumstances; it had a basis in his prior moral beliefs. The Cold War pacts conflicted with Nehru's vision of international relations, which rejected power politics, denounced colonialism, advocated non-exclusionary international and regional cooperation, and demanded equality and justice for the newly independent states. As a leading biographer of Nehru puts it, collective defence pacts were to him a reminder of India's 'long experience with colonial rule'; they represented 'an indirect return of Western power to an area from which it had recently retreated'.[20]

While Nehru's opposition to collective defence invoked the principles of sovereignty, particularly the equality of states and non-intervention, it would be wrong to view it as a simple borrowing of Westphalian doctrines. Though a lawyer, Nehru did not think about international affairs in legalistic terms (there was no Nehru doctrine comparable to the Calvo or Drago doctrines in Latin America). His writings do not suggest the influence of Western legal scholars like Hugo Grotius or Emer de Vattel who had developed the norms of sovereignty. Indeed Nehru rejected the notion that international law was basically a Western idea, insisting that there was an indigenous Indian tradition of international law.[21] His moral beliefs about India's foreign policy and international order, instead of simply reflecting Westphalian and European legal doctrines, were shaped by other experiences, which included his involvement in India's nationalist struggle and the Gandhian doctrine of non-violence.[22] It is these prior beliefs, especially anti-colonialism, which helped to define his attitude towards non-intervention, thereby strengthening and extending an emerging international norm and laying the basis of a norm against collective defence in Asia.[23] In particular, the political ideas of actors like Nehru infused and strengthened the legal norms of state sovereignty prevailing at the international level.

In early post-war Asia, non-intervention could be best described as an emerging international norm, because although not novel, it had not become salient in international relations of states outside of Europe and Latin America (mainly because much of the rest of the world was still under colonial rule). Comparing the agenda, proceedings, and outcomes of the 1947 and 1955 conferences, one finds that while in 1947 (and in the 1949 Conference on Indonesia), non-intervention was not a key issue and domestic affairs of states were a fair game for discussion, it came to dominate the agenda of the 1955 Bandung Conference that avoided any discussion of domestic politics of the participating states.

The agenda of the 1947 conference covered eight issues: National Movements for Freedom, Racial Problems, Inter-Asian Migration, Transition from Colonial to National Economy, Agricultural Reconstruction and Industrial Development, Labour Problems and Social Services, Cultural Problems, and Status of Women and Women's Movements.[24] The conference decided on a set of principles over political matters, including an agreement not to provide any assistance for the continuance of 'foreign domination' in any part of Asia, and the provision of assistance to national movements wherever possible. A third point of agreement was that 'people belonging to one country and living in another should identify themselves with the latter'.[25] It extracted assurances from countries such as India, China, Indonesia, Sri Lanka, and Myanmar that their existing or proposed constitutions would not contain any provision for discrimination on racial grounds. The principle of equality between all citizens irrespective of race and creed 'should be the rule in all countries'. This notion of equality was divided into four components: '(i) complete legal equality of all citizens, (ii) complete religious freedom, (iii) no public social disqualification of any racial group, and (iv) equality before law of persons of foreign origin who had settled in the country.'[26]

What is striking about these principles is that they were essentially concerned with the domestic jurisdiction of states. The 1947 conference was technically 'non-official', because it was organized by the non-governmental Indian Council on World Affairs (ICWA). But this should not be overemphasized. The chairman of the conference was Nehru, already the prime minister-designate of India. The fact is that in 1947, non-intervention was not the focus of the political agenda of Asian and African states. The ARC participants, united by a common opposition to colonialism and concerned mainly with self-determination and racial equality, could find it acceptable to debate and set common rules for their domestic affairs. That this would be unthinkable in a few years' time attests to the fact that the norms of sovereignty, such as non-intervention, evolved through post-war Asian interactions in response to local ideas about how to manage the escalating superpower rivalry and maintain regional order.

The 1947 ARC excluded defence cooperation from its agenda. An Asian defence system was originally envisaged by Nehru in 1946.[27] However, by the 1947 ARC Nehru had stopped pursuing this idea, mainly due to the concern that any Asian defence system would draw in outside powers ('the security of Asia had more than an Asian incidence'[28]) and rekindle big-power rivalry in Asia. This concern foreshadowed and formed the basis of Nehru's opposition to SEATO, displayed in 1954–5, as well as a more general reluctance in Asia to engage in any form of collective defence, including that limited only to Asian states, because of the realization that an indigenous collective defence system would become entangled with great-power interests and encroachment.

Faced with an escalating crisis in Indochina that they saw as a consequence of outside power involvement, the prime ministers of five southern Asian countries—India, Pakistan, Myanmar, Indonesia, and Ceylon—organized themselves into a group known as the Colombo Powers, and held their first meeting in April 1954 in Colombo. In proposing the terms of a settlement in Indochina, the drafting committee of the Colombo Conference, prodded by India and Myanmar, suggested 'a solemn agreement of non-intervention' by the USA, the Union of Soviet Socialist Republics (USSR), the UK, and China 'to refrain from giving aid to the combatants or intervening in Indo-China with troops or war material' as a specific clause in a draft joint communiqué to be issued by the Colombo Powers.[29] Pakistan, while not being 'opposed to the principle of non-intervention', objected to the inclusion of the clause (presumably because that would have delegitimized US assistance to South Vietnam at a time when Pakistan had decided to join a collective defence pact with the US). In the end, softer language was used and the outside powers—China, the US, the USSR, and the UK—were urged to agree on 'steps necessary to prevent the recurrence or resumption of hostilities' so that 'the success of ... direct negotiations [as opposed to the prospects for a ceasefire] will be greatly helped'.[30]

It was at this Colombo meeting that the idea of an 'Asian-African Conference' was proposed by Indonesia to be held under the sponsorship of the Colombo Powers. The final preparations for the conference were made in a second meeting of the Colombo Powers held in Bogor, Indonesia, in December 1954. The objectives of the Asian-African gathering would be to consider the 'problems affecting national sovereignty and racialism and colonialism', 'to explore and advance' the 'mutual and common interests' of Asian and African nations, and 'establish and further friendliness and neighbourly relations'. The period leading to the Bandung Conference was also a time when 'the word and the idea of intervention was everywhere, especially in Southeast Asia'.[31] The principle of non-intervention was advanced in three key decisions of the Colombo Powers at Bogor. The first was their position that 'acceptance of the invitation by any one country would in no way involve or imply any change in the status of that country or its relationship with other countries'. Second, they recognized the 'principle that the form of government and the way of life of any one country should in no way be subject to interference by any other'.[32] Third, Nehru successfully opposed the idea mooted by Indonesia to issue invitations to representatives of independence movements in dependent countries, because 'that would mean an interference in internal affairs, while the Colombo countries had advocated the principle of non-interference'.[33]

Nehru also viewed collective defence pacts organized by great powers as a new form of intervention and hence a violation of state sovereignty. Krishna Menon told the British high commissioner in Delhi on 14 April 1954 that 'collective defence under United States auspices would mean renewed intervention by the West in the East which would in principle be repugnant to all decent Asian opinion'.[34] At the Bogor conference, Nehru attacked SEATO for introducing 'quite a new conception' in international relations, because unlike NATO, 'members of this organization are not only responsible for their own defense but also for that of areas they may designate outside of it if they so agree; this would mean creating a new form of spheres of influence'. Nehru contrasted it with the Geneva Agreement on Indochina, which he endorsed 'because of its clause that no outside interference will be allowed in Indo-China'.[35] Indian officials described SEATO as 'a roving commission to protect people who did not want to be protected, affecting the sovereignty of the nations of the area'[36] in response to the British overtures to take a more sympathetic view of the proposed pact. This growing emphasis on non-intervention would combine with Nehru's ideas about international order to set the tone and agenda of the Bandung Conference and to create a normative injunction against participation in collective defence pacts in Asia that would prove resilient.

## 'Dulles the Menace': 'Colombo Powers' and SEATO

The Colombo Powers were a group of leaders (of India, Ceylon, Pakistan, Indonesia, and Myanmar) that were officially known as 'Conference of Southeast Asian Prime Ministers'. They were convened for the first time during 28 April–2 May 1954 in Colombo and Kandy by the prime minister of Ceylon (now Sri Lanka) Sir John Kotelawala to discuss the deteriorating situation in Indochina. Part of the reason for the worsening crisis, in the shared view of India and Indonesia at least, was outside intervention in the conflict, especially US support for the French and the anti-communist South Vietnam. But the Colombo Powers' meeting also represented the aspirations of Asia's newly independent countries to play a role in the management of security issues in their own region, rather than leave it to the hands of outside powers. Since Asia did not have a multilateral security organization as yet, the Colombo Powers represented an effort by a group of Asia's nationalist leaders to undertake regional diplomatic action as an alternative security approach to great-power intervention and management.

The Colombo Powers also represented the emerging Asian 'neutralism'. And this was a major reason for Dulles's antipathy towards them. Dulles had condemned non-alignment, an extension of Asian neutralism, in no uncertain terms. Aggravating Dulles's anger was the strong stance of four of the five Colombo Powers against collective defence pacts. India's Nehru articulated this opposition most vigorously. It should be noted that Nehru's position against collective defence pacts was formulated well before the creation of NATO, the first post-war collective defence pact, or the partition of India by the British. Hence, it could not be simply regarded as a self-serving response to Pakistan's membership in both SEATO and CENTO.[37] Nehru opposed collective defence pacts for three reasons: (a) they harked back to great-power dominance at the expense of smaller states, (b) they undermined the sovereignty and even 'dignity' of the newly independent states, and (c) they brought the Cold War to Southeast Asia's (a region which at this point included India) doorsteps. Nehru was also repulsed by the fact that the proposed Southeast Asian collective defence treaty offered to protect not only its signatories against communist aggression and subversion[38] but also states that were not members of the pact.

Nehru's position, which was shared by Myanmar and Indonesia and somewhat less clearly by Ceylon, was inspired by nationalism, ideology, as well as pragmatism. Nehru frequently called his opposition to pacts as a 'realistic' position. It should be noted that in proposing a conference to discuss the creation of the Southeast Asian collective defence system (which was to be held in September 1954), the Eisenhower government was not opposed to the participation of Colombo Powers in the Manila Conference. On the contrary, both Eisenhower and Dulles told the American ambassador George V. Allen in Delhi in May 1954 of 'the extreme importance they attached to carrying Indian and Asian opinion' on the matter of SEATO.[39] Dulles even told the ambassador that 'nothing will suit the Americans better than that the Indians should not only share but actually take the initiative'. And he asked, 'Could they not organise a scheme of collective defense among South East Asian countries with the United States and United Kingdom standing behind in support?' But the matter of inviting India and the other Colombo Powers to the Manila Conference was left to be handled by Britain, apparently at the suggestion of Ambassador Allen. A direct US approach to India, Allen had told Eisenhower and Dulles in May 1954, would not be welcome to India because it regarded the US as a country of 'extreme right', while an approach from Britain would be regarded more favourably since the latter could be expected to have modified the proposal to suit its 'middle position'.[40]

The above shows a fundamental misreading by the Eisenhower administration of India's (along with those of Indonesia, Ceylon, and Myanmar) position on collective defence pacts. This had to do with a failure to appreciate Asian nationalism and its offshoot—Asian neutralism and non-alignment. Moreover, while the Eisenhower administration seemed to be keen on the participation of the Colombo Powers, it did little to assuage Indian concerns about the implications of the proposed pact for Asian security. Whether direct US–India talks might have delivered a different outcome is moot, since one of India's grounds for objections to the treaty, which Ambassador Allen had correctly recognized, was that 'India would never join in any scheme proposed whether in Washington or elsewhere without full consultations with her'.[41]

British Foreign Secretary Anthony Eden wrote to Nehru (as well as the other Colombo Powers) asking them whether they would 'find an invitation to be represented at the proposed meeting [Manila Conference] ... acceptable'.[42] But Dulles had asked the British not to formally *invite* the Colombo Powers to the Manila Conference unless they had indicated prior willingness to accept the invitation.[43] Nehru's position was unambiguous. In his response to Eden, Nehru stated:

We have, after due thought and not always without anxieties, adopted for ourselves on the one hand a policy of what has been sometimes called non-alignment with the power blocs and on the other hand sought to pursue by a conciliatory and peaceful approach and methods to establish and promote reasonably friendly and peaceful relations with countries far and near. To this end, we seek to establish our relations with others on a firm basis on non-interference with each others affairs, non-aggression and the promotion of neighbourliness and conciliation.

The South East Asian and South West Pacific Organisation would be an organic military arrangement the participants in which are some states in the area and a larger number outside [the] area who seek to align themselves with one another for the avowed purpose of safeguarding peace and promoting the stability of the participating countries or of the area as a whole against other countries and peoples in the area or elsewhere. It is therefore far from being a collective peace system; it is rather a military alliance. This may possibly result in the formation of a counter-military alliance. If on the other hand this is not considered the likely result then the raison d'être of the arrangement fails.

Participation in and our lending support to any such policy or arrangement is not merely to abandon our well considered policies on international relations and our basic national outlook but to help to extend the area of the cold war with its attendant progressive armed preparedness and the psychosis of hatred and suspicion in this part of the world.

You have referred to the role of the Asian powers in the defence of South East Asia and mentioned its vital importance. Yet the majority of Asian countries, overwhelming majority of Asian peoples will not be participants in the organisation. Some it may be anticipated would even be strongly opposed to it, thus rendering South East Asia a potentially explosive theatre of the cold war.[44]

## The Bandung Injunction

The secretary-general of the Bandung Conference, Roselan Abdulghani, saw the purpose of the conference as not only being 'to continue the struggle toward a full materialization of national independence',[45] but also 'the formulation and establishment of certain norms for the conduct of present-day international relations and the instruments for the practical application of these norms'.[46] If the ARCs of 1947 and 1949 were mainly concerned with colonialism, the Bandung Conference's goal was to bring about an 'agreement on general principles' of conduct in international affairs.[47] Participants in the Bandung Conference would regard the Declaration on World Peace as a 'most important resolution', because it defined 'the principles regulating their relations with each other and the world at large'.[48]

A review of the debates of the closed sessions of the all-important political committee shows that self-determination issues, such as in Africa, Palestine, and West Irian, attracted less passion and preoccupied the leaders to a much less extent than intramural debates about non-intervention and non-involvement (in regional pacts).[49]

On 23 April 1955, speaking before the political committee of the Asian-African Conference in Bandung, Nehru launched into a bitter denunciation of collective defence pacts being promoted by the US in Asia and the Middle East. Membership in such pacts, argued Nehru, rendered a country a 'camp follower' and deprived it of its 'freedom and dignity'. He stated, 'It is an intolerable thought to me that the great countries of Asia and Africa should come out of bondage into freedom only to degrade themselves or humiliate themselves in this way.'[50] Responding to Nehru's attacks, Prime Minister Mohammad Ali of Pakistan, a member of both CENTO and SEATO, asserted that as 'an independent sovereign nation', Pakistan followed its 'national interest' and did not find it 'necessary for us to justify our actions to anybody except to ourselves'.[51] A more eloquent response to the Indian prime minister's harsh words came the next day from Carlos Romulo, the lead delegate of the Philippines, a SEATO member. In a barely disguised dig at Nehru, Romulo urged delegates to be 'realistic and not be starry-eyed visionaries dreaming utopian dreams'. He reminded Nehru that as a smaller nation, the Philippines could not follow India's path in renouncing collective defence to safeguard its new-found independence.[52]

Nehru drew a link between intervention and traditional European-style rivalries. Consistent with his view that regional pacts under great powers would be 'a continuation of power politics on a vaster scale', and Krishna Menon's proposition cited earlier, that 'collective defence under United States auspices would mean renewed intervention by the West in the East', it is not difficult to conclude that Nehru viewed Cold War pacts as a threat to the sovereignty of Asian and African countries. Indeed at Bandung, Nehru bitterly condemned NATO as 'one of the most powerful protectors of colonialism'.[53] (He was showing his anger over pressures on India from some European members of NATO to leave Portugal alone in Goa.) Advocates of the regional pacts at Bandung, however, countered Nehru's argument that collective defence was necessary against the threat of communist meddling. Romulo pointed out that the communists were routinely violating their own professed doctrine of non-intervention. For the pro-pact group, the key challenge to the sovereignty of the new states was communist subversion and infiltration. They defended SEATO as the first pact to cover such threats. They also argued that the pact could not violate their sovereignty, since the consent of the party concerned was required before the alliance's mutual assistance provisions could be activated. Nehru's position on pacts not unexpectedly invited Pakistan's ire; its prime minister Mohammad Ali took Nehru's comments about the 'camp followers' being 'degraded' and 'humiliated' as an affront to its own sovereignty.

The Bandung Conference resolved the debate over military pacts in the 10 principles contained in its final communiqué. Principle 5 allowed collective defence, but a subclause to principle 6 (6.a) urged the 'Abstention from the use of arrangements of collective defence to serve the particular interests of any of the big powers'.[54] This formulation broadened the meaning of non-intervention by urging newly independent states to cope with superpower interventionism through abstention from the Cold War collective defence pacts. Guy Pauker describes the 'injunction' against the 'use of arrangements of collective defence to serve the particularistic interests of any of the big powers' as the 'most significant aspect' of the conference.[55] The injunction would further discourage Asian participation in collective defence arrangements under the great-power umbrella and had much to do with the delegitimation and ultimate demise of SEATO.

## Who Lost India? The US Cold War Strategy and the Path Not Taken

While Nehru's diplomacy in the lead up to, and during, the Bandung Conference marked a decisive break with India's ties with the US, those who regret this should not lay the blame on Nehru alone. It is also clear that the strategic approach taken by the US under the Eisenhower administration, masterminded by its secretary of state Dulles, extracted substantial and long-term costs both for the US image and influence in Asia and for its relations with India. Despite the considerable initial goodwill generated by the position of the US as a non-colonial power (except the Philippines), its support for decolonization, and the vast amount of economic assistance it provided to the newly independent countries, the dogged pursuit of military pacts to fight communism and its implacable hostility towards alternative approaches promoted by the Colombo Powers alienated important nationalist leaders of Asia and created suspicions about the US intentions.

The ultimate weakness of SEATO was not due to the military ineffectiveness of such pacts as many analysts have claimed.[56] It was due to the diplomatic and political costs and consequences of the Dullesian policy. The Dullesian collective defence policy in Asia had important and adverse regional and global consequences for the US. The US lost a historic opportunity to cultivate Asian nationalism to further its influence in the region. The Dullesian alliance policy caused frictions with Britain, US's most important post-war global ally, over Asian security. A more general result of the Dullesian alliance policy was to accentuate ideological polarization and conflicts in Asia and the Middle East, culminating in the costly descent into the war in Vietnam. An opportunity to engage communist China was missed. Moreover, India, the world's largest democracy, which ought to have been a natural ally of the US, was severely alienated and so it drifted towards the Soviet Union. A similar result could be seen in the Middle East in the US's relations with Egypt, which participated in, and was influenced by, the Bandung debates over collective defence pacts in Asia. Furthermore, the chief object of this alliance policy which sparked such negative outcomes for the US was a failure to a large extent. SEATO was a weak and ineffectual organization that lacked regional legitimacy and participation and eventually collapsed in 1976.

At the global level, the policy of promoting collective defence pacts contributed in no small measure to NAM, which would challenge US interests and policies throughout the Cold War period. The seeds of NAM were planted at Bandung, which the US, along with Britain, actively and openly sought to undermine by influencing the positions—even to the extent of providing anti-communist background papers and draft resolutions to its friends and allies, such as the Philippines, Pakistan, Turkey, Thailand, and Lebanon. It remains an important question that whether NAM would have taken a different, less anti-American course had the administration treated the Asian neutrals with greater empathy and tactfulness, and engaged them directly (rather than relying on Britain).

This would have required the US to engage and support the indigenous efforts by Asian nationalist 'neutrals' led by India, Myanmar, Indonesia, Ceylon, and even Pakistan before SEATO (but not by its Cold War allies such as Elpidio Quirino, Syngman Rhee, and Chiang Kai-shek, whose efforts to create an Asian NATO the Truman administration wisely rejected) to establish a regional security architecture. By aborting its efforts to create a Southeast Asian collective defence system, immediately following the Geneva Agreement on Indochina (the haste was part of the problem), the US would have found more common cause with India, then by far the most influential regional power in South and Southeast Asia, whose opposition to Dullesian pacts did shape the attitude of Indonesia, Myanmar, and Ceylon.

Instead of seeking to manipulate the Bandung Conference through its proxies, the US might have shown more diplomatic tolerance for the event, which was by no means an anti-Western talk fest, and sought dialogue and understanding with the Asian neutrals that were the official sponsors of the meeting. A logical extension of this alternative might have been US support for the creation of a multilateral regional system led by India and Indonesia, involving Japan and Australia and with the eventual participation of the PRC. Instead the US chose to base its East Asian security strategy on SEATO and its bilateral alliances (the 'hub-and-spoke' system).

The collective defence system (by which I mean a multilateral security treaty directed against a commonly perceived and pre-identified threat from outside the group, not to be confused with a collective security system that protects any member state against a threat from within the grouping and where no state is pre-identified as a threat) being promoted by Dulles was not the only policy dealing with the security challenges facing the US in East Asia. Other and, arguably, more important instruments were the US–Japan alliance and other bilateral treaties, but it was an integral element of Dulles's 'Domino theory' and the US response to the perceived threat of communist subversion. It is not clear whether and to what extent President Eisenhower himself supported this policy, although he did share Dulles's antipathy, if not the extent of his revulsion, towards the Colombo Powers and a fundamental suspicion of communist

China. Dulles himself was an avid supporter of collective defence, which he saw as a necessary part of US response to communism.

One interesting question is whether the troubled US–India relationship was the source or the consequence of the mutual personal antipathy between Dulles and Eisenhower on the one hand and Nehru, on the other. But that it was quite pronounced is beyond doubt and of consequence. Eisenhower treated Nehru with courtesy but 'seemed to sense, under the very plausible and highly idealistic tone that he [Nehru] adopted, a pretty tough Oriental who would stick at very little'.[57] Eisenhower also refused an invitation from Nehru to visit India.

Later Dulles would grow even more bitter about the Colombo Powers. He was so put off by the very term 'Colombo Powers' that in 1956, while commenting on the Colombo Plan—conceived in 1950 under the auspices of the British Commonwealth with primarily economic objectives for southern Asia—he welcomed it as 'the best multilateral approach to the problem of the area' but saw 'disadvantages in that the name did not have a very good connotation in this country because of the recent Colombo Conference'. He was referring to the inaugural meeting of the Colombo Powers in 1954.[58] The Eisenhower administration refused to reconsider its policy of promoting military pacts. After Nehru visited the US in December 1956, the British ambassador in Washington who monitored the visit observed:

[I]t is clear that Mr Nehru's arguments against the United States Administration's policy of military alliances and defence pacts carried little conviction, and the interval between Mr Nehru's departure and the proclamation of the 'Eisenhower Doctrine' for the Middle East was no more than barely adequate to meet the needs of ordinary politeness. The United States may be prepared to consider some adjustment of their own policies, for instance over China, but if there is to be a real rapprochement between India and the United States, the major adjustment will have to come from the Indian side.[59]

That Nehru's dislike for Dulles's foreign-policy approach went beyond philosophical disagreements may be discerned from the record of his conversation with Mao in Beijing on 23 October 1954, where he said: 'A man like Dulles is a great menace. He is a Methodist or a Baptist preacher who religiously goes to Church and he is narrow-minded and bigoted. He thinks everyone must agree with him and a man like him might take any move.'[60]

Personal antipathies among leaders need not always cause a decisive breakdown in international relationships. But there can be little question that it was a factor in the US–India relationship. The relationship also suffered due to ideological differences between the US and India and the Eisenhower administration's failure to recognize India's importance in Asia. This brings us to the question of alternative course of action, *the path not taken*. This path had been articulated during the Truman administration both within and outside the administration. That administration had accorded a much greater respect to India. When Nehru visited Washington, D.C., in October 1949, President Truman sent his personal plane to fetch him from London. Truman was at the airport to personally greet Nehru as he stepped off the plane. 'Few visitors arriving in this country for the first time can have received a warmer welcome,' noted a British diplomatic dispatch from its embassy in Washington to London. In his welcome address, Truman noted that '[d]estiny willed it that our country should have been discovered in the search for a new route to yours'.[61]

More importantly, alternative ideas to an American-sponsored collective defence pact for Asia were circulating both within and outside the administration. This called for the US to refrain from setting up an Asian security organization and instead encourage cooperation led by Asian states. A state department Policy Planning Staff paper in March 1949 had argued that the US should avoid setting up an 'area organization' in the Pacific and focus on 'joint or parallel action' until there was 'a pragmatic and desirable basis for intimate association' for a 'formal organization'. In the meantime, the US 'should encourage the Indians, Filipinos and other Asian states to take the public lead in political matters', while its own 'role should be the offering of discreet support and guidance'.[62] Yet the Eisenhower administration, spurred by the Chinese revolution and the Korean War and its own understanding of, and approach to, world affairs, took the opposite course, insisting on a formal collective defence organization for Southeast Asia.

On the related issue of dealing with India, Hubert Humphrey, the newly elected senator from Minnesota, had offered an alternative approach (to the path taken by the Eisenhower administration). He recognized India's strategic location and political influence, the strength of its commitment to democracy and the quality of its leadership. Calling India one of the two great powers of Asia (China being the other), Humphrey noted:

India is strategically located for purposes of geopolitics.... She is a republic with a constitution that points in the direction of individual freedom and responsible government. The recent conference of southeastern Asiatic states [the ARC of 1947 and the conference on Indonesia in January 1949] called by Pandit Nehru is ample testimony as to her strategic and vital role in Asiatic affairs.[63]

In another statement, Humphrey contrasted India with China:

Not only is India a nation of ever-increasing democracy, but her leaders are among the great and wise men of our time.... China is an enigma. No one can be sure what is happening—what we ought to do about it or what will happen if we do nothing. There is no question about India.... In maintaining Asian stability, India is essential.[64]

The Eisenhower administration's policy towards India did recognize its strategic importance and regional influence but not to the extent of considering these to be 'essential' compared to its perceived imperative of military pacts to contain communism. While, as noted above, the administration would have been happy if India had joined SEATO or even led the organization at the behest of the 'free world', this did not mean Indian participation would be regarded as indispensable for the organization to go ahead. The US was determined to go ahead with SEATO with or without India (as well as Indonesia, Myanmar, and Ceylon). Of course, important strategic developments had intervened between 1949 and 1954 (the latter being the year in which the Eisenhower administration could have been said to have 'lost India'), including the communist takeover in China, the Korean War, as well as the French defeat in Dien Bien Phu. But whether these developments called for a policy of promoting pacts at the expense of the policy directions outlined and available since 1949—that is, avoidance of a formal area organization with direct US involvement pending 'a pragmatic and desirable basis for intimate association', and respect for the Indian (as well as Indonesian) positions on regional security—is questionable to say the least. The path not taken would prove costly for the US.

The Eisenhower administration's distrust of the Colombo Powers is also striking because none of the Colombo countries were actually communist allies or sympathizers. On the contrary, they were afraid of communist China and wary of its subversion. Nehru did raise the issue of the fear of China among its neighbours to Chou En-Lai when the latter visited Delhi in 1954 for a remarkable five rounds of conversations on Asian and world affairs. Myanmar had supported Mao's forces during the Chinese revolution, but had later grown wary of Chinese influence on, and support for, its domestic communist groups. Ceylon's Kotelawala turned out to be the harshest critic of communism at Bandung, accusing the Soviet Union of enforcing a new kind of colonialism over Eastern Europe. His formulation that communism might be regarded as a new form of colonialism ruffled even the Chinese premier, who had until then been a model of affability and calm. But Kotelawala was hardly a sympathizer of SEATO. 'What was wrong about SEATO,' he wrote in his memoirs, 'was that the opinion of Free Asia had not been sought in regard to the troubles in Vietnam and Korea…. The Colombo Conference [of April–May 1954] was going to demonstrate to the world that the people of Asia knew what was good for them.'[65]

In sum, the Eisenhower administration failed to appreciate that China's neutral friends were seeking to use their political leverage over China—secured by inviting it to participate in the Bandung Conference—in order to induce restraint on Chinese policies in the region. They were seeking to remind Beijing that it was more Asian than communist and thereby wean it away from the Soviet bloc which the US still regarded as monolithic.

The clash between the Colombo Powers (minus Pakistan) and the Eisenhower administration's collective defence strategy in Asia continued beyond the establishment of SEATO, whose founding was boycotted by the other four Colombo Powers. In fact, the gap between the administration and the segment of Asian opinion represented by the Colombo Powers and their friends (which came to include Egypt's newly anointed president Gamal Abdel Nasser) was further stretched by the Bandung Conference.

The Eisenhower administration was almost immediately and instinctively fearful of the Bandung Conference. It believed that the conference 'will offer Communist China an excellent propaganda opportunity before the representatives of countries not formally committed to either the Free World or the Communist Bloc', and 'enhance the Communist prestige in the area and weaken that of the West'.[66]

Although Dulles publicly took the position that the US attitude towards the Bandung Conference should be one of 'benevolent indifference',[67] the administration's position was anything but indifferent. After the British abandoned their initial idea of encouraging a boycott of the conference by their allies and friends in favour of pushing them to send 'strong' delegations to argue against the neutrals' positions, lest the floor is left entirely to the neutrals and communists, the US, too, followed the course. The administration did, however, adopt a policy of trying 'to discourage attendance discreetly' on the part of Liberia and Ethiopia, as did the British with respect to Ghana and Singapore. In Asia and Arab countries, the administration believed that the 'attendance of friendly governments at the conference would, on balance, be desirable' and hence it moved to encourage them to 'send the strongest possible delegations'.[68]

The US state department issued a guidance to its mission on how to deal with friendly delegations attending Bandung.

> The Guidance advises United States Missions to avoid an open show of interest. They should however seek to put friendly and neutral delegations on their guard against Communist misrepresentations, and against Communist attempts to put down for discussion subjects which could be used to discredit the West. Friendly delegations should be warned against acrimonious exchanges, and advised to take non-provocative lines of argument which 'non-committed' delegations can accept, so that some positively beneficial result could come out of the conference.[69]

In reality, the US did not have to do much since most of the propaganda work was done by the British. The British carried out an extensive effort consisting of supplying 'guidance' papers on subjects ranging from communist colonialism to nuclear disarmament to pro-Western delegations going to Bandung, including, it appears, the supposedly neutral Ceylon. For example, Kotelawala's famously controversial formulation of communism as a new form of colonialism was crafted in London, not Colombo. And there was plenty of coordination between the US and Britain over the effort: 'Her Majesty's Ambassador in Washington should also tell the State Department that we hope that ... British and United States representatives will work in close cooperation and exchange documents. We do not, however, consider it either necessary or desirable that the actual guidance given by our respective representatives to foreign governments should be identical on all points.'[70]

## Nehru: Winner or Loser?

When the Bandung Conference was over, the US ambassador to Indonesia told his Australian counterpart that '[t]he Conference was, in the words of one of his friends there, an 85 per cent victory for us (that is, for the West or the United States).'[71] Among the positive effects from the US viewpoint was the diminishment of Nehru's image (he was believed to have been eclipsed by Chou and came out as arrogant and overbearing during the conference, even losing his temper publicly), the acceptance of the principle of collective defence in the final communiqué of the conference, and what the US might have thought to be the alleged disunity within the neutralist camp while the pro-Western participants functioned as a dynamic, cohesive group. Yet this view could be challenged, both with and without the benefit of hindsight. The Asian-African Conference had the following consequences, which supported Nehru's objectives:

a) Although the principle of '[r]espect for the right of each nation to defend itself singly or collectively, in conformity with the Charter of the United Nations' was accepted by the Bandung Communiqué, it was neutralized by another principle in the final communiqué that called for 'abstention from the use of collective defense to serve the particular interests of any of the big powers'. Moreover, SEATO lost out in the sense that its hopes for acquiring new members were dashed by the Chinese show of moderation at the conference.

b) The advancement of neutralism and its mutation into NAM, Nehru's chief global foreign policy platform. Although Marshal Tito of Yugoslavia did not attend Bandung (he was not invited) and Kwame Nkrumah of Ghana—then still a British dominion, but soon to be the first sub-Saharan African nation to gain independence—was prevented from doing so by the British (which still controlled Ghana's foreign and security policy pending full independence), Bandung had a profound influence on the latter, especially as he organized a group of African countries oriented towards non-alignment.

c) Perhaps the most satisfying outcome for the US was relief that the conference did not turn out to be as much a clear-cut victory for the communists and neutrals as it had feared. But these fears were largely unfounded to begin with and were based on a misreading of the neutrals' intentions.

d) The pacts policy also damaged US relations with Egypt. Prior to the conference, a US state department memo had assessed Egypt's Nasser to be: 'Friendly to West, especially to the United States.' It also noticed that Nasser had, since the Suez agreement and UK arms shipment to Egypt, become 'increasingly friendly' to the UK. However, it also warned that Nasser had become more 'reserved' towards the West since the signing of the Baghdad Pact, which he 'believes will damage Egypt's position of leadership among the Arab states'.[72] This resonated with Nehru's warning before Bandung that the Middle East Pact split the Arab League and made an otherwise friendly Egyptian government wary of US intentions.[73] The warning was prophetic, as within months of the Bandung Conference, Nasser would sign an arms deal with Czechoslovakia and nationalize the Suez Canal, thereby setting the path for a major confrontation with the US and the West.

The alternative path for the US, the path not taken, would have been to: (a) directly engage the Colombo Powers (despite the strong possibility that the British would not have liked this too much, even though they were asking the administration to take the Colombo Powers seriously on matters pertaining to collective defence), (b) abort the creation of SEATO in favour of a more informal approach to regional defence cooperation, (c) show greater tolerance and respect for the Asian-African Conference, and (d) patiently and indirectly encourage the development of an indigenous regional grouping (as did the Johnson administration that encouraged the formation of ASEAN in 1967).

The Dullesian alliance policy was based on fears about communist advance in Asia that seemed quite exaggerated, to say the least, to Asian neutrals like India and Myanmar. The US view of communism as a monolith or the assumption of a tight Sino-Soviet bloc was contrary to the evidence at Bandung that China was prepared to act on its own when it proposed talks with the US on Taiwan without apparently consulting the Soviet Union. The Dullesian obsession with collective military pacts alienated an important segment of Asian and Third World nationalist opinion, the reversal of which proved to be a far more difficult, politically costly, and time-consuming affair. Hence, while Nehru might have shown less charm and tactfulness at Bandung, his foreign policy objectives did shape the outcome of the conference and its consequences for international order.

# Notes and References

1. 'Speech of Jawaharlal Nehru at the Closing Session of the Bandung Conference', in *Asia–Africa Speaks from Bandung* (Jakarta: Department of Foreign Affairs, 1955), p. 175.

2. Ali Sastroamidjojo, *Milestones on My Journey* (Brisbane: University of Queensland Press, 1979), p. 278.

3. Inward Telegram, U.K. High Commission, Ceylon, to Commonwealth Relations Office, 'Afro-Asian Conference', 2 May 1955, FC 1041/828, FO 371/115049, UK National Archives.

4. John K. Franklin, 2006, 'The Hollow Pact: Pacific Security and the Southeast Asia Treaty Organization', PhD dissertation, Texas Christian University.

5. 'Memorandum for the Secretary's File, Subject: Conference with Congressional Leaders Concerning the Crisis in Southeast Asia', 3 April 1954 (5 April 1954, Dulles Papers, Library of Congress, Washington, D.C.).

6. 'Memorandum of Conversation with the President', 19 May 1954 (Dulles Papers, Library of Congress, Washington, D.C.).

7. A total of 29 countries participated in the Bandung Conference held between 18 and 24 April 1955. They included the five 'Colombo Powers'—Myanmar, Ceylon, India, Indonesia, and Pakistan—as well as Afghanistan, Cambodia, China, Egypt, Ethiopia, the Gold Coast (Ghana), Iran, Iraq, Japan, Jordan, Laos, Lebanon, Liberia, Libya, Nepal, the Philippines, Saudi Arabia, Sudan, Syria, Thailand, Turkey, the Vietnam Democratic Republic, South Vietnam (later reunified with the Democratic Republic of Vietnam), and Yemen (Republic of Yemen).

8. Jawaharlal Nehru, *The Discovery of India*, 23rd Impression (New Delhi: Oxford University Press, 2003), p. 539.

9. Nehru quoted in V.S. Mani, 'An Indian Perspective on the Evolution of International Law', in *Asian Yearbook of International Law, 2000*, Vol. 9 (Netherlands: Brill, 2004), p. 66.

10. Judith Brown, *Nehru: A Political Life* (New Haven: Yale University Press, 2003), p. 246.

11. Nehru's interview cited in B. Shiva Rao, *India's Freedom Movement: Some Notable Figures* (New Delhi: Orient Longman, 1972), pp. 139–40.

12. Mohammed Ayoob, *The Third World Security Predicament: State-Making, Regional Order and the International System* (Boulder: Lynne Rienner, 1995), p. 104.

13. Cecil Crabb, *The Elephants and the Grass: A Study of Non-Alignment* (New York: Praeger, 1967), p. 67.

14. Menon quoted in Sisir Gupta, *India and Regional Integration in Asia* (Mumbai: Asia Publishing House, 1964), p. 59.

15. *Speeches of Jawaharlal Nehru, 1953–57* (New Delhi: Government of India, 1957), p. 20.

16. *Speeches of Jawaharlal Nehru*, p. 60.

17. Bharat Karnad, *Nuclear Weapons and Indian Security: The Realist Foundations of Strategy* (New Delhi: Macmillan, 2002), p. 80.

18. As Martha Finnemore and Kathryn Sikkink write: '[F]requently heard arguments about whether behavior is norm-based or interest-based miss the point that norm conformity can often be self-interested, depending on how one specifies interests and the nature of the norm.' See Martha Finnemore and Kathryn Sikkink, 1998, 'International Norm Dynamics and Political Change', *International Organization*, 52(4): 887–917.

19. For example, Jaswant Singh has criticized Nehru's 'idealistic romanticism'. See Jaswant Singh, *Defending India* (Basingstoke: Macmillan, 1999), p. 34.

   K. Subrahmanyam argues that Nehru was influenced by Gandhian non-violence during the freedom struggle and was thus not attuned to defence preparedness. Subrahmanyam cited in Singh, *Defending India*, p. 41. And drawing upon Nehru's own words that India would provide '"leadership [to] a large part of Asia"…without joining in "the old game of power politics on a gigantic scale", or having anything to do with …"realism and practical politics"', Bharat Karnad concludes that the Nehruvian vision 'eschewed all the means of traditional statecraft and international relations, like a strong military, primary and subsidiary alliances, buffer states, security *cordons sanitaire*, secret understandings and defence pacts, and still hoped to lead'. See

Bharat Karnad, 'India's Weak Geopolitics and What to Do about It', in Bharat Karnad (ed.), *Future Imperiled: India's Security in the 1990s and Beyond* (New Delhi: Viking, 1994), p. 21.

20. Michael Brecher, *Nehru: A Political Biography* (New Delhi: Oxford University Press, 1999), pp. 555, 584.

21. Mani, 'An Indian Perspective on the Evolution of International Law', p. 66.

22. As Karnad points out, 'Nehru admitted three main influences on his foreign policy thinking. Derived from his experiences during the freedom struggle and his study of history, these were anti-imperialism, anti-racism and, specially, the Gandhian emphasis on truth and morality as arbiters of individual and collective behaviour.' See Karnad, 'India's Weak Geopolitics and What to Do about It', p. 32. Hence, Karnad concludes: 'Little surprise that he reacted viscerally to geopoliticians.' K. Subrahmanyam points to the influence of Gandhian non-violence on Nehru's world view and approach to defence. See K. Subrahmanyam, 'Evolution of India's Defence Policy 1947–64', in *A History of the Congress Party* (New Delhi: All India Congress Committee and Vikas Publishing House, 1990).

23. This is consistent with the notions of 'grafting' and 'localization', which hold that the impact of emerging norms is facilitated by the existence of a prior receptive norm. See Amitav Acharya, 2004, 'How Ideas Spread: Whose Norms Matter? Norm Localization and Institutional Change in Asian Regionalism', *International Organization,* 58(2): 239–75.

24. A. Appadorai, 1979, 'The Asian Relations Conference in Perspective', *International Studies*, 18(3): 275–85.

25. Appadorai, 'The Asian Relations Conference in Perspective', p. 279.

26. Appadorai, 'The Asian Relations Conference in Perspective', p. 280.

27. B. Shiva Rao's interview with Nehru, transcript found in the files on the Asian Relations Conference, ICWA, New Delhi, 28 January 2003.

28. Appadorai, 'The Asian Relations Conference in Perspective', p. 4; George H. Jansen, *Afro-Asia and Non-Alignment* (London: Faber and Faber, 1966), pp. 43, 48, 49.

29. 'Southeast Asian Prime Ministers' Conference: Minutes of Meetings and Documents of the Conference', Colombo, April 1954 (hereafter cited as 'The Colombo Conference Minutes').

30. 'The Colombo Conference Minutes'.

31. Abdulghani, *The Bandung Spirit,* p. 49.

32. 'Joint Communique by the Prime Ministers of Burma, Ceylon, India, Indonesia and Pakistan', in 'Conference of the Prime Ministers of the Five Colombo Countries, Bogor, December 1954, Minutes of Meetings and Documents of the Conference' (hereafter cited as 'The Bogor Conference Minutes').

33. 'The Bogor Conference Minutes', First Session, p. 6.

34. Inward Telegram, UK High Commissioner in Delhi to Commonwealth Relations Office, 14 April 1954, FO 371-112053, File F1071/229, UK National Archives.

35. 'The Bogor Conference Minutes', Second Session, p. 6.

36. Cited in Gupta, *India and Regional Integration in Asia,* p. 59.

37. On this, see Acharya, *Whose Ideas Matter?* Nehru was also irked by Portugal's reference to the NATO umbrella in dealing with India on the issue of Goa, then still a Portuguese colony.

38. Dulles was concerned not just about communist subversion, as is commonly assumed, but also about 'armed attack and invasion by forces which serve international communism' against the State of Vietnam, Laos, and Cambodia. See 'Declaration of Common Purpose' (given informally to Denis Allen [UK] as indicating present US thinking), (12 April 1954, Dulles Papers, Library of Congress, Washington, D.C.).

39. This is quoted from a British memo based on a conversation with Allen. See Inward Telegram, UK Foreign Office, UK High Commissioner in India to Commonwealth Relations Office, 27 May 1954, FO-371-111863, UK National Archives.

40. Inward Telegram, UK Foreign Office, UK High Commissioner in India to Commonwealth Relations Office, 27 May 1954, FO-371-111863, UK National Archives.

41. Inward Telegram, UK Foreign Office, UK High Commissioner in India to Commonwealth Relations Office, 27 May 1954, FO-371-111863, UK National Archives.

42. Inward Telegram, UK Foreign Office, UK High Commissioner in India to Commonwealth Relations Office, 2 August 1954, FO 371-11875, UK National Archives.

43. Inward Telegram, UK Foreign Office, UK High Commissioner in India to Commonwealth Relations Office, 2 August 1954, FO 371-11875, UK National Archives.

44. Inward Telegram, UK Foreign Office, UK High Commissioner in India to Commonwealth Relations Office, 2 August 1954, FO 371-11875, UK National Archives.

45. Abdulghani, *The Bandung Spirit,* p. 72.

46. Abdulghani, *The Bandung Spirit*, p. 103.

47. *The Report of the Arab League on the Bandung Conference* (Cairo: League of the Arab States, 1955), p. 23.

48. *The Report of the Arab League*, p. 151.

49. This made Arab and African representatives less than satisfied with Bandung, and might have contributed to their lack of enthusiasm for a permanent Asian-African regional organization.

50. Nehru's speech in the political committee dated 23 April 1955 cited in 'Proceedings of the Political Committee Meetings of the Asian-African Conference', Bandung, 20–24 April 1955 (hereafter cited as 'Bandung Political Committee Proceedings').

51. Mohammed Ali's speech in the political committee dated 23 April 1955 cited in 'Bandung Political Committee Proceedings'.

52. Mohammed Ali's speech in the political committee dated 23 April 1955 cited in 'Bandung Political Committee Proceedings'.

53. 'Bandung Political Committee Proceedings'.

54. 'Final Communiqué of the Asian-African Conference', available at http://franke.uchicago.edu/Final_Communique_Bandung_1955.pdf (accessed on 15 November 2016).

55. Guy J. Pauker, *The Bandung Conference* (Cambridge: Centre for International Studies, MIT, 1955), p. 18.

56. In a refreshing new assessment, Franklin concludes: 'Ultimately, SEATO did fail, but not due to military reasons. The treaty failed because the Eisenhower administration mismanaged its Asian policy.' See Franklin, 'The Hollow Pact', p. 8.

57. 'Extract from the Prime Minister's Note of His Conversation with the President in Bermuda', PREM 11/1877, UK National Archives.

58. 'Memorandum of Conversation with Mr John Cowles' (13 May 1956, Dulles Papers, Library of Congress, Washington, D.C.); 'Memorandum of Conversation between the Secretary and Governor Stassen, August 24, 1954' (25 August 1954, Dulles Papers, Library of Congress, Washington, D.C.).

59. 'Mr Nehru's Visit to the United States', Sir Harold Caccia to Mr Selwyn Lloyd, 15 January 1957, PREM 11/1877, UK National Archives.

60. Jawaharlal Nehru, *Selected Works of Jawaharlal Nehru*, Vol. 27 (New Delhi: Jawaharlal Nehru Memorial Fund, 2000), p. 34.

61. 'Visit of Pandit Nehru to the United States', 31 October 1949, FO-371-76096, UK National Archives.

62. Cited in Chintamani Mahapatra, *American Role in the Origin and Growth of ASEAN* (New Delhi: ABC Publishing, 1990), p. 48.

63. Hubert Humphrey, 'American Foreign Policy in the Asiatic Area', Statement before the United States Senate, 11 April 1949, *Congressional Record* (Appendix), 25 April 1949.

64. Hubert Humphrey, 'India—A Bulwark of Democracy', Statement before the United States Senate, 8 April 1949, *Congressional Record* (Appendix), 25 April 1949.

65. P.K. Balachandran, 'Kotelawala Placed Sri Lanka on the World Map', *Daily News* (Colombo), 5 October 2006, available at http://www.dailynews.lk/2006/05/10/fea01.asp (accessed on 27 April 2009).

66. British Embassy, Tokyo, 'Extract from the United States Intelligence Report No. 4448 of 6/1/55', 17 Jan 1955, D2231/85, FO 371/116977, UK National Archives.

67. *Washington Post*, 6 May 1955, D2231/235, FO 371/116980, UK National Archives.

68. Roger Makins, British Embassy, Washington, to Foreign Office, London, 27 January 1955, D2231/78, FO 371/116976, UK National Archives.

69. Roger Makins, British Embassy, Washington, to Foreign Office, London, 'Addressed to Foreign Office Telegram No. 132 Saving

of February 26, 1955', 26 February 1955, D2231/119, FO 371/116977, UK National Archives.

70. Foreign Office, London, to Ankara, 15 March 1955, D2231/136, FO 371/116978, UK National Archives.

71. Personal Impressions by the Australian Ambassador to Indonesia, W.R. Crocker: Far Eastern Dept., DO35-6099: Afro-Asian Conference, 44/232, UK National Archives.

72. British Embassy, Washington, to Foreign Office, London, US Department of State Intelligence Report No. 6830.3, 'Developments Relating to the Bandung Conference', 18 March 1955, D2231/283, FO 371/116982, UK National Archives.

73. In a speech to the Indian Parliament just before the Bandung Conference, Nehru had warned of the consequences of the Baghdad Pact: 'Take the effect of this very Middle East pact [Baghdad Pact].... The first result has been the weakening and also the breaking up of the Arab League, which has brought the Arab countries together for cooperative effort. The second effect is that there is great bitterness. Egypt, for instance, is greatly opposed to this.' He also mentioned that the signing of the pact had led to a change of government in Syria, with the new government 'very much opposed to these pacts', thus implying that the pacts are radicalizing politics in the region. See Jawaharlal Nehru, 'India and World Affairs', in Ravindar Kumar and H.Y. Sharada Prasad (eds), *Selected Works of Jawaharlal Nehru*, Vol. 28 (New Delhi: Jawaharlal Nehru Memorial Fund, 2000), p. 310.

# 4.

# Chou En-Lai at Bandung: The Origins of Sino-Indian Rivalry?

'It was in Bandung that the seeds of Indo-Chinese misunderstanding were sown,' writes B.K. Nehru, a senior Indian government official who accompanied Jawaharlal Nehru to the Asian-African Conference in Bandung in 1955. Elaborating,

B.K. Nehru (a relative of the prime minister) contends that the misunderstanding might have had two sources:

> This was Chou-en-Lai's first exposure to the international community. Jawaharlal was then a recognized world leader. He consequently took it upon himself to 'introduce' the lesser known Prime Minister of China. Chou-en-Lai seems to have regarded this as an attitude of condescension and 'big brotherliness' towards China and resented it.... Though relations remained outwardly cordial and *'Hindi-Chini'* continued for some time to be *'Bhai-Bhai'*, there was an unmistakable rift in the lute. The roots of this may well have been as much in the differing interests of the two countries as in the umbrage taken by a powerful personality at what he considered as being patronized.[1]

If Chou did really take umbrage at Nehru's patronizing introductions, he certainly made little show of it during the conference or in his post-conference debriefings. B.K. Nehru might also have mentioned that aside from competing interests, the Bandung episode was also symptomatic of the differing identities of two Asian powers that were emerging from centuries of decline. Almost five decades after the Bandung Conference, in a personal conversation with me on 22 April 2004, Roselan Abdulghani, the secretary-general of the conference, noted that to wean China away from the Soviet Union was one of the main diplomatic objectives of Indonesia in proposing the Bandung Conference. Making China a responsible Asian power and player was also a goal pursued by Nehru.

The Bandung Conference was the first major international conference in which communist China participated without the presence of the Soviet Union. The Chinese leadership had no doubt that 'the participation of the People's Republic of China will greatly affect the conference'.[2] Bandung provided China with an unprecedented opportunity to engage with its Asian neighbours and dispel suspicions and fears about Chinese intentions. As a secret Chinese planning document for the conference put it, the Chinese delegation to the conference led by Premier Chou was to 'make effort to let the participating countries know our peace aim and good-neighbour policy so as to spur some of the Asian states to dispel their doubts and fears of China as far as possible'.[3] The Chinese placed utmost emphasis on behaving and performing well at the conference. They included a Muslim delegate to demonstrate religious tolerance under the communist regime. Chinese experts advised the delegation under Chou about the necessity of wearing Western clothes at the conference.[4] This was carried out faithfully to great effect by the Chinese delegation, whose heroic performance has been documented in the popular film *Zhou Enlai in Bandung*.

## Nehru: Founder of the 'Engaging China' Strategy

China's presence at the Bandung Conference was a triumph for Nehru and his policy of 'engaging' China. Nehru's approach to China was conceived in the context of his regionalist approach to Asian security, evident in his leadership of two previous Asian conferences: the ARC of 1947, an unofficial event that was attended by the Republic Of China (which had offered to host the second such conference that was never held), and the Conference on Indonesia in 1949, which discussed Indonesian independence. By the time of Bandung, however, much in the region had changed: a communist regime had come to power in China, the Cold War was in full swing after the Korean War, and the US was escalating its intervention in Indochina in response to the defeat of the French. The main issue was no longer just decolonization, but also great-power intervention. The strategy of containment and military alliances pursued by the Eisenhower administration was in full swing with the establishment of SEATO in September 1954. India—which was only the second country after Myanmar, outside the communist bloc, to recognize the PRC—opposed US Secretary of State Dulles's policy of setting up military pacts. This position was inspired by Nehru's general philosophical dislike of great-power spheres of influence, which he took SEATO to be. But it was also due to his specific approach to dealing with communist China, which rejected containment and favoured a policy that in contemporary Asian diplomatic parlance might be called a policy of engagement or 'constructive engagement'.

Nehru's alternative engagement policy was premised on several assumptions. The first was that China's main goal was regime legitimation through rapid economic development, and that it was for this that it needed a period of peace and stability in its neighbourhood. At a press conference in New Delhi on 13 November 1954 following his visit to China, Nehru said:

> I am convinced that China, entirely for its own sake, wants peace, wants time to develop its country and thinks in terms of at least three or four five-year plans—fifteen or twenty years' time to lay the foundations of a socialist state. So all this question of aggression, internal or external, has to be seen in that context, of their not desiring to get entangled.[5]

A second assumption underlying his approach was that China had serious concerns about the US policy in the region, which threatened Chinese regime security as well as its claim on Taiwan. Moreover, the US was getting China's neighbours involved in this plot through containment measures such as SEATO. Hence, it was important for China to know more about the policies of its neighbours. As an official account of Nehru's statements at the second session of the Bogor Conference goes:

> The Indian Prime Minister was convinced that China is anxious to avoid war, anxious even to avoid friction and possibilities

of conflict. China urgently desires peace, because she is passionately concerned about the problem of economic uplift. She would like to be left in peace and to develop relations with other countries. So no attack will come from China. She fears, however, that the neighbouring countries could be used to endanger her security. It is important for her to know what the neighbouring countries are doing. That is why the Geneva Conference is so important, because of its clause that no outside interference will be allowed in Indo-China.[6]

The same report cites Nehru questioning the prevailing American assumption of international communism as a monolithic entity. He recognized the contingent nature of the Sino-Soviet alliance. Hence:

As for China, she was logically and practically thrown in the arms of Russia. The Prime Minister of India reminded the Conference of the history of China during the Second World War and after, when she had to cope with the Korean War and the embargo. During the War when Chiang Kai-shek was in power, Russia even told Mao Tse-tung to tone down. Of course it became a different matter after Mao's success. The Indian Prime Minister was of the opinion, after what he saw in China, that the people in China are essentially Chinese.[7]

This led to Nehru's belief that the best chance of living in peace with China was through a regional normative framework of interaction in which China's neighbours would not only become familiar with the Chinese regime but also be assured of its peaceful intentions, while China itself felt comfortable in dealing with its neighbours. Such a framework, however, would have to be developed around certain norms of international conduct, especially the Westphalian principle of non-interference in the internal affairs of states. The prospects for regional order depended not on Cold War pacts such as SEATO, but on a regionalist framework through which China made a commitment of non-interference in return for a place at the Asian table. Nehru believed that the elements of such a framework had already been established in the form of the Five Principles of Peaceful Coexistence developed as part of a Sino-Indian agreement over Tibet.[8] Nehru believed that this would constrain China from exporting its ideology and arrest the spread of communism in Asia, including India. 'The establishment of friendly relations with China on the basis of the Five Principles would definitely tend to weaken the danger of internal communism.'[9]

The proposed Bandung Conference fitted well into this Nehruvian strategy. While Nehru, chastened by his earlier experiments at Asian regionalism, such as the ARCs, was initially sceptical of the idea of an even wider Asian-African Conference, he eventually succumbed to Indonesian pressure for holding such a conference. He saw in the proposed Bandung Conference an opportunity to introduce communist China to the region and pursue his normative engagement strategy. To his mind, there was no doubt that China had to be invited to the forum. When the Bogor Summit of the Colombo Powers in December 1954 discussed the issue of Chinese participation and the prime minister of Sri Lanka expressed some misgivings about inviting China, Nehru intervened forcefully. According to a note written by Nehru on the Bogor Conference:

It has been said that if the People's Government of China is invited, this will displease the U.S.A. and I understand that some pressure has been brought to bear on some of the countries which might be invited, in regard to China. I feel that it would be out of the question for us to leave out China. Most of us are pressing for the inclusion of China in the UN and for us not to invite China would be opposed to our entire policy. It would also be a little absurd for Asian countries to meet and the biggest Asian country to be left out. Nobody can accuse us of inviting countries belonging to one group of nations when we are inviting, at the same time, the other group fully; but we will be accused of partiality if we do not invite China and there will be no answer to that accusation. Therefore, I feel that China has to be invited even though this might displease some people. It must be remembered that we are likely to invite Japan, Thailand, the Philippines and Turkey which are definitely aligned with the opposite group. Some countries of Western Asia may also perhaps be said to be inclined that way.[10]

It is important to bear in mind that China and India did not agree on all matters of geopolitical significance related to the conference. The areas of disagreement included the need for setting up a permanent regional organization out of the Bandung Conference. China supported such a move as early as in January 1955. As an internal Chinese official document noted: 'It seems that we do not have to take the initiative to raise this issue, but can encourage other countries to propose the establishment of a permanent institution for economic and cultural cooperation or the permanent institution of Asian-African Conference in the meeting.'[11]

But the issue came up during a conversation among Chou, Nehru, and U Nu in Bandung on 16 April 1955, apparently to coordinate their positions at the conference. Nehru, unaware that this was an official Chinese goal, expressed himself against a permanent regional organization. According to the minutes of that meeting:

Nehru said, now some people [believed] that political and economic permanent institutions should be set up after the conference. In regard to the political permanent institution, he said that the 29 countries must doubtlessly have their representatives, but the 29 countries had much difference in opinion so that it was unimaginable how this institution would effectively perform its function.... He said again that the permanent institution must have [a] headquarter, and if the headquarter was in Jakarta, many of the participating countries had no representatives in Indonesia....

U Nu said that ... the only purpose of this conference was to provide an opportunity for the delegations of various countries to meet. He continued that this conference could announce several general principles to the world, and after this conference, the countries supporting these principles would hold another conference and then set up a permanent institution. He continued that this institution would consist of those countries with concerted views on important issues and be consequently effective; however, the present conference could not make any resolutions on important issues and even if it set up a permanent institution, this institution would have no effective way to implement the resolutions....

Premier Chou said that if the conference could succeed in two matters, it would be of great significance. The first was to use a document, no matter what form it would be, to express our common aspirations, including the Five Principles stressed by Prime Minister Nehru in Rangoon talks. The second was to set up a permanent institution. We could find a way that would not bind the participating countries too tightly, such as a liaison institution. Such an institution could facilitate the governments of the participating countries to contact each other; especially some of the participating countries of the conference were not the UN members. If the headquarters of the institution was set up in Jakarta ... the participating countries with diplomatic envoys there could join the institution, and the countries without diplomatic envoys in Jakarta could dispatch their secretaries to join it, and the too faraway countries might contact by mail.... Such [an] institution not only did not contradict with the UN Charter, but also was in conformity with the purpose of this conference, i.e. the friendly and good-neighborly relations among the Asian-African countries.

Nehru still doubted that such institution could be effective and said that it was not wise if the conference did anything to enter into rivalry with UN. U Nu said again that even if an institution could be set up after the conference, it could not win respect from the world due to its ineffectiveness so that it would be much better to form a small but effective institution later.[12]

China implicitly disagreed with India's soft stance on colonialism. From China's perspective: 'The eight-item agenda put forward by India confines the colonialist issue to the specific colonies and trustee states, which seem to have an attempt of absolving US from the blame. We should still take US as the main target of attack.'[13]

China was wary of India's willingness to compromise on the Five Principles. The Chinese goal was to 'strive to confirm the Five Principles in the final communique or declaration'. Nehru preferred to tread softly, aware that the Five Principles were viewed with suspicion by many Asian nations as a communist ploy, reflecting the policy of the Soviet Union—a view that would be expressed by the pro-Western nations during the Bandung Conference. The Chinese anticipated that India might soft-pedal the principles, but were willing to accept this if it facilitated a compromise at the conference. Hence according to a Chinese document: 'India may propose to list both the Five Principles and the UN Charter side by side, or list the Five Principles in a changed appearance, but not the essence in order to reach [a] unanimous agreement. If such happens, we may compromise.'[14]

China also had some misgivings about Indian attempts at dominating both the conference and the emerging Afro-Asian bloc. The Chinese appeared to be concerned about India's growing international influence, including in the Middle East. But they were also careful about not competing with India, realizing how much they needed Nehru's support to make their debut at an Asian regional conference. One Chinese document urged the delegation to 'take a special cautious attitude towards India in order to avoid the impression of contending for leadership with it, which will give a chance to the imperialism and its lackeys to sow discord between China and India'.[15]

## Chinese Expectations and Apprehensions

China saw the Bandung Conference to be both an opportunity and a challenge. When the plan for holding such a conference became known, China was not sure whether it would be invited. Among the five Colombo Powers that sponsored the conference, India, Indonesia, and Myanmar were seen by Beijing as likely 'to invite our country to take part in and Pakistan and Ceylon may oppose us'.[16] Another Chinese report noted that while Indonesia in August 1954 had sent invitations for attendance to 17 countries, including the seven member states of the Arab League, Abyssinia, Iran, Afghanistan, Pakistan, Ceylon, Myanmar, Thailand, and the Philippines, China was not on the list. This was attributed to the fact that China was not a member of the UN. It did, however, hold out hope that China would eventually be invited.[17]

As noted, there was some disagreement among the sponsoring Colombo Powers (India, Pakistan, Ceylon, Myanmar, and Indonesia) over whether China should be invited, but this was quickly dispelled by Nehru. When the invitation did arrive, China saw it as a huge diplomatic opportunity. In his reply to the Indonesian premier Ali Sastroamidjojo, Chou noted while accepting the invitation:

> The Asian-African Conference is the first of its kind in history convened to promote goodwill and co-operation among the countries of Asia and Africa, to explore and advance their mutual as well as common interests and to establish and further friendliness and neighbourly relations.... The convocation of this Conference also affords a good opportunity for making it possible for the Asian and African countries with different social

systems to coexist in peace under the principle that the form of government and the way of life of any one country should in no way be subject to interference by another, and also for these countries to make contributions towards the promotion of world peace and co-operation.[18]

Still, China remained concerned about pressure from Asian countries, including its good friend India, to adhere to a strict doctrine of non-interference. The Chinese believed that Nehru's push for non-interference was as much directed at Chinese subversion as at Western intervention. A pre-conference memo from the Ministry of Foreign Affairs noted that Nehru's interpretation of 'one of the Five Principles related to noninterference ... admitted that ... interference with other nations' affairs by communism was also valid [concern]'. This, along with Ceylon's demand that the Bandung Conference must 'absolutely adhere to mutual noninterference' and that this would require that 'China should guarantee against any subversive activities in the form of penetration', could be seen as evidence 'that some states in Asia did have doubts towards our country, which were taken advantage of by U.K. and the U.S.A. for rumour-mongering or provocation'.[19]

But the Chinese had no plan to abandon their stance of distinguishing between interference in the internal affairs of a state and support for communist ideology and party-to-party relations. This was clear from a document:

> The so-called Communist subversive activities: Strictly distinguish the internal affairs from the Communist ideology.... If somebody mentions this issue, we should point out that the internal affairs [of a country] is not allowed to be interfered with, but the influence and spread of the Communist ideology can not be prevented; revolution can not be exported, but at the same time the people's common will of any country is also not allowed to be interfered with by any external forces.[20]

What were the Chinese objectives for the conference? A top-secret working plan signed by Chou on 13 January 1955 outlined five key objectives:

Task (Added by Zhou Enlai: forbid using the atomic weapons, hydrogen weapons, chemical weapons and all the exterminating weapons.)

(1) Develop the Five Principles of Peaceful Co-Existence, promote the friendly relations among the Asian-African countries, expand the peaceful zone, oppose the formation of the warring cliques, and relax the international tension.
(2) Support the movements of national independence, oppose colonialism, the interference in the internal affairs and the violation of the sovereignty of other countries.
(3) Develop the normal trade and economic cooperation, and strengthen the cultural exchange among the participating countries.
(4) Strive to establish the diplomatic relations with a number of Asian-African countries.[21]

The same working plan divided the participants at Bandung into four categories and adopted the following goals for each of them:

In addition to China and the Democratic Republic of Vietnam, the participating countries may be generally divided in several categories as following:

(1) 'Peaceful and neutral' countries
India, Burma, Indonesia and Afghanistan.
(2) Close to 'peaceful and neutral' countries
Egypt, the Sudan, Nepal, Syria, Lebanon, Yemen, Saudi Arabia, Jordan, the Gold Coast, Cambodia, Laos, Ceylon and Pakistan.
(3) Close to 'anti-peaceful and anti-neutral' countries
Japan, South Vietnam, Libya, Liberia, Iran, Iraq, and Abyssinia.
(4) 'Anti-peaceful and anti-neutral' countries

Thailand, the Philippines and Turkey.

Under the general line of expanding the peace and united front, it seems that we should unite the countries of the first category, win over the second, influence the third and isolate the fourth in the conference.

Outside the conference, we should select some key countries from each category as our work target and solve some specific issues. Besides the Colombo countries, Egypt and Japan are the other key countries.[22]

A key goal of the Chinese was to counter the US influence. Beijing was concerned about Western attempts to sabotage the conference. 'Apart from performing the above conspired activities, the U.S. might as well incite other countries like the Philippines, Thailand and Pakistan to attend the Asia–Africa Conference (AAC) in order to impose pressure from both the outside and the inside, so that the effect on peaceful strengths would be minified to force them to give in.'[23] 'In the process of the conference, we should concentrate our efforts to isolate the American force, actively win over the "peaceful and neutral" countries, and try to split the countries closely following USA and hostile to China.'[24]

On the evening of the conference, a 'Group of Experts' consulted by the Chinese government outlined some more specific goals for China to work towards at the conference: 'To strive for establishment of diplomatic relations between China and other participating nations, especially between China and Egypt; to make the most of every opportunity to contact with delegates from different participants, and even invite some delegations to pay a visit to China, so as to expand our political influence.'[25] It would seem that by this time, China had recognized the potential for developing ties with Egypt, which was still thought to be under Western influence. This would assume considerable significance during the conference, where

President Nasser would turn out to be a popular and influential figure, and a few months later, when Egypt would sign an arms deal with Czechoslovakia.

Another key Chinese objective was resolving the dual-nationality issue, beginning with Indonesia. One document, referring to the 'Overseas Chinese' issue noted: 'First of all, reach an all-round agreement with Indonesia, and then seize opportunities to discuss the solution of the overseas Chinese issue with other countries on the basis of this agreement.'[26] Another stressed the political benefits of this move: 'We might as well strive for a signing ceremony for dual nationality with Indonesia before the conference; and try our best to relieve the doubts of Southeast Asia countries and increase their trust on us.'[27]

## Chou En-Lai's Performance

Chou En-Lai emerged as what Nehru called the 'star performer' of the Bandung Conference. But this did not mean he did not have to make some major concessions. One of the concessions involved dropping the term 'peaceful coexistence', which came under fierce attack from the pro-Western camp (both 'anti-peaceful and anti-neutral' countries and 'close to anti-peaceful and anti-neutral' countries) that considered it a communist ploy. Chou quickly came up with a new formulation—'living together in peace'—which subsumed the Five Principles while changing the overall phrasing, as follows:

> In order to achieve and to safeguard the national independence of the Asian and African countries, in order to maintain and strengthen international peace,
> The Asian-African Conference declares
> We Asian and African countries
> Are determined to *live together in peace* and in friendly cooperation with one another on the basis of mutual respect for the right of self-determination of peoples, mutual respect

for sovereignty and territorial integrity, non-aggression, non-interference in each other's internal affairs, and equality and mutual benefit,

Advocate the settlement of international disputes by peaceful means,

Call on the big powers to reach agreement on the reduction of armaments, and

Maintain that atomic energy be used only for peaceful purposes and demand the prohibition of the use of atomic weapons and other weapons of mass destruction.[28]

A second area where China came under intense pressure was from a member of what the Chinese called 'close to peaceful and neutral' countries—Ceylon. This occurred during discussions on the 'problem of dependent peoples' in the all-important political committee of the conference and was somewhat unexpected, since the Chinese had anticipated criticism mostly from the pro-Western camp, rather than from the 'neutrals' group, of which Ceylon was considered to be a member. Yet Ceylonese Prime Minister Sir John Kotelawala's description of communism as a new form of colonialism and his reference to the east European countries as de facto colonies of the Soviet Union took Chou (and Nehru, who castigated Sir John for not consulting him, only to be told by the latter that he did not expect Nehru to clear with him before making speeches) by surprise. Chou's response the next day to this attack was conciliatory and prompted a moderate response from Sir John, but the issue continued to fester and came close to wrecking the whole conference. A joint proposal presented by Libya, Sudan, Iran, Iraq, Lebanon, Pakistan, the Philippines, and Turkey on 22 April 1955 regarding the problem of dependent peoples had proposed the following language:

The Asian-African Conference, having considered the problem of dependent peoples and the evils resulting from *domination, exploitation and subjugation in any of their forms*

1. declares its faith in the dignity and worth of the human person, and in the right of peoples to freedom and independence;

2. condemns all modes of political, social, economic, cultural, intellectual and spiritual domination of peoples;

3. condemns all types of colonialism, including international doctrines resorting to the methods of force, infiltration and subversion;

4. calls upon every member of this Conference as well as every other nation to refrain from the practice of colonialism in any form.[29]

The reference to 'all types of colonialism, including international doctrines resorting to the methods of force, infiltration and subversion' was, of course, an affront to China. In the end, the Chinese won an interpretive victory of sorts—thanks to a formulation attributed to Egypt's Nasser—which would remove the last remaining obstacle to the conference statement (communiqué) that Chou had regarded as one of the two outcomes signalling the success of the conference. (The other, a standing institution, was never seriously pursued at the conference, except by the less significant economic committee). This compromise phrasing prepared by a subcommittee on Problems of Dependent Peoples set up by Ali Sastroamidjojo (who, as the chairman of the conference, had resorted to the habit of creating a subcommittee every time a deadlock loomed) substituted colonialism in 'all its forms' with colonialism in 'all its manifestations'. It read as follows:

The Asian-African Conference discussed the problems of dependent peoples and colonialism and the evils arising from the subjection of peoples to alien subjugation, domination and exploitation ... the Conference is agreed:

(a) in declaring that colonialism in all its manifestations is an evil which should speedily be brought to an end;

(b) in affirming that the subjection of peoples to alien subjugation, domination and exploitation constitute[s] a denial
of fundamental human rights, is contrary to the Charter of
the United Nations and is an impediment to the promotion
of world peace and cooperation;

(c) in declaring its support of the cause of freedom and
independence for all such peoples, and

(d) in calling upon the powers concerned to grant freedom and
independence to such peoples.[30]

## Post-Bandung Assessments

Many observers of Chou En-Lai believed that China scored a
major victory at the Bandung Conference at the expense of
India and Nehru. American Congressman Clayton Powell,
who personally observed Bandung, described Nehru as the
'greatest loser' at the conference, a man who came across
as 'jumpy and touchy', while Chou used a 'Dale Carnegie
approach to win friends'.[31] Lebanese Foreign Minister Charles
Malik's own verbatim impressions of a conversation he had
with Chou just after the conclusion of the conference further
attest to this:

Malik: I think it can be said, Mr. Prime Minister, that you
came out of this Conference winning every important battle.
Others made mistakes; for instance, Mr. Nehru lost his temper
once or twice and he had to apologize. Others may have won
a point or a battle here and there, but they didn't win every
important battle. I think it can be said of you that you won every
important battle in which you wanted or you allowed yourself
to be engaged. Here we argued with you for hours in the subcommittees and in the Political Committee, we gained some
understanding of your mind; although we differed on many
points, some very important, we developed a sort of intimate
relationship with you. You had many pleasant and even perhaps
fruitful contacts with important leaders of Asia and Africa. We

have had a chance to see the Chinese Communists in action and they appear to be human beings like the rest of us. The strange mystery that was surrounding you is partly dispelled. You made a good hit at the Conference, perhaps, as I say, the best hit of all. And you crowned all this magnificence with your offer the other day to negotiate your differences with the United States. Thus throughout, this Conference has been pouring gain for you. No man can ask for more. Now please do not do anything that will mar this impression or compromise your victory. I assure you I have no axe to grind. On the contrary, you will recall that I disagreed and argued vigorously with you on many a point. My words must therefore be taken as honest and sincere words. Conserve and consolidate the good impression you made all around in this gathering and rush to no acts in the Far East that will compromise your gains.

Chou: I too have made many mistakes in this Conference. You will remember when I asked for responding of a certain matter relating to a text on the United Nations because the text has been adopted in my absence. I too had to crave the indulgence of the Committee and even later to apologize. But I thank you for your words.

Malik: Oh, about that question of the United Nations, that was nothing. Those of us who have worked for so long at the United Nations know well how such matters always turn up. Texts are not adopted in a hurry or in our absence or when we are not paying close attention, and we often ask that the matter be reopened and be re-determined. Even after we ourselves have voted for a text, it happens that on second thoughts we change our mind and we think it was a bad provision. So when a new chance arises we move for the reopening of the question. It never occurred to anybody. I assure you that what happened to you the other day was not a defeat. I repeat therefore my sincere opinion that you ought to be congratulated on your performance which I believe could not have been better. In every major encounter you came out with banner flying. May nothing be done to mar this record.[32]

One may disregard this as a sort of platitude expected at a direct face-to-face conversation between two leaders. A more sober assessment of Chou's performance was provided by Indonesia's Antara news agency: 'It is generally conceded that the attitude of the Chinese premier contributed much to the success of the conference. The Chinese delegate time and again proved to be prepared to meet his counterpart halfway, or even much farther.'[33]

The British showed more scepticism about Chou's performance at Bandung. According to the memo of a British official sent to monitor the conference: '[A]lthough Chou En-Lai scored an outstanding success by his personality as much as by his consistent moderation and flexibility, he probably failed materially to lull the suspicions of any key nation.'[34] Another British assessment argued:

> While Chou En-Lai's deliberate attitude of conciliation undoubtedly brought him enhanced status in the eyes of Asians, it must have been brought home to him that all Asians are not prepared to take Chinese statements at their face value, and how diverse their attitudes are. The extent to which he is prepared to negotiate over Formosa has yet to be seen, but in subsidiary matters (for example his formal witnessing with Mr Nehru of the joint declaration signed by the Laotian and Viet Minh representatives on Laos) he has committed himself further, at least vis-à-vis Mr Nehru, on non-interference.[35]

Some British and Australian officials also doubted if Nehru was diminished vis-à-vis Chou. According to a British intelligence assessment:

> Mr Nehru seems deliberately to have remained rather in the background, though he was extremely active in promoting informal contacts and understandings between Chou En-Lai and the representatives of the S.E. Asian countries. He regards the fruitfulness of these contacts as his principal contribution

at Bandung. There are no substantial reasons for believing that his own standing in Asia has in fact suffered as a result of the Conference, the conclusions of which were broadly in line with India's avowed policies.[36]

The Australian watchers of Bandung agreed with this view. According to a report by the Australian external affairs ministry, 'Mr. Nehru played a relatively subsidiary role by choice and that he was not simply "pushed into the back seat" as a result of Chou En-Lai's appearance.'[37] And the Australian ambassador in Jakarta, who had closely monitored the conference and 'debriefed' some of the leaders, including Nehru, as they returned from the conference through Jakarta, noted:

It is commonly said at Djakarta to-day that Chou's rise in prestige was proportionate to, and indeed the cause of, Nehru's decline in prestige. Some at least of this argument originates from identifiable sources, some of it is wishful, and some is exaggerated. It was, after all, Nehru who insisted on Chou's being invited, who indoctrinated him carefully before the Conference, and who sponsored him in the difficult opening days at Bandung. Mr. Nehru did not strike me as feeling that he had been supplanted by Chou. He might of course have been concealing his feelings but during the time I spent with him after the conference he spoke highly of Chou's performance and he seemed to be pleased with it. But this does not change the fact that sooner or later India and China will find themselves in rivalry and that the only dangerous potential enemy of India is China. Nehru is also aware of this fact. It is one reason for his plea for co-existence and the Five Principles.[38]

The Australian's assessment was borne out by Nehru's own impressions of Chou's performance. In a letter to Edwina Mountbatten, Nehru compared his own performance with that of Chou:

Chou En-Lai was a star performer. As a matter of fact, he did not say very much, but naturally he attracted most attention. He was the mysterious figure representing a country which was playing an important and perhaps dangerous part in the world, and both, those who were favourably inclined to him and those who were bitterly opposed, were anxious to see him and measure him. The Chinese in Bandung, and there was a large number of them, gathered in the streets to cheer him. Chou En-Lai did not speak much, but what he said was to the point and authoritative. He was quiet and restrained and obviously determined to do everything in his power to make the Conference a success. He did not bring forward any controversial proposition. If, however, anything was said, which was objectionable from his point of view, he spoke firmly but quietly. He spent long hours in subcommittees and went to every party there. There were dozens of parties, sometimes three or four a day. Apart from this, he met small groups of individuals. Altogether he created a very good impression. Even his opponents melted somewhat and agreed that he was an attractive person. Only once, in a subcommittee, did he speak rather curtly and said that China was not going to be bullied. He had some reason to feel irritated because Pakistan and some others were creating every kind of difficulty. So far as I was concerned, I behaved generally. Once I lost my temper, but regained it soon after. On two or three occasions I spoke with some vigour. It is true, however, that I was often very irritated and it was with some difficulty that I restrained myself.[39]

What about China's own assessment of the impact of Bandung? Chou's report to the National People's Congress dismissed the view that the formulation 'communist colonialism' had won the day:

[D]uring the course of discussion on opposition to colonialism there were certain persons who for ulterior motives strangely distorted colonialism. Because the evils caused by the Western colonial rule practiced in Asian and African countries in the past few hundred years can never be erased, these persons went to the length of using the term so-called colonialism of all forms in order to slander socialism as another form of colonialism. This was an attempt to confuse the objective of the Asian and African peoples in their struggle against colonialism. Nevertheless it is well known to us that socialist countries having overthrown capitalism in their own countries, have thus destroyed the basis for preserving or giving rise to colonialism in these countries. The relationship among the socialist countries is entirely a kind of relationship based on respect for each other's sovereign rights and national independence. It is a new kind of relationship among nations based on equality and mutual assistance to work for common economic growth. The control of one state by another has nothing in common at all with the system and policy of the socialist countries. One may like or dislike certain social systems, but views and interpretations contrary to the truth could not be accepted by the conference. Prime Minister Nehru rightly said on April 30, 1955, in his report to the House of Peoples of India: 'Such views could not become part of any formulation on behalf of the conference.' ... In the Resolution on the Problems of Dependent Peoples, the Asian-African Conference declared that colonialism in all its manifestations was an evil which should be speedily brought to an end. The phrase 'in all its manifestation' here denotes colonialism in its political, military, economic, cultural and social manifestations and thus there cannot possibly be any other interpretation.[40]

The Chinese also thought that the principle of neutralism has been advanced and claimed that this also vindicated the Five Principles. 'The Five Principles declared by China and India has won support from many Asian-African countries of the world, demonstrating that the possibility of expanding the Asian-African peace region is increasing and the tendency to peace and neutrality from India to Egypt is developing day by day.'[41]

From the Chinese perspective, SEATO suffered a major defeat. 'In Southeast Asia, the countries that didn't join the "Southeast Asian Alliance" still don't want to join it, such as Ceylon, so that USA is unable to expand it.'[42] Moreover, '[e]ven the countries that have joined the American military alliances don't want to completely follow the steps of USA and have signs to change their attitude.' The conference confirmed that the newly independent countries '[o]ppose the military alliances formed by imperialism. For example, the Manila Treaty, Turkey–Pakistan Treaty, US–Pakistan Treaty, Turkey–Iraq Treaty, etc. have suffered strong opposition from the Asian-African people and the main Asian-African countries have adopted the policy of peace and neutrality, refusing to join any military alliances.'[43] This assessment by the Chinese was broadly consistent with the fact that SEATO attracted no new members after Bandung. In addition, the Chinese assessment of their diplomatic victories as a result of the Bandung Conference was listed down in a post-conference assessment by the Chinese Ministry of Foreign Affairs as follows:

After the Asian-African Conference, the tendency to anti-colonialism, peace and neutrality in the Asian-African countries has further strengthened, their relations with China and Soviet Union have obviously developed, and even Thailand and the Philippines, the extremely and persistently pro-American countries, have had some signs of changing their attitude.

Egypt's purchase of weapons from Czech and India's position on Goa won universal support from the Asian-African countries.

Even the countries that have joined the American military alliances don't want to completely follow the steps of USA and have signs to change their attitude.

Thailand: a) Agreed to the Five Principles of Peaceful Co-existence after the Asian-African Conference; b) Recognized the importance of China's international status and estranged its relations with Chiang Kai-shek clique; c) Actively considered and discussed the direct trade with China.

Even the Philippines has changed its attitude to some extent.

As for Pakistan, its prime minister declared in the Asian-African Conference that he would visit China, and when its new prime minister came into power, he didn't change the decision and declared to come to Beijing next spring.[44]

A good deal of this assessment holds true. Thailand initiated secret diplomatic contacts with China, despite being very fearful of US reaction to such a move.[45] My argument, however, is that Chou's diplomatic gains at Bandung were both short-term and short-lived. These gains were contingent on adherence to a strict policy of non-interference. As China supported communist insurgencies in Southeast Asia, it continued to remain isolated from the region, including the regional association ASEAN formed in 1967. It was not until China had abandoned this support that it could enjoy stable political relations with Southeast Asian countries. In this sense, Nehru's strategy of socializing China through a set of norms had a long-term impact even though it might have cost India dearly in the short-term.

Bandung might have showed that China could act as an Asian power and influence Asian events without the presence and backing of the Soviet Union. Chou's acceptance of 'colonialism in all its manifestations' was essentially a face-saving device. It was seen as implicitly accepting a criticism of the Soviet Union. A US state department assessment of the conference noted 'apparent variations' between Chinese and Soviet positions (for example, on Formosa) because Chou had not dissociated publicly from communist colonialism and/or Formosa and had accepted negotiations over Taiwan. The same report also noted that at Bandung China had been 'accepted as an established state fully participating in international life without subservience to anyone'.[46] At the conference, the Pakistani premier Mohammed Ali insisted that the criticism of communism as a new form of colonialism applied to the Soviet Union, and not China (presumably because it was the former that had acquired satellites in Eastern Europe). Indeed at Bandung Nehru's defence of the Eastern European countries as genuinely sovereign states was more vigorous than Chou's defence of the Soviet Union. Western reports of Bandung noted the disappointment and displeasure of the Soviet embassy in Indonesia with the outcome of the Bandung Conference. Moreover, the Chinese offer of talks on Taiwan with the US was apparently undertaken without prior consultation with the Soviet Union. Even Dulles, who strongly believed in monolithic communism, recognized a degree of Chinese independence from the Soviet Union. In all, as the on-the spot observer Homer Jack noted, 'Bandung saw the emergence of China as a great Asian power and not merely as an isolated partner of Russia.'[47]

Evidence suggests that the Nehru–Chou rivalry, which was perceived by many of the participants in the conference—thanks partly to the Western media's coverage of the conference—was somewhat exaggerated. To be sure, there were some important areas of disagreement over approach between the two countries, as mentioned earlier. But in general, the Chinese respected and trusted India. The Chinese had accepted the idea that the second Asian-African conference would be held in India, despite differences with Nehru over the need for setting up a permanent institution. A top-secret memo that Chou sent to Mao on 4 April 1955 to serve as the basis for Mao's discussion with the politburo noted one of the Chinese goals at the conference to be to 'strive to establish the permanent institution of the Asian-African Conference and convene a conference every another year, and the next conference shall be held in India'.[48]

In reality, both India and China came out as 'losers' at the Bandung Conference. Nehru's perceived arrogance at the conference might have reinforced existing concerns in Southeast Asia about Indian leadership (and hence domination) of an Asian regional organization, even though, as the evidence suggests, Nehru himself was opposed to such an organization. While China was able to dispel some of the fears about its foreign policy at the conference, this was not sufficient for its neighbours to contemplate a regional grouping under Chinese leadership. Indeed the perceived rivalry between India and China might have put off the smaller and weaker Asian nations to join either or both in forming any regional association. With the two largest Asian countries unacceptable as a regional leader, the space opened for the region's smaller and weaker countries to take the initiative in forming ASEAN—Asia's first viable regional association—more than a decade after Bandung (although ASA, which was a direct precursor to ASEAN, was formed in 1960).

## Implications for Asian and World Order

What might be the implications and lessons of the Bandung era of Sino-Indian relationship for the contemporary Asian and international order? One of its most powerful and obvious lessons seems to have been forgotten by those who conceive of the absurdity called 'Chindia'. India's relationship with China is unlikely to ever resemble the pre-Bandung era relationship. Another lesson of Bandung was that Asia-wide regionalism would be wrecked when its two civilizational powers are not in agreement over the goals and direction of that regionalism. Today both India and China share membership in various Asian regional groupings, especially the ARF and the EAS. But neither is occupying the 'driver's seat' of these organizations. That place belongs to ASEAN, which can be explained as another aspect of Bandung's legacy. At Bandung, while Nehru and Chou disagreed over the need for a permanent organization, other states, including the smaller Southeast Asian neighbours represented there, worried about the prospects of Sino-Indian domination over Asian regionalism. In the end, India and China, whether individually or jointly, were not acceptable as the leaders that could bring about the permanent structural unity of Asia, as some pan-Asianists had earlier hoped for. Hence, an enduring legacy of Bandung was that the leadership of Asian regionalism passed to the smaller and weaker states, which came to be grouped in 1967 as ASEAN. Some argue that ASEAN's role as the driver of Asian regionalism is coming to an end now that both India and China are asserting themselves. But without a dramatic transformation of the Sino-Indian relationship (as well as China's relations with Japan), and in the absence of sufficient trust in each of these powers by the Southeast Asian states, the key role of ASEAN in the Asian regional architecture is unlikely to fade away.

Bandung was a blow to India's image in the sense, as noted earlier, that its representatives (especially Nehru and Krishna Menon) were widely perceived to have acted in an arrogant and heavy-handed manner. Indian diplomacy took decades to recover from that image and it still arouses misgivings in Southeast Asia, at least in terms of its style, if not substance. The lesson for China was different. While the image of 'Chou the charmer' in contrast to a frowning and arrogant Nehru was the talk of the town, the subsequent Chinese support for communist insurgencies in Southeast Asia fundamentally undermined those gains. Hence, Bandung is a powerful reminder of the fragility of China's charm offensive and the transience of its soft power in the absence of behaviour that conforms to declared principles.[49]

But perhaps the most important lesson of Bandung may be that it provides a useful context for understanding the nature and implications of the simultaneous rise of China and India as world powers. To conclude, Bandung brought India and China, both as individual Asian nations and as a joint entity through the then seemingly unshakeable Nehru–Chou partnership, to regional and global limelight. Today both India and China are enjoying the limelight as Asia's two rising powers (Japan at Bandung was a minor presence and while it remains on the scene as a major Asian power today, the idea of 'Japan rising' seems perhaps as unrealistic today as it might have been for entirely different reasons in 1955).

While China is a fast-rising power today, its transformation into a legitimate superpower remains incomplete and is far from guaranteed. Great-power status, especially as the world number one, requires not only hard power but also legitimacy. To have the kind of legitimacy that the US has enjoyed since the Second World War, China needs to have three things: an attractive ideology, an ability to provide international public goods, and exercise restraint towards smaller states, partly by creating and maintaining multilateral institutions. The US has had all these three attributes despite periodic deviations (for example, McCarthyism during the early Cold War period and unilateralism under George W. Bush). It provided the public goods such as market access, incurring trade deficits with Asian and European countries, and a security umbrella in Europe and the Asia Pacific. By contrast, China's ideology and its domestic political system can hardly be considered attractive to most people in the world. While China's economic growth contributes to regional prosperity, unlike Japan which has been a net provider of investment to Southeast Asia, China in the 1990s diverted significant investment from Southeast Asia. Most importantly, many countries in Asia and the West see China as a security challenge, even a threat, not a security provider. Moreover, China has no real alliances, compared to the dozens of alliances the US has. And as recent events proved, claims about China's soft power were vastly exaggerated.

How does India compare with China? Just as the West mistakenly saw Bandung as a diplomatic victory for China over India, it might be making a similar mistake in assuming that the current regional order in Asia is for China to dominate. Some analysts believe that all great powers are alike—in the sense that they all behave and engage in power politics in a similar fashion. This view, while always simplistic and misleading, is even more so in the case of China and India. While China and India are both rising, they are not growing into being similar type of world powers. The difference is both quantitative and qualitative. China is a much stronger economy and more militarily powerful actor, and expectations that India would catch up or even overtake China are somewhat far-fetched, at least for the next three decades. China could conceivably emerge as a great power or even a superpower. Neither status is guaranteed for India. But even if it does emerge as a great power, it would likely be fundamentally a different type of great power than China. For one thing, India is likely to be much more oriented towards the status quo than China. China, while not a revisionist player as it was under Mao, is still likely to question many aspects of the prevailing world order to a greater extent than India, notwithstanding its permanent membership of the UN Security Council (which would otherwise give it a stake in preserving the status quo).

In contrast to China, India has a domestic political system that is much more attractive to the international community at large and which no amount of self-serving and cynical dismissal of democratic politics (for example, the argument that 'democracy is bad for development') can credibly dent. The fact that India is unlikely to be a *superpower* in the manner of the US, the USSR, and perhaps China of the not-too-distant future is in some ways a blessing, as it creates less fear in the international community about its rise. India will not have a global-power projection capability. To a much greater extent than China's, India's rise will be based on both material and ideational or normative factors. Overall, by and large, all other major powers of the world (perhaps with the exception of China) and the international community at large are overwhelmingly likely to cheer, not fear, India's emergence as a world power. Yet India also needs to eschew diplomatic hype and arrogance of the type that distracted from Nehru's otherwise constructive and visionary role in 1955.

Finally, today Asia and the world are going through another period of 'engagement' with China. While the circumstances are different, some of the underlying expectations and challenges remain similar. Nehru was criticized in India and the West for putting too much trust on China while neglecting the Indian defence preparedness. But whatever the circumstances and causes of the subsequent Sino-Indian conflict, few today would deny the fundamental idea that engaging China is likely to yield more benefits in the long term than isolating and containing it. China, too, needs to heed a political lesson from the Bandung era about how to engage its neighbours: violating principles (then it was non-interference in the internal affairs of other states) it professes to be sacred under whatever pretext would invite regional suspicion and isolation. Today China has emerged as a more restrained (compared to Mao's China, so far at least, the developments in the South China Sea notwithstanding) actor in Asia and it has carefully avoided seeking regional leadership. In this sense, at least, the Bandung Conference and the so-called 'Nehruvian idealism' were the precursors of the 'new realism' in Chinese foreign policy and the contemporary 'engaging China' policy adopted by China's neighbours. But a real lesson from the fate of the Sino-Indian relationship of the Bandung era would be not only to dismiss the pathetically nonsensical idea of 'Chindia', but also to be careful about accepting the very notion of a rising Asia, rising India, or rising China as a historic inevitability. It would also mean embracing the fact that India and China are going to develop fundamentally different identities as world powers, at least judging by their current developmental approaches and political systems. This will be a key factor in the prospects for a peaceful Asia and it critically underscores the value of the present situation in which ASEAN, rather than India or China, occupies the multilateral leadership of Asia.

## Notes and References

1. B.K. Nehru, *Nice Guys Finish Second: Memoirs* (New Delhi: Viking, 1997), p. 296.

2. 'Draft of the Tentative Working Plan for Participating in the Asian-African Conference', 16 January 1955, Department of Asian Affairs (PRC foreign ministry archives, obtained by Amitav Acharya, English translation). These and other Chinese documents used in this chapter are from the PRC foreign ministry archives that were obtained by the author and translated. Some, but not all, of these documents are available at the Cold War International History Project of the Woodrow Wilson Center, Washington, D.C. (http://digitalarchive.wilsoncenter. org/collection/16/bandung-conference-1955). Some of the documents used in this book which are also in the Wilson Center archives are from an earlier translation commissioned by me; hence their texts may differ.

3. 'Views and Suggestions of the Experts on the Asian-African Conference', 5 April 1955 (PRC foreign ministry archives, obtained by Amitav Acharya, English translation).

4. 'The members of the Chinese delegation may wear the Western-style clothes, must not necessarily wear the Chinese tunic suit, so as to avoid the difference from others' and 'invit[e] all the delegations (including the hostile states) to attend our banquet, and shak[e] hands and hav[e] conversations with all representatives'. See 'Views and Suggestions of the Experts on the Asian-African Conference', 5 April 1955 (PRC foreign ministry archives, obtained by Amitav Acharya, English translation).

5. Jawaharlal Nehru, 'Impressions of the Visit', in *Selected Works*, Vol. 27, p. 73.

6. Jawaharlal Nehru, 'Discussions on the International Situation', Statement at the Second Session of the Conference of the Prime

Ministers of the Five Colombo Countries, Bogor, 29 December 1954, in *Selected Works*, Vol. 27, pp. 116–17.

7. Nehru, 'Discussions on the International Situation', pp. 116–17.

8. The Five Principles of Peaceful Coexistence are: mutual respect for sovereignty and territorial integrity, mutual non-aggression, non-interference in each other's internal affairs, equality and mutual benefit, and peaceful coexistence. See 'The Five Principles of Peaceful Co-existence', available at http://news.xinhuanet. com/english/2005-04/08/content_2803638.htm (accessed on 15 November 2016).

9. Jawaharlal Nehru, 'Collective Security in Southeast Asia', in *Selected Works*, Vol. 27, p. 71.

10. Jawaharlal Nehru, 'Thoughts on Afro-Asian Conference', 20 December 1954, in *Selected Works*, Vol. 27, p. 110.

11. 'The Existing Issues of the Asian-African Conference and Suggestions', 1 January–31 March 1955 (PRC foreign ministry archives, obtained by Amitav Acharya, English translation).

12. 'Summary of the Talks between Premier Zhou and Nehru and U Nu', Bandung, 16 April 1955 (PRC foreign ministry archives, obtained by Amitav Acharya, English translation).

13. 'The Existing Issues of the Asian-African Conference and Suggestions', 1 January–31 March 1955 (PRC foreign ministry archives, obtained by Amitav Acharya, English translation).

14. 'The Existing Issues of the Asian-African Conference and Suggestions', 1 January–31 March 1955 (PRC foreign ministry archives, obtained by Amitav Acharya, English translation).

15. 'The Existing Issues of the Asian-African Conference and Suggestions', 207-00004-06 (PRC foreign ministry archives, obtained by Amitav Acharya, English translation).

16. 'On the Asian-African Conference (AAC) Issues', 15 December 1954, pp. 52–3 (PRC foreign ministry archives, obtained by Amitav Acharya, English translation).

17. 'About the Asian-African Conference', 4 September 1955 (PRC foreign ministry archives, obtained by Amitav Acharya, English translation).

18. 'Premier Chou En-Lai's Telegram to Ali Sastroamidjojo, Prime Minister of the Republic of Indonesia, Concerning China's

Acceptance of the Invitation to Attend the Asian-African Conference', in *China and the Asian-African Conference (Documents)* (Peking: Foreign Languages Press, 1955), pp. 65–6.

19. 'Different Attitudes among Nations Worldwide on the Eve of the Conference', Confidential Documents, Secret Code No. 103, edited by the Information Office of the Ministry of Foreign Affairs (PRC foreign ministry archives, obtained by Amitav Acharya, English translation).

20. 'The Common Issues of the Asian-African Conference', circulated to senior leaders before the conference, 4–5 April 1955 (PRC foreign ministry archives, obtained by Amitav Acharya, English translation).

21. 'Draft of the Tentative Working Plan for Participating in the Asian-African Conference', signed by Chou En-Lai on 16 January 1955, Department of Asian Affairs (PRC foreign ministry archives, obtained by Amitav Acharya, English translation).

22. 'Draft of the Tentative Working Plan for Participating in the Asian-African Conference', signed by Chou En-Lai on 13 January 1955, Department of Asian Affairs (PRC foreign ministry archives, obtained by Amitav Acharya, English translation).

23. 'On the Asian-African Conference (AAC) Issues', 15 December 1954 (PRC foreign ministry archives, obtained by Amitav Acharya, English translation).

24. 'Draft of the Tentative Working Plan for Participating in the Asian-African Conference', 16 January 1955, Department of Asian Affairs (PRC foreign ministry archives, obtained by Amitav Acharya, English translation).

25. 'Views and Suggestions of the Experts on the Asian-African Conference', 5 April 1955 (PRC foreign ministry archives, obtained by Amitav Acharya, English translation).

26. 'The Common Issues of the Asian-African Conference' (PRC foreign ministry archives, obtained by Amitav Acharya, English translation).

27. 'Views and Suggestions of the Experts on the Asian-African Conference', 5 April 1955 (PRC foreign ministry archives, obtained by Amitav Acharya, English translation).

28. 'Proposal by the Delegation of the People's Republic of China', 22 April 1955 (PRC foreign ministry archives, obtained by Amitav Acharya, original in English).

29. 'The Asian-African Conference, Joint Proposal Presented by: Libya, Sudan, Iran, Iraq, Lebanon, Pakistan, Philippines, and Turkey', 22 April 1955 (PRC foreign ministry archives, obtained by Amitav Acharya, original in English).

30. The Ministry of Foreign Affairs, Republic of Indonesia (ed.), *Asia–Africa Speak from Bandung* (Jakarta: Ministry of Foreign Affairs, 1955), pp. 161–9.

31. *The Washington Post*, 6 May 1955, D2231/235, FO 371/116980, UK National Archives.

32. 'Record of Interview between Charles Malik of Lebanon and Mr. Chou En-Lai, Prime Minister of the People's Republic of China', 25 April 1955, Bandung, Indonesia (Dulles Papers, Library of Congress, Washington, D.C.).

33. 'Bandung: Text of Selected Speeches and Final Communique of the Asian-African Conference', *Far East Reporter*, New York, 1955, p. 9.

34. 'Some Impressions of the Bandung Conference by R.W. Parkes': Memo from Bandung Conference sent by O.C. Morland to Macmillan at the British Foreign Office, CO 936-35025/42, UK National Archives.

35. D.J.D. Maitland, Foreign Office Minute, 'Afro-Asian Conference', 29 April 1955, D2231/329, FO 371/116984, UK National Archives.

36. Joint Intelligence Committee Assessment: Far Eastern Dept., DO35-6099: Afro-Asian Conference, 81/232, UK National Archives.

37. 'Australian Dept of External Affairs Report by Mr. Shann': Far Eastern Dept., DO35-6099: Afro-Asian Conference, 2/232, UK National Archives.

38. 'Personal Impressions by the Australian Ambassador to Indonesia', W.R. Crocker: Far Eastern Dept., DO35-6099: Afro-Asian Conference, 41/232, UK National Archives.

39. Kumar and Prasad, *Selected Works*, Second Series, Vol. 28, pp. 141–2.

40. 'Premier Chou En-Lai's Report on Bandung to the Standing Committee of the National People's Congress, People's Republic of China', in *Texts of Selected Speeches and Final Communique of the Asian-African Conference, Bandung, Indonesia, April 18–24, 1955* (New York: Far East Reports, 1955), pp. 49–50.

41. 'The Asian-African Conference', 207-00086-03.

42. 'The Asian-African Conference', 207-00086-03.

43. 'The Asian-African Conference', 207-00086-03.

44. 'The Asian-African Conference', 207-00086-03.

45. Sirin Phathanothai, 'Chapter 3', in *The Dragon's Pearl: Growing Up among China's Elite* (London: Pocket Books, 1995).

46. Roger Makins, British Embassy, Washington, to Foreign Office, London, 'United States Views on the Bandung Conference', 11 May 1955, D2231/350, FO 371/116985, UK National Archives.

47. Homer A. Jack, *Bandung: An On-the-spot Description of the Asian-African Conference, Bandung, Indonesia,* a Toward Freedom pamphlet, April 1955, p. 36.

48. 'Draft Plan for Participating in the Asian-African Conference.'

49. Amitav Acharya, 'China's Charm Offensive in Southeast Asia', *International Herald Tribune*, 8 November 2003, available at http://www.nytimes.com/2003/11/08/opinion/08iht-edacharya_ed3_.html (accessed on 11 September 2016).

# 5.

# India and China in Southeast Asia: Competition and Convergence*

$C$hina's relentless rise has prompted different scenarios of Asian and global order. One perspective likens China today with

* This chapter uses extracts from Amitav Acharya, 'India's "Look East Policy", in David M. Malone, C. Raja Mohan, and Srinath Raghavan (eds), *The Oxford Handbook of Indian Foreign Policy* (Oxford: Oxford University Press, 2015). By permission of Oxford University Press.

the rising Germany of the late nineteenth and early twentieth centuries. It anticipates a spiral of great-power competition leading to a major war. Europe's past becomes Asia's future. For others, China's ascent can be compared with America's in the nineteenth century. Like the US, which pursued regional expansion and imposed a sphere of influence (known as the Monroe Doctrine), China could seek regional, if not global, hegemony. If so, America's past becomes Asia's future. In the third scenario, China's ascent will return Asia to the China-centred tributary system that served as a mutually beneficial framework for commerce and peace for the East Asian countries before the entry of European powers. Here, Asia's future is seen not from the prism of Europe's or America's past, but its own.

However, the likelihood of any of these scenarios materializing in the twenty-first-century Asia is remote. In the absence of a rivalry over overseas colonies, and thanks to economic interdependence based on trade, investment, and production networks, the German parallel for China in Asia is implausible. A Chinese Monroe Doctrine would be vigorously resisted by the US and others (no European power was in a similar position to challenge US expansionism in the nineteenth century). The revival of a benign China-centric regional order would be thwarted by the US, Japan, India, and Russia. A regional order based on Confucian notions of hierarchy and deference may appeal to some inside China, but not outside. And it is inconsistent with China's own professed emphasis on sovereignty and equality.

Since this book is about the India–China–Southeast Asia triangle, I will discuss the so-called Chinese Monroe Doctrine as a take-off point in understanding China's attempt at reshaping Asian order in general and Southeast Asia in particular. I will also examine India's 'Look East' policy, which has the potential to compete with and complicate the Chinese influence in the region. ASEAN's engagement of both China and India as an approach to regional cooperation and legitimation will also be discussed as providing ample room for the two Asian powers to have a legitimate stake in the region as they pursue their grand interests.

## A Chinese Monroe Doctrine?

As the Cold War came to an end, the outlook on China's relations with Southeast Asian countries was hardly a positive one. The refocusing of Chinese military from the border region with Russia to its eastern maritime frontiers, its build-up of naval and air-force projection capabilities, its refusal to negotiate multilaterally with ASEAN on the Spratly Islands dispute, its perceived policy of creeping encroachment in the South China Sea, and its growing relationship with Myanmar have sparked concerns in Southeast Asia about China's strategic intentions in the region. Although Southeast Asian states, mindful of their own diplomatic culture, refrained from calling China a 'threat', security officials in several of them, including Singapore, Malaysia, Indonesia, Vietnam, and the Philippines, held deep private misgivings about the strategic implications of China's rise. Apart from the question of direct Chinese expansion into Southeast Asia in pursuit of its territorial claims, they also worried that competition between China and the US would present them with uncomfortable choices. If they take sides in the US–China rivalry, Southeast Asia would be engulfed in a wider Asian disorder.

Later analysts and policymakers in the region have projected the idea of a Chinese Monroe Doctrine over Southeast Asia. The former president of the US–ASEAN Business Council, Ernest Bower, warned of such a doctrine being 'built here in the region'. Others have spoken of the likely emergence of a Chinese sphere of influence in Southeast Asia. S.D. Muni, an Indian scholar, has argued that China's close relations with the new ASEAN members—Cambodia, Laos, and Myanmar—have 'all the characteristics of a centre-periphery relationship'.[1] The *New York Times* fears that China has been 'grabbing much of the new foreign investment in Asia, leaving its once-glittering neighbours—Thailand, South Korea, Singapore—with crumbs....' If the trend persists, Southeast Asia may be reduced to 'the role of supplier of food and raw materials to China in exchange for cheap manufactured goods....'.[2] Stephen Walt, an American academic, for his part argues:

> [W]hen China's economy overtakes that of the US, 30–40 years down the road, Southeast Asian states may develop special relations with China so much so that the US may chose not to compete with China for influence in the region. It may leave Southeast Asia to China, in exchange for a Chinese understanding not to interfere in Latin America.[3]

And according to Australian analyst Owen Harries, one of the most critical challenges for Asian security in the twenty-first century is 'what sort of sphere of influence will China have and will there be agreement between it and other powers on what it will be entitled to'.[4]

In his 2001 book, *The Tragedy of Great Power Politics*, John Mearsheimer argued: 'A wealthy China would not be a status quo power but an aggressive state determined to achieve regional hegemony.' He argues that rising powers seek hegemony, especially regional hegemony, in order to ensure their survival. If China continues its meteoric rise, a confrontation with the US would be inevitable, rendering Asia deeply unstable, the growth of regional economic interdependence and institutions notwithstanding. Note a key difference between Friedberg and Mearsheimer: the former did not think Asia had enough interdependence and institutions (along with democracy) to mitigate anarchy, while the latter simply dismissed them as inconsequential to prospects for peace and stability as evident by the following statements:

[A]ll states like to be regional hegemons, they like to dominate their backyard and make sure that no other state can interfere in their backyard. This is the way the United States has long behaved in the Western Hemisphere, it's what the Monroe Doctrine is all about. Well, if China continues to grow economically and militarily, why should we expect China not to imitate the United States? Why should we expect that China won't want to dominate its backyard the way we dominate our backyard? Why should we expect that China won't have a Monroe Doctrine, when we have a Monroe Doctrine?[5]

Chinese military modernization appears to be headed exactly in such a direction, developing what military analysts term 'anti-access, area denial' capability. In March 2010, the commander of the US Pacific Command, Admiral Robert Willard, warned: 'China's rapid and comprehensive transformation of its armed forces ... challenge[s] our freedom of action in the region', and 'potentially infringe[s] on their [US allies'] freedom of action'.[6] Evidence of a Chinese Monroe Doctrine can be seen from its recent actions in the South China Sea. In fortifying its territorial claims in the South China Sea, China has built seven new islets in the disputed areas by piling sand on to reefs, thus claiming a portion of the sea for its own use. As a consequence, China's island-building (albeit claimed to be late in the game compared to the other East Asian claimants) has further strained geopolitical tensions, fuelling suspicions of a Chinese military agenda. The US, for one, is concerned about the security of its commerce since about US\$ 1.2 trillion worth of its annual bilateral trade passes through the South China Sea.[7]

In light of the foregoing, is a Chinese Monroe Doctrine possible in Southeast Asia? The Monroe Doctrine had two principal elements. The first, its nineteenth-century version, was to exclude European powers from hemispheric affairs. The second, its twentieth-century extension, was to sanction US intervention in the internal affairs of Latin American nations to arrest internal instability and injustice (including economic injustice) done to foreigners. The first element was not just aimed at preventing any further European conquest of the Americas beyond their existing possessions, but was also an ideological effort to prevent European powers from exporting their political systems (monarchy) into the Americas.

Of these, the extended Monroe Doctrine, which allows the hegemon's interference in the internal affairs of the weaker states, will be inconsistent with Chinese notions of state sovereignty. Unlike the US in the nineteenth century (it did not accept non-interference until the 1930s), China has accepted this principle, at least since the 1970s, when it stopped supporting insurgencies in Southeast Asia. In fact, this principle is central to China's efforts to delegitimize US support for the secession of Taiwan and any US attempt at 'peaceful evolution' within China. The prospects of Chinese intervention for the ethnic Chinese in Southeast Asia in the event of their persecution by local authorities cannot be completely ruled out (despite Chinese restraint during the anti-Chinese riots in Indonesia in 1998). This, though, is likely to be undertaken through diplomatic pressure rather than military action.

Could a Chinese Monroe Doctrine take shape with the purpose of preventing the spread of American values and democracy into the region? Remember Asian values? China has a shared interest with some ASEAN nations, especially Vietnam, Myanmar, Laos, and perhaps even Malaysia and Singapore (both of which had endorsed Asian values), to limit the spread of democracy in the region. China not only resists regime change in Myanmar and North Korea but its support has also been crucial to the survival of these regimes. A Chinese ideological Monroe Doctrine, however, is unlikely to materialize beyond China's current efforts to prevent further democratization of Hong Kong and thwart 'peaceful evolution'. China cannot expect to apply this approach to ASEAN generally, not the least because it will be inconsistent with its professed adherence to non-interference. In fact, a Chinese ideological Monroe Doctrine attempted through efforts to block democratic transitions in the region would undercut its own arguments against US and Western efforts to promote democracy in the region and 'peaceful evolution' within China itself.

But there are major differences between the two historical contexts that make the Monroe Doctrine parallel less than apt. First, in the early-nineteenth century, there was no countervailing force available, be it another regional power or an offshore balancer, to block US regional hegemony over its backyard. The rivalry between Britain and France constrained America in the Western Hemisphere. China today not only faces the US—an offshore, although some say a 'resident', balancer—but also regional balancers such as India, Japan, and Russia, should it seek regional hegemony.

Second, the Monroe Doctrine came at a time of a historic shift in the US economic development. From December 1807 to March 1809, the Congress imposed a near-total embargo on US international commerce, a policy that, along with the 1812 US–British war, helped the development of US domestic industry and lowered the overall international economic interdependence for the US. In this climate of reduced dependence on foreign trade, US policymakers did not need to worry about any damage to their economic interests if European powers cut off their trade routes to the US.

Compare this to the interdependent global economic order of today that China depends on. According to a recent report in *China Daily*, over 60 per cent of China's GDP now depends on foreign trade. Imported oil accounts for 50 per cent of its oil needs. China's commerce, and hence prosperity, depends very much on access to sea routes through the Indian Ocean, the Malacca Straits, and other areas over which it has little control and which are dominated by US naval power. India, too, has significant naval power in the Indian Ocean.

So if push comes to shove, an aggressive Chinese denial of trade routes in the South China Sea to world powers and the resulting disruption of maritime traffic would be immensely self-injurious to China. It would provoke countermeasures that will put in peril China's own access to critical sea routes in the Indian Ocean and elsewhere. Chinese leaders are not oblivious to this fact. The truth is that they may not have the option of pursuing an aggressive posture. The costs will simply be too high.

Can a Chinese Monroe Doctrine evolve on the basis of ASEAN members' voluntarily jumping on the bandwagon with China? Despite their desire to cultivate Beijing and their weaker economic and strategic position, the core ASEAN countries are unlikely to collectively bandwagon with China— contrary to the argument made by Korean-American scholar David Kang.[8] Except Myanmar, there is no military alignment (a key indicator of bandwagoning) between China and any of the original members of ASEAN. Defence relations between China and ASEAN members remain rudimentary and are aimed at confidence-building rather than operational issues. Though security relations with Vietnam have improved since the two countries reached border agreements (a land-border agreement in 1999, an agreement on the delimitation of the Gulf of Tonkin, and an agreement on fishery cooperation on 25 December 2000),[9] the two countries are not in a bandwagoning relationship. Recent joint statements involving China and Singapore, and China and the Philippines have included modest proposals for defence exchanges.[10] The main ASEAN members are yet to develop defence links with Beijing involving arms transfers, joint exercises, or operational planning. This is partly explained by domestic politics (in Malaysia and Indonesia) and close security ties with the US (in the case of

Singapore, the Philippines, and Thailand). At the same time, ASEAN countries have not completely eschewed a balancing posture towards China. While the arms build-up in Southeast Asia is by no means solely geared to countering China, the possibility of China developing an expansionist security approach is an important factor for Malaysia, Singapore, and especially the Philippines.[11] The kind of convergence of threat perception between China and the major ASEAN members that led to Thailand buying some Chinese weapons is not likely to be replicated in the post-Cold War period. It is highly unlikely that the rhetorical opposition to US hegemony by some ASEAN members such as Malaysia, a concern they ostensibly share with China, would translate into military alignment with China.

While economic considerations and the new Chinese diplomacy explain ASEAN's reluctance to balance China, this could change in the event of a Sino-US confrontation. An aggressive US policy of containment will force ASEAN to choose sides and provoke conflict between Southeast Asian states and China. This could be aggravated by US policies encouraging or endorsing Taiwanese independence. ASEAN countries do not support an independent Taiwan, but they will not necessarily acquiesce with an unprovoked Chinese military takeover of Taiwan. In the event of a cross-Straits confrontation, ASEAN members will be forced to make unpleasant choices if the US endorses unilateral Taiwanese independence. Singapore, in particular, is caught in the Sino-US conflict over Taiwan. Some Chinese defence officials would regard Singapore's provision of military facilities to the US in such a crisis as 'an act of war'. But this is unlikely to deter Singapore.

Resentment of the Bush administration's unilateralism might have put Beijing in a better light as a regional diplomatic partner. But ASEAN countries such as the Philippines, Singapore, and Thailand have considerably enhanced their security cooperation with the US. Manila and Bangkok now enjoy major non-NATO ally status in Washington. While ostensibly geared towards countering the threat of terrorism and separatism in Mindanao, Manila also seeks to rebuild its defence links with the US with a view to responding to Chinese military provocations in the Spratly Islands. Singapore has recently signed security cooperation agreements with both the US and India. Malaysia has cooperated more quietly with the US on defence, developing extensive security links with it. Despite not having a formal military relationship, there have been more than 75 US ship visits to Malaysia in the last two-and-a-half years, more than 1,000 overflights annually, as well as US army and Navy SEAL training in Malaysia.[12] In coping with the most pressing security challenge facing the region—terrorism—ASEAN remains dependent on Washington's help. In contrast, Beijing's role in Southeast Asia's war on terror has been rather marginal. There is little chance of Southeast Asia subjecting itself to a Chinese Monroe Doctrine in which Beijing denies the region to 'outside' powers such as the US.

Singapore's former prime minister Goh Chok Tong, upon being asked by the author at a public forum to comment on how Singapore and ASEAN would deal with a militarily powerful, economically prosperous but geopolitically assertive China, replied that a regional 'balance' would be important in countering such a development. '[W]e need to have a US presence over here. We need to have a strong Asean, we need Japan to be present in the region. We need Europeans to be here.'[13] It is also noteworthy that China's growing ties with ASEAN have been accompanied by closer ASEAN–India cooperation.[14] This was originally reflected in ASEAN's decision to let India into the ARF. More recently, ASEAN invited India to hold a summit meeting with itself, the first of which was held in Cambodia in 2002.[15]

Another route to a Chinese sphere of influence in Southeast Asia could be in the form of a return to the old Chinese world order. Attacking Western scholars for 'getting Asia wrong' because of their Euro-centric perspectives, Kang put forth an elaborate argument centred on the notion of a benign China-centric order in Asia. 'Historically,' he suggests, 'it has been Chinese weakness that has led to chaos in Asia. When China has been strong and stable, order has been preserved. East Asian regional relations have historically been hierarchic, more peaceful, and more stable than those in the West.'[16]

But the evidence for a benevolent Chinese hierarchy in historical Asia—the Chinese world order[17]—is not convincing. The noted Chinese historian of Southeast Asia Wang Gungwu observes that the Chinese employed an authority relationship with their neighbours that included the idea of 'impartiality' (that China did not 'discriminate among foreign countries and treated everyone equally').[18] This did not mean they were 'equal to the emperor, but they were equal in the eyes of the emperor'.[19] As a consequence, '[i]t was seldom feasible to establish equal relations ... for long'.[20] The core principle of the Chinese world order was thus a belief in Chinese superiority: 'China was the superior centre and its ruler had duties toward all other rulers as his inferiors.'[21] This notion of hierarchy, in marked contrast to the European system of nation states 'equal in sovereignty and mutually independent within the cultural area of Christendom',[22] survived despite challenges such as defeat at the hands of, or conquests by, foreigners or the penetration of foreign ideas into China. But the concept of Chinese superiority and the belief in the essential inequality of states was not always reflected in practice; the Chinese were pragmatic enough to accord equal status to powerful overseas rulers whom they could not subjugate by force.[23] Wang and others argue that the belief in Chinese superiority was not rigid; it was subject to considerations of security.[24]

Power was a deciding factor in the management of the historical hierarchy of the Chinese world order. When dealing with powerful states (this is especially true of states across China's land borders such as the Han emperors in dealing with the Xiongnu federation, Tang rulers with Tibet, and Song rulers with Mongols), the Chinese would tone down the imperial rhetoric and treat them with respect. Against lesser states the Chinese did not refrain from threatening or using force. Thus, the Yuan dynasty threatened Vietnam and Champa in demanding subjection. Although 'the language used [was] couched in Confucian terms, the demands were obviously accompanied by threats, and force was in fact used wherever feasible and necessary'.[25]

Where it demanded only tribute, such as with Siam, Khmers, and Quilon, rather than subjection, it was because of the lack of power or capability to subjugate—that is, 'only where power was irrelevant'. The Ming emperor Yongle invaded Vietnam, reversing his father's edict not to attack certain countries that included Vietnam. The fact that the use of force was mostly limited to frontier areas such as Vietnam is explained by a lack of capability rather than imperial benevolence; where Chinese did have the capability, they did not hesitate from resorting to force. Yongle threatened to attack Siam and Java (even reminding their rulers of his successful attack on Vietnam) and 'could certainly follow up his threats because the Zheng He expeditions were roaming around Southeast Asia and the Indian Ocean'.[26] In general, Yongle maintained an 'aggressive policy towards China's neighbours overseas',[27] while his famed admiral Zheng He 'did intervene in local politics in Sumatra as well as Ceylon'.[28] Commenting on the Qing dynasty's relations with its neighbours, Warren Cohen writes: 'With lesser powers, when they perceived force to be effective, as with the Zungaris and Nepalese, they did not refrain from applying it as ruthlessly as circumstances required.'[29] The non-coercive relationships in the tribute system were more due to the Chinese inability to coerce those states rather than a policy of benign and voluntary restraint. The Chinese world order did not prevent war and expansion in the periphery, as in the case of Southeast Asia, which saw major wars despite being supposedly under Chinese 'protection'.[30] The Chinese simply did not have the power to back up their protection. Against this backdrop, the peaceful and tranquil nature of the Chinese world order can be overstated.

A sceptic could further ask: whatever might have been the mix of coercion and benevolence in the hierarchical East Asian order of the past, can it be translated into a world of nation states that Asians live in today? Can one say that Asians find security in hierarchy, since one could argue that 'they always have, and they do now'? To say that an awareness of the past can and should inform one's analysis of the present is by no means misguided.[31] Nevertheless, this does not validate assertions that the conditions that prevailed in the past and the instruments that produced stability then could work in similar ways today and should therefore be welcomed. There exist serious differences in objective and normative conditions between Asia's past and its present, which must be accounted for in any cultural and historicist argument about the Asian security order. For example, there is no reason to believe that China's neighbours will accept hierarchy today as they did in the days of the Chinese world order. The norms of Asia's postcolonial international relations are too different to support a return to its precolonial past. How does one reconcile hierarchy with the overwhelming identification of Asian countries with the Westphalian norms of equality and non-interference? A return to the past seems especially unlikely when Asian states today remain among the most vocal defenders of Westphalian sovereignty.

The challenge to the prevailing thinking about Asian security, especially the (mis)application of the European-derived theoretical models to Asia, is both welcome and persuasive. A focus on the East Asian international system as an indigenous framework for investigating the Asian security order opens the door to interesting new research and analysis. Yet there are several problems with the view that Asia might be developing a Sinocentric regional order.

First, the argument that some Asian countries are not balancing China may well be right, but that they are bandwagoning with China seems incorrect. The attitude of Vietnam and South Korea, not to mention Japan and India, towards China is certainly not one of bandwagoning. Second, one could overstate the Chinese imperial benevolence that underpinned a supposedly stable classical East Asian order. The tributary system did not preclude major wars involving the Chinese use of force, and the voyages of Admiral Zheng He in the first half of the fifteenth century were themselves a symbol of imperial (though not colonial) militarism. Moreover, the image of China pursuing its peaceful rise and recreating its benevolent imperial past risks stoking Chinese (and overseas Chinese) nationalism. Third, the conditions that sustained the benign Chinese world order during the Ming and Qing dynasties are not replicated in the twenty-first century. The notion of a formal hierarchy is incompatible with the norms of non-intervention and sovereign equality of states that are hallmarks of Asian neo-Westphalianism that China itself keenly champions.

Against this backdrop, it seems unlikely that China can build a regional sphere of influence by excluding America and other extra-regional powers from Southeast Asian affairs. Such a Chinese sphere of influence, or a Chinese version of the Monroe Doctrine, is unlikely to develop as an automatic by-product of the rise of Chinese economic and military power. There is little likelihood of a neo-Confucian Chinese world order developing spontaneously because of any cultural–historic tendency of East Asia to bandwagon with China. Moreover, in an era of transnational production, intra-firm trade, and high capital mobility (which means capital can flee as easily from China as it came, should there be a major political and security crisis involving China, such as a war in the Taiwan Straits), a Chinese economic dependency in Southeast Asia is unlikely as a natural outgrowth of Sino-ASEAN economic relations.

For a Chinese Monroe Doctrine to emerge, China has to consciously manipulate regional relations so as to create a sphere of influence to exclude the US and assert its geopolitical weight in a coercive manner. Yet such an attempt by Beijing would almost certainly backfire. Its ability—military, diplomatic, and ideational—to 'deny' the region to the US is highly doubtful. It can hope to gain little by assuming a coercive posture towards ASEAN. It is easy to forget the extent of its recent diplomatic gains due to its willingness to play by the rules (mainly set by ASEAN).

For example, a good test of a Chinese Monroe Doctrine or a sphere of influence would be a successful effort by Beijing in getting a core ASEAN member to deny military facilities to the US, either in peacetime or in a crisis. Some have speculated that Chinese pressure led Thailand to deny an American request for prepositioning of military equipment off Thailand, but the evidence for this is not available. Beijing has not tried to persuade ASEAN members not to cooperate with the US in the war on terror by denying facilities or overflight rights. Apart from the fact that China itself supports the war on terror (though not the attack on Iraq), any such pressure by Beijing on an ASEAN member would almost certainly have been rejected out of hand. Also, most, if not all, ASEAN members have not shared Beijing's discontent for the US 'pivot' or 'rebalancing' policy; thus, China has been unable to make a case for the negative strategic consequences of such US military and diplomatic strategy in the region. Things may be different in the event of a Sino-US confrontation over Taiwan, but even then, it is doubtful if all ASEAN members, especially Singapore and the Philippines, would deny the US access to their facilities or air space for force deployments in such a crisis.

Although Sino-ASEAN relations seem unequal at present and hence conducive to a hierarchical pattern reminiscent of the past, ASEAN is not without a bargaining clout in its dealings, especially collective dealings, with China. To sustain its economic growth, China needs Southeast Asian resources and markets as well as a stable regional environment, which ASEAN can help provide. China also requires Southeast Asia's acquiescence and cooperation to realize its leadership ambitions in Asia and the world. Its relationship with ASEAN is a test case of Beijing's credibility as an engaged and constructive world power. While Beijing remains wary of ASEAN's pressure on the South China Sea dispute and the pro-US defence orientation of many ASEAN members, there are also reasons for it to view Southeast Asia as a relatively 'safe' and 'benign' area within which to cultivate positive and mutually beneficial relationships. Beijing is also mindful that an adverse relationship with Southeast Asia could move many of them towards closer alignment with China's competitors, such as Japan and the US. This offers an opportunity to Southeast Asian states—provided they can stay united and purposeful—to extract strategic restraint from China and develop cooperative security strategies.

## India's 'Look East' Policy and Southeast Asia

As noted in Chapter 2, after the Cold War and the collapse of the socialist model, India began the process of 'returning to Asia', marking the fourth stage in its evolving relationship with East Asia. It is during this stage that the 'Look East' policy was articulated.[32] But the forces driving this return were quite different from those that underpinned India's diplomacy in East and Southeast Asia in the 1940s and 1950s. In a speech at Harvard University in 2003, Jaswant Singh, who was India's external affairs minister during 1998–2002, outlined this difference:

In the past, India's engagement with much of Asia, including South East and East Asia, was built on an idealistic conception of Asian brotherhood, based on shared experiences of colonialism and of cultural ties. The rhythm of the region today is determined, however, as much by trade, investment and production as by history and culture. That is what motivates our decade-old 'Look East' policy.[33]

Another difference is that the new 'Look East' policy was, at least initially, more of a one-way street with India courting ASEAN than the other way around. In the early post-Second World War period, many Southeast Asian leaders, including Lee Kuan Yew of Singapore that was still under British colonial rule, looked to India and Nehru for inspiration. In this respect, India's engagement with ASEAN was different from China's engagement with it. While ASEAN sought to engage China because of its rising economic and military power, it was India that initiated its engagement with ASEAN due to pressing domestic economic and, to a lesser extent, strategic reasons. ASEAN would reciprocate India's 'Look East' policy, but slowly and warily, in contrast to its initially enthusiastic engagement of China. After being excluded from its founding, India would be invited to become one of ASEAN's dialogue partners and accepted as a member of the ARF.

The immediate factors contributing to the emergence of India's 'Look East' policy had much to do with India's domestic economic liberalization drive that was forced upon the Rao government (1991–6) by harsh domestic economic and political realities. In 1991, India's balance-of-payments situation was precarious, with foreign exchange reserves at a mere 1.2 billion, sufficient only to pay for three weeks' worth of imports, and the country was on the verge of default. In response, Rao initiated a series of economic reforms and articulated the 'Look East' policy in the context of these reforms, especially with a view to promote economic integration with East Asia and the Pacific countries.[34] As Rao would explain in 1994, the objective of the 'Look East' policy was 'to draw, as much as possible, investment and cooperation from the Asia-Pacific countries, in consonance with our common concept and solidarity and my faith in our common destiny'.[35] But it is important to recognize that the 'Look East' policy was also supported by strategic and diplomatic developments that changed the outlook of both India and its Southeast Asian neighbours in engaging each other. These developments included the end of the Cold War, the settlement of the Cambodia conflict, the rise of China, and the emergence of new multilateral institutions in the Asia-Pacific region. Because of these strategic developments, the 'Look East' policy, while it was initiated by India, came to reflect the changing attitudes and imperatives of its eastern neighbours as well. Hence, unlike many other accounts of the 'Look East' policy, I would like to underscore its two-way dynamic.

India's 'Look East' policy was, at its initial stages, not really pan-Asian but largely focused on Southeast Asia and ASEAN. This is not surprising because not only was ASEAN closer to India in terms of geography (although Myanmar would become a full member of ASEAN only in 1999), but it had also gained international recognition as a respected regional grouping. The end of the Cold War and the collapse of the Soviet Union removed a major political obstacle in the way of India–ASEAN relations. India's close ties with the Soviet Union had made some of the pro-Western ASEAN countries such as Thailand and Singapore (as well as Japan and South Korea in Northeast Asia) wary of embracing it. For India, the end of the Cold War also lessened the strategic rationale for the non-alignment approach that had been a cornerstone of its foreign policy. Indeed, in the past ASEAN had been viewed in some Indian circles as too pro-Western a bloc. The pursuit of regionalism, such as that developed by ASEAN, became more appealing to India than before. The settlement of the decade-long Cambodia conflict by the Paris Peace Agreement in 1991 also helped India's 'Look East' orientation. That conflict, triggered by the Vietnamese invasion of Cambodia in 1979 and its occupation of the country until 1989, had been a source of rift between India and ASEAN, as the former had recognized the Vietnamese-installed regime in Cambodia whereas the latter was actively supporting the coalition resisting that regime.

Another element is the changing strategic climate in the Asia-Pacific region that favoured the development of closer political and security ties between India and the Southeast Asian countries. With the end of the Cold War, ASEAN diluted its earlier policy of ZOPFAN that had sought to minimize the involvement of outside powers, India included, in Southeast Asian affairs. The more inclusive turn in the ASEAN posture created space for India to seek greater engagement in Southeast Asia. And ASEAN's instrumental role in resolving the Cambodia conflict (albeit in partnership with Western nations and Japan) gave it the diplomatic clout to pursue an agenda of expanding not only its own membership but also the network of its dialogue partners by inviting China, South Korea, and India, among others, to be part of it. In the context of such widening, ASEAN also launched a wider regional security forum in 1994, the ARF, comprising the key players affecting the security of the Asia-Pacific region, including the US, China, and Australia. While India had to wait for two years before it was accepted into the ARF, the new framework of 'cooperative security' gave it an opening to advance its 'Look East' policy beyond its initial economic focus.

Finally, the rise of China, although less pronounced in the early 1990s than a decade later, did create more common ground between India and its eastern neighbours. India itself saw the rise of China both as a security challenge and an economic opportunity. Apart from sensing possibilities for expanding trade and other economic links with China directly, India also found ASEAN's policy towards China—a mix of diplomatic engagement through regional institutions and strategic hedging through closer ties with other greater powers such as the US, Japan, EU, Australia, as well as India—to be consistent with its own interest and approach. Unlike China, India did not have any outstanding border or land disputes in Southeast Asia. It had already marked out her maritime boundary with Indonesia and Thailand. Despite the wariness caused by the memories of India's diplomatic style (a reputation for lecturing, moralizing, and arrogance), no Southeast Asian nation considered India to be a threat to its security. For its part, India did not and still does not expect any major challenge to its security interests from a Southeast Asian nation, with the exception of its concerns about Chinese military presence and activities in the military-ruled Myanmar. China's development of naval and surveillance installations along the Myanmar coast provoked concern and anxiety in India. It was reasonable to see the growing military ties between Myanmar under the junta and China as a source of shared concern for both India and ASEAN and thus a basis of India's 'Look East' policy. ASEAN's decision to grant full membership to Myanmar in 1997 in the face of widespread international condemnation of the move was partly an effort to reduce Myanmar's dependence on China. Like ASEAN, India opposed the isolation of Myanmar and welcomed its entry into ASEAN, despite pressure from human rights groups in India.

India's contemporary 'Look East' policy has three main dimensions: economic, strategic, and institutional. Political, demographic, and cultural factors are also part of India's 'Look East' policy, and there is possibly a fourth, a somewhat historical dimension, that adds ballast to the three others. But the changing context of India's 'Look East' approach is driven mainly by strategic, economic, and institutional factors. And these are closely linked. Economic calculations are vital if India is to be a credible player in the East Asian security architecture, since India's neighbours see its potential as a strategic partner mainly due to its economic growth and capability. The following sections outline these briefly.

## The Economic Dimension

Economic necessity and opportunity were primary factors not only behind India's initial articulation of its 'Look East' policy but also behind ASEAN's desire to embrace that policy. In 2005, Singapore's prime minister Lee Hsien Loong told the ASEAN Business and Investment Forum:

> The rise of China and India is transforming the entire region. China has already overtaken the US as the major trading partner of many Asian countries, including Japan, Korea and several ASEAN economies. India opened up several decades after China—the initial pace of reform was slow, but India has made significant progress in recent years. Combined, these two economic powerhouses will shift the centre of gravity of the world economy towards Asia.[36]

India's economic attraction to ASEAN countries such as Singapore was initially, and to some extent continues to be, based on a desire not to become too dependent on China. Moreover, the economies of India and ASEAN are complementary in a number of respects. ASEAN's resource intensity and higher per capita income provide India with opportunities for meeting its food and energy security needs. India's leadership position in information technology provides ASEAN with an opportunity to benefit from forging stronger economic links with it through greater economic integration. Despite this, India has found it hard to catch up with the broader economic trends in Asia in order to cement the economic side of its 'Look East' policy. Although India is far behind China in strengthening economic relations with its eastern neighbours, there are positive developments resulting from its competitive economic policy. For example, India's impressive economic growth in the 2000s has led to expansion of trade with ASEAN. ASEAN–India bilateral trade jumped from a mere US$ 2.9 billion in 1993 to US$ 12.1 billion in 2003, and to US$ 71.8 billion in 2012. At the tenth ASEAN–India Summit in November 2012, the leaders set the target of US$ 100 billion by 2015 for ASEAN–India trade. But this target was missed; in 2015, the trade volume between ASEAN and India reached only US$ 58.7 billion.[37] Indian foreign direct investment (FDI) in ASEAN was US$ 2.6 billion in 2012.[38] By comparison, China–ASEAN trade increased from US$ 280.4 billion in 2011 to US$ 318.6 billion in 2012—a rise of 13.6 per cent—with a target of US$ 500 billion by 2015.[39]

India–China bilateral trade increased from US$ 2.92 billion in 2000 to US$ 66.5 billion in 2012. China has emerged as India's largest trading partner. For example, in 2012, while India was the fifteenth largest trading partner of China, it was also its seventh largest export destination.[40] But India's massive trade deficit with China, which stood at US$ 29 billion in 2012, has been a sore point in the relationship and led to fears that China is using India as a dumping ground for cheap manufactured goods. During his visit to India in September 2014, the Chinese president Xi Jinping pledged US$ 20 billion in investment in India's infrastructure with the possibility of more to come.[41]

What about economic relations with Japan? Does it contribute to India's relative economic power? On the surface, the economic ties between India and Japan have considerable potential. India's Ministry of External Affairs notes:

In the economic sphere, the complementarities between the two countries are particularly striking. (i) Japan's ageing population (23% above 65 years) and India's youthful dynamism (over

50% below 25 years); (ii) India's rich natural and human resources and Japan's advanced technology; (iii) India's prowess in services and Japan's excellence in manufacturing; and (iv) Japan's surplus capital for investments and India's large and growing markets thanks to the burgeoning middle class.[42]

Yet the potential is far from realized. Japan–India bilateral trade stood at $ 18.6 billion in FY 2012–13, amounting to only 1 per cent of Japan's total foreign trade and between 2.2 to 2.5 per cent of India's total trade. It is far lesser than China–India trade. But Japan is a bigger investor in India, at least until now. Between April 2000 and June 2012, Japanese companies invested US$ 12.66 billion in India, accounting for 7 per cent of the total FDI inflow into India. In 2012, Japan was the fourth largest investor in India. Japanese FDIs in India accounted for only 2.3 per cent of Japan's overall FDI outflow in 2012. But Japan has been a major investor in Indian infrastructure. It has invested in several high-profile projects, including the New Delhi metro network, the Western Dedicated Freight Corridor (Western DFC), the Delhi–Mumbai Industrial Corridor (DMIC) with eight new industrial townships, and the Chennai–Bengaluru Industrial Corridor (CBIC) that are described as 'mega projects on the anvil which will transform India in the next decade'.[43] Narendra Modi's four-day visit to Japan in August 2014 and the Japanese prime minister Shinzo Abe's visit to India in December 2015 resulted in economic agreements that might lead to major increases in Japanese investment in India.

India is not yet integrated into the East Asian production network but the potential is there, especially in the automobile sector, where Japanese (as well as South Korean) companies continue to play a leading role. India is also part of the Regional Comprehensive Economic Partnership (RCEP), which is a proposed free trade agreement (FTA) between the 10 member states of ASEAN as well as Australia, New Zealand, China, India, Japan, and South Korea.

An important, if as-yet-unrealized aspect of India's 'Look East' policy concerns the development of its Northeast Asian region through foreign investment from Southeast Asia as well as assistance from multilateral institutions such as the ADB. But security concerns related to the persisting insurgency in the Northeast have limited the progress of this initiative. The political and economic opening of Myanmar, following a downturn in its deep economic and military ties with China, offers new opportunities for India's 'Look East' policy and its more recent 'Act East' policies. India has been stepping up its investment in port development, energy, and transport sectors.

## The Strategic Dimension

As noted, India's 'Look East' policy was initially driven by economic calculations mainly on its own part. But strategic considerations have become increasingly dominant and may now be driving the relationship. Moreover, this policy now reflects imperatives from both India and its eastern neighbours, especially the ASEAN countries. India's lack of territorial disputes with ASEAN members, and, in the contest of the rising Chinese naval power, India's growing security ties with the US (which are a plus for ASEAN), and its naval power in the western Southeast Asian and Indian Ocean waters make it a 'strategic asset' for ASEAN.

Of late there has been much talk about India being a 'balancer' in Asia or East Asia. To be sure, some ASEAN members such as Singapore hope that drawing India into Southeast Asia would balance China's diplomatic and strategic influence. But the idea of 'balancing' here must be a qualified one, resting more on the political, economic, and diplomatic elements than on the military. A more traditional conceptualization of 'balancing' resting on military power and alliances is problematic for several reasons. First, it is not clear whether India would seek such a role for itself. Some Asian strategic analysts have cast India and China as 'natural rivals' for influence in Southeast Asia. But Indian officials were critical of any move towards a pre-emptive containment of China, preferring instead to talk about the 'engagement' of China, which would bring it into a system of regional order. This policy might have changed with the growing assertiveness of China, but India is unlikely to fully embrace a doctrine of containment. At least Indian elite opinion is divided over a balancing role for India in East Asia, partly due to confusion over what a 'balancer' role might actually involve. India is not ready to see the formation of an Asian 'NATO'. An Asian NATO against China might be in contradiction with the lingering ethos of non-alignment that exists among sections of India's foreign-policy elite.

Does India as 'balancer' mean physically challenging China by registering a credible military presence in East Asia? This is unlikely, despite the occasional forays by the Indian navy into the South China Sea and East Asian waters. Might India pursue a policy akin to what Britain did in continental Europe during the eighteenth and nineteenth centuries, that is, become an offshore balancer? Apart from a lack of political resolve, India also may not have the resources—military and economic—that such a balancing role would require.

Balancing can also occur through increased defence cooperation with like-minded nations in Southeast and East Asia. India has increased its defence contacts with the ASEAN countries. In the 1990s, the Indian navy began conducting 'friendship exercises' with some ASEAN navies, including those of Singapore, Indonesia, Thailand, and Malaysia. India and Malaysia briefly cooperated in a programme to provide familiarization and maintenance training for the Russian-supplied MiG aircraft to the Malaysian air-force personnel. India has stepped up its defence cooperation with the ASEAN countries and others through initiatives such as intelligence-sharing, joint or coordinated naval patrolling to combat piracy and other maritime security threats, and bilateral and multilateral military exercises. Examples include the Regional Cooperation Agreement on Combating Piracy and Armed Robbery against Ships in Asia (ReCAAP) and the Milan exercises that are held every alternate year since 1995. Among the 15 participants in the 2014 Milan exercise held off the Andaman and Nicobar Islands were seven ASEAN member states (that is, Cambodia, Indonesia, Malaysia, Myanmar, the Philippines, Singapore, and Thailand) as well as Australia. Exercise Malabar, which began in 1992 as an annual bilateral exercise between the Indian and US navies, has in recent years included Japan, Australia, and Singapore and has been conducted both in the Indian Ocean and East Asian waters (such as the 2014 exercises held in the Sea of Japan).

India has also increased its defence diplomacy with the Asia-Pacific countries through its participation in the Shangri-La Dialogue (SLD), held annually in Singapore, and the ASEAN Defence Ministers' Meeting Plus (ADMM Plus), which brings together the defence ministers and officials of ASEAN countries and a number of key Asia-Pacific nations including the US, China, Japan, and Australia. Modest but growing defence contacts were also established between India and the Northeast Asian countries, which have since expanded, especially with Japan. India also conducted joint patrols with the US navy in the Straits of Malacca in 2002 to curb the risks of piracy and terrorist attacks, a move that was welcomed by the Southeast Asian countries. Indeed, joint military activities between India and the US in Southeast Asia and the Indian Ocean are part of the US calculus as it pursues a 'pivot' or 'rebalancing' strategy in Asia.

The India navy has also registered a presence in the South China Sea, which has become a major flashpoint of conflict in

East Asia due to competing territorial claims involving six parties: China, Taiwan, the Philippines, Vietnam, Malaysia, and Brunei—the last four of whom are ASEAN members. Increased deployments to South China Sea might signal an Indian intent to act as a balancer to China, but this would be fraught with risks as the latter would see such a move as highly provocative. While part of the reason for the increased Indian military presence in Southeast Asia has to do with concern over the growing Chinese military power, India is unlikely to play a dyadic balancing role vis-à-vis China in the latter's own backyard.

Until now, the Indian navy remained the only one in Asia with medium-sized aircraft carriers. China has recently acquired its first aircraft carrier. India also has a relatively modern submarine force and has an active programme to build principal surface combatants. China, too, is building up a long-range naval force. This might set the stage for a growing naval rivalry between the two powers, especially in the Indian Ocean where Chinese naval presence is growing.[44]

But India's balancing role as part of an overall 'Look East' approach is both cautious and limited. While Indian strategic planners recognize the importance of global trade routes through Southeast Asia and share a concern about the rise of Chinese military power, there is little indication that India has any grand plans for assuming a major security role in East Asia. Instead of balancing in its traditional sense of military measures and alliances, India is more interested in extending its involvement in the cooperative protection of regional sea lanes, such as being part of the 'Eyes in the Sky' programme for patrolling the piracy-infested Straits of Malacca.

As noted, India features in the US 'pivot' or 'rebalancing' strategy in Asia. This strategy, outlined by President Barack Obama during his second term, seeks to redeploy US strategic assets from the Middle East and Europe towards Asia and the Pacific in order to counter the growing Chinese assertiveness.

But India maintains an uncertain or ambiguous stance towards the US strategy. US–India ties have improved markedly in the past decade, especially after Washington lifted economic sanctions against India imposed after its nuclear tests in 1998 and allowed the transfer of nuclear technology to India for civilian purposes. The two countries conduct regular military training and exercises and India is now a major buyer of US arms such as the C-130 Hercules and also has access to advanced US fighter jets should it decide to acquire them. These might have been unthinkable during the Cold War. Both US and India are worried about the rise of China and the threat it might pose to Asian security, including India's territorial integrity. But as already noted, India is also wary of any US strategy of pre-emptively containing China that would provoke the latter and complicate Sino-Indian relations.

Nonetheless, with the exception of China, where significant tensions over border issues and a sense of strategic competition remains, India's bilateral ties with all the major Asian neighbours to the east, notably Indonesia and Japan, have registered significant improvements. In the past, right from the time of the Bandung Conference, India and Indonesia did not agree on the management of regional security matters. But in 2005, the then Indonesian president Susilo Bambang Yudhoyono visited India to sign a strategic-partnership agreement. President Yudhoyono was the chief guest at India's Republic Day celebrations in January 2011. Security cooperation, especially over maritime affairs, between the two countries has also improved. C. Raja Mohan argues that India and Indonesia can develop a new relationship as each country leaves behind the North–South divide as the main basis of its foreign policy. Both are democratic nations now and have the capability to play the role of 'potential consensus-builders' on the world stage through their membership in the G20, as well as shape East Asia's balance-of-power and security architecture. Adding to this is the emerging notion of an 'Indo-Pacific Region'. India's desire to raise its profile in the Pacific part of the 'Indo-Pacific' would require Indonesia's political support and, if successful, will 'end the artificial separation between the two oceans and help construct a new Indo-Pacific region'.[45] But the 'Indo-Pacific' concept, which is explicitly designed to bring India into the Asia-Pacific security architecture and thereby make up for its lack of membership in APEC, has strong authorship and support from Indonesia (although one might think that too much of an Indian role here might spark misgivings from Indonesia). Indian maritime doctrine's declaration that the entire Indian Ocean region, from the Persian Gulf to the Straits of Malacca, is its 'legitimate area of interest' might raise concerns in Indonesia. India's maritime strategy document released in 2009 listed the Sunda and Lombok straits as falling within the Indian navy's area of strategic interest. It did note, however, that 'cooperation with Indonesia is a prerequisite to enable the navy's operations in these waters'.[46]

It is arguable whether Nehru's embracing of Communist China over what turned out to be a democratic and wealthier Japan during the 1950s was a strategic blunder, as some of Nehru's critics allege. For long, India–Japan ties suffered from Cold War polarization as well as from India's socialist economy and hostile attitude towards foreign investment at a time when Japan had emerged as a major source of investments in Asia. Their ties seem poised to take a major uplift with the advent of the Modi government in New Delhi. This came on the heels of the Abe government's clear move to relax the restrictions on the Japanese defence posture set in its post-Second World War constitution and push for a more visible and forward Japanese military presence in East Asia and the Indian Ocean. Japan was the first overseas destination of Prime Minister Modi outside of South Asia. The warming Indo-Japanese relations reinforce similar trends in India's ties with the US and Australia, thereby fuelling talk of an emerging alliance of democracies, although that idea may be a little far-fetched as India does not want to use ideology as the basis of its foreign policy and is careful not to antagonize China.

## India and Asian Regionalism

ASEAN has been the lynchpin of India's engagement with regional institutions in the Asia-Pacific and East Asia. Prior to the 1990s, the Asia-Pacific region had an institutional deficit. ASEAN was the only regional group of any consequence. But the region witnessed a proliferation of regional bodies beginning with the creation of APEC in 1989. India was excluded from APEC mainly because of its protectionist economic policies and on the ground that it was not a part of the Asian production networks forged by Japanese investments in the 1980s. But this changed subsequently with India's economic liberalization drive initiated by the Rao government.

India's relations with ASEAN have been facilitated by New Delhi's participation in a number of common regional forums. In 1992, India became a sectoral dialogue partner of ASEAN. Although restricted to areas concerning trade, investment, tourism, and science and technology, this represented India's first formal involvement with ASEAN activities. In 1995, India was made a full dialogue partner by ASEAN. This new status meant that India became eligible to participate in a wider range of sectors, including infrastructure, civil aviation, computer software, as well as in the ASEAN Post Ministerial Conference (ASEAN-PMC). India was invited for the first time to summit-level talks with ASEAN in Cambodia in November 2002. At the second ASEAN–India Summit in Bali in October 2003, India signed a framework agreement for creating an ASEAN–India FTA in a decade's time, which includes FTA in goods, services, and investment. In the same year, India also signed a framework agreement for creating an FTA with Thailand and started negotiations for the Comprehensive Economic Cooperation Agreement (CECA) with Singapore.

In 1996, India joined the ARF, the first multilateral security organization in Asia-Pacific under the ASEAN leadership. Until then, ASEAN members had been opposed to Indian membership. India, as with the rest of the South Asian countries, was considered to be outside of the geographic scope of the Asia-Pacific region. A more important, if not publicly stated, factor was ASEAN's fear that South Asian membership would saddle the ARF membership with the seemingly intractable India–Pakistan rivalry, including the Kashmir problem. ASEAN's motive in inviting India into the ARF has something to do with the perceived importance of India as a counterweight to China. After the end of the Cold War, the Southeast Asian community was reassured about India's participation based on the decline in India's defence expenditures and naval modernization efforts. The inclusion of India is a successful outcome of the 'Look East' policy. I.K. Gujral's July 1997 speech to the ASEAN-PMC expressed the hope that the ARF process will produce a congruity of world view and strategic interests between India and the Asia-Pacific nations. According to an Indian official, India's expectations concerning the ARF are no different from those held by ASEAN, that is, 'to ensure through some kind of dialogue mechanism [the] security, stability, and predictability' in the Asia-Pacific environment.

While successful in gaining entry into the ASEAN-PMC and the ARF, India was disappointed by its continuing exclusion from APEC, an institution that was once highly valued by Indian officials. But this is offset by APEC's declining importance and India's growing links with ASEAN and sub-ASEAN groupings. India has participated in the launching of a new subregional grouping called BIMST-EC involving economic cooperation between Bangladesh, India, Myanmar, Sri

Lanka, and Thailand. In 2004, the grouping changed its name to the Bay of Bengal Initiative for Multi-Sectoral Technical and Economic Cooperation (BIMSTEC). The BIMSTEC was originally a Thai initiative whose objectives included regional cooperation in transport and infrastructure. India had entered into a framework agreement for creating a BIMSTEC FTA. BIMSTEC could become a bridge between India and ASEAN. India also engages the newer ASEAN members through the Mekong–Ganga Cooperation (MGC) initiative, which involves building transport links between India and the newer ASEAN members.

In 2005, India got invited to the EAS despite Chinese objections and it came to be seen as a key player in the Asian balance of power. The exact functions of the EAS are still contested; the US which joined the EAS in 2010 wants to turn this into a security forum, a move opposed by China. India's inclusion into the EAS, despite not being an East Asian country, is symptomatic of the view held in Southeast Asia that it is an important player in the Asian balance of power. Indeed, India got a seat at the EAS over Chinese objections—thanks to support from some ASEAN countries, especially Singapore and Indonesia. Justifying the participation of India, New Zealand and Australia in the EAS, Lee Kuan Yew commented:

We agreed that we should also invite India, Australia and New Zealand and keep the center in ASEAN; also, India would be a useful balance to China's heft. This is a getting-together of countries that believe their economic and cultural relations will grow over the years. And this will be a restoration of two ancient civilizations: China and India. With their revival, their influence will again spread into Southeast Asia. It would mean great prosperity for the region, but could also mean a tussle for power. Therefore, we think it best that from the beginning, we bring all the parties in together. It's not Asians versus whites. Everybody knows Australia and New Zealand are close to the U.S. There shouldn't be any concern that this is an anti-American grouping. It's a neater balance.[47]

It should be stressed that Lee's use of the term 'balance' ('useful balance' and 'neater balance') was not to call for a military role for India (or Australia and New Zealand) in ASEAN or a formal strategic alliance between India and ASEAN. It was rather a diplomatic manoeuvre. This approach would be construed as 'balancing' only if one interprets balance of power in diplomatic and political terms. In other words, the meaning of 'balance' here is institutional rather than military. This may reflect the inherent ambiguities and multiple meanings of the term—but is hardly compatible with the conventional notion of power balancing.

For its part, in these ASEAN-led multilateral forums, India's role has been relatively low-key, instead of a repeat of its 1940s and 1950s behaviour when it tried, often arrogantly, to lead Asia. India has now tended to be a junior and rather passive partner in contemporary Asian regional institutions. It has been a listener and constructive player and has raised few controversies with its participation.

The US and Japan are also wooing India. There have been suggestions that the three could form an 'alliance of democracies' against a rising China. But India may not be amenable to this. Unlike the early post-war period, India is not in a position to lead Asian regional institutions. Moreover, while in the 1950s India championed limiting the US role in the region and overshadowed Southeast Asian leaders and diplomats, today its role in Asia is being carried out in association with ASEAN's diplomatic framework and with the backing of the US and pro-Western players like Australia and Japan. Also, economic rather than purely strategic factors dominated India's 'Look East' policy. India can make a contribution to Asian regional order by being a key player in the Asian power balance and by using its growing economic and strategic resources to promote Asian community-building.

There has been much progress in India's 'Look East' policy since it was first formulated in the early 1990s. It is no longer a one-way street, as it originally seemed to be. After a slow start, India's eastern neighbours have rediscovered and engaged India. This was due to a growing recognition of India's economic potential and rising strategic power. While economic factors initially drove India's 'Look East' policy, now it is shaped by both strategic and economic considerations. Moreover, the 'Look East' policy was extended beyond the original ASEAN-6 to include Vietnam (which joined ASEAN in 1995) and beyond to cover the Northeast Asian region, especially China, Japan, and South Korea. At the same time, India's 'Look East' policy came to be recognized and welcomed by other major powers in the region, including the US, Australia, and Japan who have actively embraced India, partly due to their concerns over a rising China. The Modi government has pledged to intensify its eastern engagement; in August 2014, Indian External Affairs Minister Sushma Swaraj pledged to turn India's 'Look East' to an 'Acting East' policy.[48]

Moreover, there are challenges, both old and new, to India's 'Look East' policy. Asian neighbours, including the major champions of India's greater engagement in the region such as Singapore, are sometimes exasperated by New Delhi's lack of attention to the region. They doubt the sincerity of Indian policymakers when they talk about the 'Look East' narrative. India, as the geographic pivot of Asia, has to pay equal, if not more, attention to its western sector if its 'Look East' policy is to be taken seriously. A second criticism has to do with misgivings stemming from a lack of resources and ability to compete with China. Another challenge is India's global ambitions as an emerging power. India's membership in BRICS (Brazil, Russia, India, China, and South Africa) as well as the G20 means it has received global recognition as a leading power of the twenty-first century. Might this, then, mean less time for, and attention to, its engagement with relatively weaker players such as ASEAN?

In the 1940s and 1950s, India had big ambitions about the future of Asia. But it did not have the ability to overcome the effects of the Cold War and regional competitions and tensions in Asia. Today India has steadily growing power potential. But New Delhi appears to be still hamstrung by a vision deficit. At a time when many of the original ideas of Nehru, such as an Eastern federation, seem realizable at least on the economic front, India seems to be still plagued by self-doubt and the burden of inherited ideologies. On the security front, India indeed has the potential to define the future security architecture of the region. There has been a tendency to sharply differentiate between two orientations of India's role in East Asia: a balancer role and a community-builder role. India can do both as a way to contribute to the Asian regional order: by being a 'swing player' in the Asian power balance and by using its growing economic and strategic resources to promote Asian community-building. India has to override the internal tension between pursuing an 'anti-Western' orientation and the new opportunities that emerge from a deeper, alliance-like relationship with the US and Japan, despite the significant recent improvement in its ties with both countries. This, however, seems far from assured.

India has traditionally focused on insulating itself from the pressures of the international and regional systems than on shaping them. The big question is: can India lend a new purpose to its newfound regional power? This is the key challenge facing the future of its 'Look East' policy.

## Is there Room for Both China and India?

What is the place of India, China, and Southeast Asia in the Asian order? If one is to get an acute sense of how the rise of

China and India is reshaping Southeast Asia in particular and Asia in general, Singapore is the place to go. 'China and India will shake the world' is how the late leader of Singapore Lee Kuan Yew put it when he addressed the inaugural conference of the Lee Kuan Yew School of Public Policy titled 'Managing Globalization: Lessons from China and India'.[49] And the Singaporean prime minister Lee Hsien Loong told the ASEAN Business and Investment Forum:

> The rise of China and India is transforming the entire region. China has already overtaken the US as the major trading partner of many Asian countries, including Japan, Korea and several ASEAN economies. India opened up several decades after China—the initial pace of reform was slow, but India has made significant progress in recent years. Combined, these two economic powerhouses will shift the centre of gravity of the world economy towards Asia.[50]

And Singapore's then foreign minister George Yeo, a key champion (and later chancellor) of the Nalanda University in Bihar, remarked: So there's China, there's India, then we see, what about ourselves? Where do we stand in the face of all this? Will we be left behind? ... [T]he rise of China and India has galvanised us both as individual economies and collectively as a region.[51]

Southeast Asia provides the key test of any thesis that holds that India and China can find accommodation in the Asian century. For much of its known history, Southeast Asia used to be an Indo-centric universe, now it appears headed to be a Sino-centric one. What is the role of India in this Sino-centric world? Today both India and China have a chance at regional leadership, even regional dominance, again. ASEAN was created when both were faced with internal disarray and external distraction. That gave space to the region's weaker countries, organized into ASEAN, to shape not only Southeast Asia's but also Asia's regional institution-building. Today both China and India are rising powers. Many analysts see them as rivals for influence in Asia, especially Southeast Asia. While this perception may be exaggerated, there is little doubt that China and India and their relationships with Southeast Asia are key factors in Asia's regional order. But it is one that has been virtually ignored by academic analysts and policy pundits interested in Asian affairs. Much of their concern about the Asian regional order remains focused on China–US relations. Intra-regional dynamics such as the India–China–Southeast Asian triangle receives far less attention and is often dismissed as a sideshow. Yet this is a gap that needs to be addressed, especially as concerns about the US's staying power in Asia grow despite its 'pivot' or 'rebalancing' policy, especially in Southeast Asia.

Multilateralism enables ASEAN to moderate, if not prevent, great-power dominance in Southeast Asia. A key element of this strategy is the engagement of China and India. The rise of China has led to speculation that ASEAN might either resort to balancing against, or bandwagoning with, China. Either could jeopardize ASEAN-led multilateralism in Asia. A balancing posture would compromise the hitherto policy of engaging China through multilateral institutions such as the ARF. Bandwagoning would mean accepting regional institutions dominated by China, which, some fear, may happen to the emerging East Asian regionalism. Either development would threaten ASEAN's own security community-building project.

China presents the greatest challenge to ASEAN. In terms of size, economic resources, and military strength, China dwarfs Southeast Asia and has the potential to deeply affect the autonomy of ASEAN. China's GDP is more than four times the combined GDP of ASEAN (in 2015, it amounted to US$ 10.87 trillion[52] to ASEAN's US$ 2.5 trillion).[53] Some analysts have spoken of the likely emergence of a Chinese sphere of influence in Southeast Asia. China's close relations with the new ASEAN members, particularly Cambodia, Laos, and Myanmar, have been perceived as having 'all the characteristics of a centre–periphery relationship'.[54] China's building of dams in the upper reaches of the Mekong River would give it the ability to control the flow of water to other riparian states, especially Laos, Cambodia, and Vietnam.[55] Before its turn to democracy, Myanmar's links with China were of major concern to ASEAN members. At one point, they covered a wide variety of activities such as the sale of military equipment, military training programmes, and the stationing of Chinese military personnel to operate sophisticated electronic communication and surveillance equipment.[56] Chinese military facilities in Myanmar reportedly support communication and logistics for Chinese air and naval (submarine) deployments.[57] While some of these reports might have been 'based on unsubstantiated rumours or idle speculation',[58] they nonetheless shaped ASEAN's opposition to Western sanctions against the repressive military junta in Myanmar and its decision to admit the country as a full member in 1997.

In the 1990s and early 2000s, concerns about China's role in Southeast Asia fed from two paradoxical developments: a growing level of comfort in Sino-ASEAN political relations and heightened economic competition. Long-term concerns about Chinese power-projection capabilities remain alive in Southeast Asia. While the main aim of China's military build-up, as a July 2002 Pentagon report noted, is to 'diversify its options for use of force against potential targets such as Taiwan and to complicate United States intervention in a Taiwan Strait conflict',[59] the report also notes that forces being developed against Taiwan can be used against other Asian states such as the Philippines. Chinese power projection in Southeast Asia remains limited. Its projection forces would allow it to pursue a 'limited harassment' of ASEAN by sea and air.[60] China may be able to seize most islands in the disputed areas in the South

China Sea, but holding on to them is another matter. Its power projection is constrained by a number of factors: limited range of force projection assets and long-range strike capabilities, and lack of combat experience and training.

Political relations between China and ASEAN improved in the 1990s—thanks partly to their convergent approaches on three of Southeast Asia's major recent challenges: the 1997 currency crisis, the threat of terrorism, and the Severe Acute Respiratory Syndrome (SARS) outbreak. ASEAN appreciated China's pledge not to devalue its currency in the wake of the Asian crisis in 1997. For its part, Beijing was grateful for ASEAN's refraining from condemning China for its initial mishandling of the SARS outbreak. Joint regional efforts to arrest the spread of the disease set a benchmark for cooperation against transnational threats to regional security.

But ironically, contentious economic issues came to the fore. Despite its widely appreciated role during the Asian economic crisis, China's increasingly powerful economy is seen both as an economic threat to Southeast Asia as well as a source of Chinese influence over the region. Singapore's former prime minister Goh Chok Tong described China's economic transformation as 'scary'. Singapore's and the region's 'biggest challenge', according to him, was 'to secure a niche for ourselves as China swamps the world with her high quality but cheaper products'.[61]

At the top of ASEAN's concerns about competition from China was the issue of investment diversion. The total FDI flows to China amounted to US$ 3.4 billion in 1990, US$ 28 billion in 1993, US$ 44 billion in 1997, and have remained around US$ 40 billion since. In comparison, FDI to ASEAN-5 was US$ 12.4 billion in 1990, US$ 27 billion in 1997, and US$ 11.4 billion in 2001.[62] In 1990, according to UNCTAD estimates, ASEAN received 52.6 per cent of the total FDI to Asia, while China received 14.4 per cent. In 2001, in a dramatic reversal of the trend, these figures stood at 14.7 per cent and 55.5 per cent respectively.

Partly to counter China's economic challenge, ASEAN developed a multilateral approach to economic relations with China, concerned that disunity within the ASEAN ranks and acceptance of selective trade concessions from China would worsen ASEAN's relative economic position vis-à-vis China. In this context, the ASEAN–China Free Trade Area (ACFTA, proposed by Beijing itself) assumed importance. The ACFTA, which came into effect on 1 January 2010, was billed as one of the largest free-trade zones in the world covering a total population of 1.9 billion and a combined GDP of about US$ 2 trillion annually. It aims at reducing and eliminating tariffs by 2010 for China and ASEAN-6, and by 2015 for Cambodia, Laos, Myanmar, and Vietnam. According to some estimates, the ACFTA could bolster ASEAN's and China's GDP by 0.9 per cent and 0.3 per cent respectively. It would also increase ASEAN's exports to China by 48 per cent and China's exports to ASEAN by 55 per cent.[63]

An FTA with China with its large domestic market might create more trade and investment opportunities for the ASEAN member states. A China–ASEAN FTA had set a model for similar concessions for ASEAN from FTAs with Japan, Korea, and India. It has made ASEAN more attractive as an FDI destination. Yet Beijing excluded two of Southeast Asia's major exports, rice and palm oil, from the 'early harvest' of tariff reductions, and the products covered in the 'early harvest' scheme amounted to less than 2.1 per cent of the total China–ASEAN trade. While ASEAN's market consisting of 580 million people and rich natural resources were important considerations for China behind its drive for an FTA with ASEAN, trade liberalization also offered potential political benefits. China could exploit it to replace Japan as the primary driving force for economic growth and integration. Indeed, China's likely political gains from its FTA with ASEAN might have prompted Japan to propose its own trade initiative in the region.

China's interest in an FTA with ASEAN was challenging to the US and put paid to any remaining hope of Washington promoting free trade through APEC. In its effort to address China's growing economic weight owing to its strategic economic partnerships such as the ACFTA and the RCEP (a proposed trade agreement between ASEAN and its six FTA partners, including China, that covers 3 billion people and a combined GDP of US$ 17 trillion accounting for about 40 per cent of the world trade),[64] the US proposed the Trans-Pacific Partnership (TPP). If realized, it would be a trade agreement among select Pacific countries aimed at stimulating a competitive rate of economic growth. Specifically, its aim was to 'enhance trade and investment among the TPP partner countries, promote innovation, economic growth and development, and support the creation and retention of jobs'.[65] But more than its economic value, the TPP would have strategic value in sustaining America's primacy in the Asia-Pacific.[66] In an interview with the *Wall Street Journal* in July 2015, when the TPP's future looked uncertain, President Obama said: 'If we don't write the rules, China will write the rules out in that region.'[67]

Despite their desire to cultivate Beijing and their weaker economic and strategic position, the core ASEAN countries are unlikely to collectively bandwagon with China. There has been no direct military alignment between China and any of the original members of ASEAN. Defence relations between China and ASEAN members remain rudimentary and are aimed at confidence-building rather than fighting a common enemy (except non-traditional challenges). Following China's accession in October 2003 to the ASEAN Treaty of Amity and Cooperation and the Joint Declaration on ASEAN–China Strategic Partnership for Peace and Prosperity, a five-year (2005–10) plan of action adopted in December 2004 called for closer security cooperation in defence and military fields;

dialogue, consultation, and seminars on defence and security issues; and cooperation in military personnel training, joint military exercises, and peacekeeping operations.[68] Although security relations between China and Vietnam have improved somewhat, they were not in a bandwagoning relationship. Security ties involving China and other ASEAN members remained relatively modest.[69]

At the same time, ASEAN countries have not eschewed a balancing posture towards China. Concerns over a possible expansionist Chinese security approach led Singapore, Malaysia, Indonesia, and the Philippines to engage in an arms build-up.[70] And there is no convergence of threat perception between China and the major ASEAN members. ASEAN members' past concern over US dominance, particularly Malaysia's, did not translate into military alignment with China. Although ASEAN states do not wish to take sides in the US–China rivalry, as a consequence of their 'hedging strategy', if push comes to shove they will make unpleasant choices, particularly in the event of a direct confrontation between the two powers. Singapore, for one, may be caught in the Sino-US conflict over Taiwan.

ASEAN's main goal remains the continuation of the engagement of China through regional institutions. Its approach seeks to ensure China's enmeshment in a system of regional order in which the costs of any use of force in dealing with problems with its neighbours will be outweighed by benefits. The key element of this approach is the ARF.[71] If China is to turn away from this framework and view and use regional institutions as instruments of leverage, they will certainly unravel. But this will cost it significant diplomatic and strategic clout.

The rise of India also affects ASEAN's engagement strategy. There has been much talk in Southeast Asia about an emerging Sino-Indian rivalry in the region. To some extent, this is evident in Myanmar. And in Southeast Asia, memories of a

Sino-Indian diplomatic competition (perceived, if not real) in the 1950s (Nehru–Chou rivalry at Bandung) are still present. In relating to Southeast Asia, China has some important advantages over India. Many economic and political elites in Southeast Asia are ethnically Chinese. China has a head start over India in economic reform and hence its economic clout in Southeast Asia is substantially stronger. Its trade with ASEAN is considerably greater than India's trade with the latter. The attraction of India in Southeast Asia is somewhat negative, linked to a desire among the ASEAN members not to put all their economic eggs in a single basket. Just as in geopolitics, it is about not becoming too dependent economically on China. But India is not without some cards. India has no territorial disputes with Southeast Asia, like the South China Sea. India's growing security ties with the US are a plus for ASEAN which is mainly pro-US. India's naval power in the western Southeast Asian waters is more substantial than China's.

China's growing ties with ASEAN have been accompanied by closer ASEAN–India cooperation. This was originally reflected in ASEAN's decision to let India into the ARF. ASEAN invited India to hold a summit meeting with the association, the first of which was held in Cambodia in 2002.[72] Against this backdrop, two possible scenarios stand out. First, ASEAN may use India to balance China. This is the most popular scenario going around in Southeast Asia today, although few say it publicly. A second scenario is that Southeast Asia will seek friendly relations with both and engage them in multilateral institutions in which ASEAN retains at least nominal leadership. These include ASEAN, the ARF, and the EAS. In reality, these are not mutually exclusive. Regional institutions can be used to strike a diplomatic, if not military, balance in the region. This was evident when some ASEAN members managed to get India invited to the EAS despite Chinese reservations. Also, this posture allows Southeast Asia to moderate Sino-Indian competition and prevent either power from dominating the region. The continued pursuit of engaging China and India as well as China and the US through regional institutions without taking sides in their potential rivalry provides the most optimal condition for the development of ASEAN's security community-building effort.

It should be noted that while ASEAN has helped India return to Asian regionalism, India's role in Southeast Asia today is quite different from that in the 1940s and 1950s. Then India was the leader of Asian regionalism; now it is following ASEAN's lead. While India's role in the earlier phase of Asian regionalism was dominated by political and strategic concerns, especially Nehru's bid to gain acceptance of Communist China in Asia and weaken the US-led SEATO, economic motives play a large part in contemporary Indian interest in Asian regionalism. In either case, ASEAN retains an important influence over the terms of India's engagement.

While ASEAN members such as Singapore hope that drawing India into its multilateral sphere will balance China's diplomatic and strategic influence, the concept of 'balancing' must be a qualified one. As mentioned earlier, Singapore's Lee Kuan Yew opined that India's participation in the EAS could be viewed as a 'useful balance to China's heft' and, together with Australia and New Zealand, a 'neater balance' for a 'tussle for power' and the pursuit of 'greater prosperity'.[73]

India and China are often described as 'historic rivals' in their bilateral relationship, or 'natural rivals' for the leadership of Asia. India is also described as a 'balancer' of China in Southeast Asia. Whatever the term, perceptions of rivalry dominate those of interdependence and coexistence between the two Asian giants.

But are China and India really historic rivals? In a 2000-year relationship, India and China have fought only one war between them—in 1962. In precolonial Southeast Asia, the two did not compete for power but represented two different kinds of influence that were actually complementary. The Chinese influence was more strategic and geopolitical; it included 'protection' for smaller states through the tribute system and occasional intervention in local affairs (as evident in Admiral Zheng He's military forays into Sumatra and Sri Lanka). The Indian influence was mainly ideational, transmitted through religious beliefs and political institutions. This did not produce the kind of big-power rivalry that small states in classical Europe were subjected to, but allowed selective and creative adaptation by Southeast Asians to suit their context and need and to enrich their own culture and politics.

To be sure, today there can be no 'back to the future', such as a return to the Chinese tribute system (despite some loose talk about this) or to the 'Indianization' of Southeast Asia. Both India and China (along with the ASEAN states) show a common belief in the rules of a modern international system, including equality of states and the doctrine of non-intervention. This regulates and limits their competition. Both are participants in regional institutions geared towards promoting cooperative security and managing economic interdependence.

The geographic factor, one of the most powerful natural causes of war between nations, is conducive to stability in India–China ties. Although the overall China–India military balance is in China's favour, their maritime-capabilities balance in the Indian Ocean may still be in India's favour. India's sea-denial and sea-control ability in waters close to the critical Southeast Asian/Indian Ocean sea lanes, through which Chinese oil imports and commerce as much as that of the rest of Asia must pass, is a critical factor in the India–China balance. The latter's strategic environment is after all mainly maritime.

Some Indian strategists would like to confront Chinese power. Memories of the 1962 war aside, they resent Chinese support for Pakistan. This and China's growing nuclear arsenal made for a major reason, if not the only one, for India's own nuclear weapons programme.

India is also concerned about Chinese influence in Myanmar. For their part, Chinese strategists see India as a rival power because of its location and power in the Indian Ocean. As China's dependence on imported oil grows, Indian naval power will bear increasingly on Chinese security concerns.

But there are good reasons why the India–China relationship is not destined to end in war. Both have common security concerns against terrorism and radical Islam in Central Asia. Both are focusing on domestic reform and economic development. India is keen to demonstrate that a democratic developing nation can achieve significant economic growth and maintain its stability. China is keen to prove that it is possible for a nation humbled by foreign intrusion and internal strife to peacefully regain its status as a world power. Pursuing these core national commitments will impose limits on their desire and ability to engage in disruptive confrontation. Indians are more likely to be slighted by China's failure to recognize India as a great power than feel intimidated by Chinese military might or economic clout.

The past decades have seen Indians being increasingly confident of their ability to withstand economic competition from China. FDI into India pales (depending on the type of statistics used) in comparison to that into China. But India's capital markets are more developed and it has a better record of attracting investment into its stock market and creating world-class companies. Some economists argue that lower dependence on FDI makes growth more sustainable and creates a more 'living economy'. The rise of China has been a blessing in disguise for India, as it provides the impetus for more domestic economic reforms that enhance Indian competitiveness.

India and China did compete for the political leadership of Asia at the ARC when China was under nationalist rule. And as discussed in chapters 3 and 4, at the 1955 Bandung Asian-African Conference, Chinese premier Chou En-Lai, with an unexpected show of moderation and compromise, was said to have 'eclipsed' Nehru who appeared aloof and arrogant. But Nehru, whose main goal was to ensure that China recognized Asian fears over its support for communist insurgencies in the region, was instrumental in securing Chou an invitation to Bandung and introducing him to sceptical leaders from non-communist Asia and Africa. And China's diplomatic gains were somewhat dissipated by its continued support, until the 1970s, for communist insurgencies in Southeast Asia. After Bandung, neither India nor China led an initiative for regional cooperation in Asia until the establishment of the Asian Infrastructure Investment Bank (AIIB, formally set up in January 2016), a Chinese-led financial institution which India has joined. Instead they have accepted participation in institutions developed by their supposedly weaker neighbours in Southeast Asia. This in itself is a moderating factor in any potential competition for regional influence between India and China in Southeast Asia. Another factor is economic interdependence. Singapore's former foreign minister George Yeo said: 'Every time, the east–west trade flourished, we prospered with it. The growth of the east–west trade in this century will dwarf anything that has ever been seen before and will open up a whole new horizon for us.'[74]

He then outlined the strategy for Southeast Asia that might result from this historical context: '[I]n every area, we have to think and act strategically so that Southeast Asia becomes a major intermediary between China and India. This is our historical position and this should also be our future.'[75]

Both India and China are rising powers. Realists believe that such powers often challenge and disrupt international order. But both India and China are behaving mostly as status-quo powers. With free trade and transnational production acting as agents of prosperity, the contemporary international system does make it possible for countries to become wealthy and satisfied without disrupting international stability, China and India included.

## Notes and References

1. S.D. Muni, *China's Strategic Engagement with the New ASEAN: An Exploratory Study of China's Post-Cold War Political, Strategic, and Economic Relations with Myanmar, Laos, Cambodia, and Vietnam*, IDSS Monographs No. 2 (Nanyang Avenue: Institute of Defence and Strategic Studies, 2002), pp. 21, 132.
2. 'Economic Juggernaut: China Is Passing US as Asian Power', *The New York Times*, 29 June 2002.
3. Comments at the IDSS–WFCIA Workshop on Southeast Asian Security, March 2004.
4. Personal communication with Owen Harries, Sydney, 3 September 2004.
5. 'Through the Realist Lens: Conversations with John Mearsheimer', interviewed by Harry Kreisler, Institute of International Studies, University of California, Berkeley, 8 April 2002, available at http://globetrotter.berkeley.edu/people2/Mearsheimer/mearsheimer-con0.html (accessed on 2 October 2016).
6. 'China's Build-up Is Affecting Regional Military Balance: US', *DNA India,* 27 March 2010, available at http://www.dnaindia.com/world/report-china-s-build-up-is-affecting-regional-military-balance-us-1364063 (accessed on 10 October 2016).
7. Derek Watkins, 'What China Has Been Building in the South China Sea?' *The New York Times,* 31 July 2015, available at http://www.nytimes.com/interactive/2015/07/30/world/asia/what-china-has-been-building-in-the-south-china-sea.html?_r=0 (accessed on 31 July 2015). See also M. Taylor Fravel, *Policy Report: U.S. Policy towards the Disputes in the South China Sea Since 1995* (Nanyang Avenue: S. Rajaratnam School of International Studies, Nanyang Technological University [RSIS], 2014), available at

http://taylorfravel.com/documents/research/fravel.2014.RSIS.
us.policy.scs.pdf (accessed on 31 July 2015).

8. David Kang, 2003, 'Getting Asia Wrong: the Need for New Analytical Frameworks', *International Security*, 27(4): 57–85.

9. 'Sino-Vietnam Border Treaties Equal to Both Countries: Spokesperson', *People's Daily*, 25 January 2002, available at http://english.peopledaily.com.cn/200201/24/eng20020124_89291.shtml (accessed on 2 October 2016).

10. Carlyle A. Thayer, 2000, 'China Consolidates its Long-term Bilateral Relations with Southeast Asia', *Comparative Connections*, 2nd Quarter: 61–72.

11. For further details, see Mely Caballero-Anthony, 'U.S.-Philippines Relations Post September 11: Security Dilemmas of a Front-Line State in the War on Terrorism', IDSS Commentaries, October 2002, available at https://www.rsis.edu.sg/rsis-publication/rsis/539-u-s-philippines-relations-po/#.V91VbJh97IU (accessed on 2 October 2016).

12. J.N. Mak, 'Malaysia and Security Cooperation: Coming out of the Closet', paper presented at the conference on Evolving Approaches to Security in the Asia-Pacific, organized by the Institute of Defence and Strategic Studies, Singapore, 9–11 December 2002.

13. Natalie Soh, 'S'pore a Friend of the US, Not a Client State', *The Straits Times*, 28 November 2002.

14. To quote Goh Chok Tong: 'We welcome India's participation in Asean for two reasons. One is strategic. We do want another big country to be actively engaged with Asean. Otherwise, Asean would be, in a sense, overwhelmed by their (*sic*) Northeast Asian countries—China, Japan. So, if we have another wing in terms of constructive engagement, and that is India, it will make for a more stable Asean.' See BBC London, 'East Asia Today', 5 November 2002, radio broadcast at 2200 hours, Foreign Broadcast Monitor, Ministry of Information and the Arts, Singapore, 6 November 2002, pp. 7–8.

15. Sujit Chatterjee, 'India, ASEAN Agree to Create Free Trade Area', *The Indian Express*, 9 January 2003, available at http://

www.expressindia.com/fullstory.php?newsid=16537 (accessed on 2 October 2016).

16. Kang, 'Getting Asia Wrong', p. 66.

17. Fairbank's notion of a Chinese world order did not make claims about its pacific nature. See John K. Fairbank (ed.), *The Chinese World Order: Traditional China's Foreign Relations* (Cambridge: Harvard University Press, 1968). Moreover, the largely culturalist arguments of its contributors emphasizing Confucian virtues such as the emperor's impartiality and benevolence towards tributary states have been challenged by a new body of work which stresses Chinese realpolitik.

    Iain Johnston, a notable contributor to this scholarship, argues that the early Ming was quite warlike in its approach to interstate relations. See Alastair Iain Johnston, *Cultural Realism: Strategic Culture and Grand Strategy in Chinese History* (Princeton, NJ: Princeton University Press, 1998).

18. Wang Gungwu, 'China's Overseas World', in *To Act Is to Know: Chinese Dilemmas* (Singapore: Eastern Universities Press, 2003), p. 306.

19. Wang Gungwu, 'Early Ming Relations with Southeast Asia', in *The Chinese World Order*, p. 50.

20. John K. Fairbank, 'Introduction', in Denis Twitchett and John K. Fairbank (eds), *The Cambridge History of China*, Vol. 10 (Cambridge: Cambridge University Press, 1978), p. 29.

21. Fairbank, 'Introduction', p. 30.

22. John K. Fairbank, 'A Preliminary Framework', in *The Chinese World Order*, p. 9.

23. Although the myth of inequality was preserved by a clever use of a two-level record system whereby letters received by the emperor from foreign rulers were translated in 'extremely polite language' showing deference to the emperor, for letters sent by the emperor to foreign rulers, the official language was 'toned down in order to preserve cordial and friendly relationships with those countries' (albeit the Chinese originals of the edicts kept at the archives were not toned down). See Gungwu, 'China's Overseas World', p. 308.

24. Gungwu, 'Early Ming Relations with Southeast Asia', p. 61.

25. Gungwu, 'Early Ming Relations with Southeast Asia', p. 49.

26. Gungwu, 'China's Overseas World', p. 303.

27. Gungwu, 'China's Overseas World', p. 302.

28. Gungwu, 'China's Overseas World', p. 303.

29. Warren I. Cohen, *East Asia at the Center* (New York: Columbia University Press, 2000), pp. 243–4.

30. This included two wars between Ayutthaya and Malacca in the fifteenth century. The Chinese world order also did not prevent the takeover of Malacca by the Portuguese.

31. I have offered similar arguments about Southeast Asia. See Acharya, *The Quest for Identity*. On the possibilities and limits of historicism, see Jack S. Levy, 'Explaining Events and Developing Theories: History, Political Science and the Analysis of International Relations', in Colin Elman and Miriam Fendius Elman (eds), *Bridges and Boundaries: Historians, Political Scientists and the Study of International Relations* (Cambridge: MIT Press, 2001), pp. 39–83; John Lewis Gaddis, 1997, 'History, Theory, and Common Ground', *International Security*, 22(1): 75–85.

32. Sultan Shahin, 'India's "Look East" Policy Pays Off', *Asia Times*, 11 October 2003, available at https://www.globalpolicy.org/component/content/article/162/27908.html (accessed on 19 September 2014).

33. Dong Zhang, 'India Looks East: Strategies and Impacts', AusAID Working Paper, AusAID, Canberra, September 2006, available at http://aid.dfat.gov.au/Publications/Documents/india_east.pdf (accessed on 19 September 2014), p. 15.

34. Zhang, 'India Looks East', p. 6.

35. Nanda, *Rediscovering Asia*, p. 320.

36. Lee Hsien Loong, 'Moving Asean Forward: Sustaining Momentum', 3rd ASEAN Business and Investment Forum, 11 December 2005, Shangri-La Hotel, Kuala Lumpur, Malaysia, available at http://www.mfa.gov.sg/content/mfa/overseasmission/wellington/press_statements_speeches/2005/200512/press_200512_4.html (accessed on 2 October 2016).

37. 'Overview: ASEAN–India Dialogue Relations', August 2016, available at http://asean.org/storage/2012/05/Overview-ASEAN-India-as-of-19Aug16-r3fn.pdf (accessed on 9 October 2016).

38. 'Overview of ASEAN–India Dialogue Relations', available at http://www.asean.org/asean/external-relations/india/item/overview-of-asean-india-dialogue-relations (accessed on 18 September 2014).

39. Association of Southeast Asian Nations, 'ASEAN–CHINA Dialogue Relations', available at http://www.asean.org/asean/external-relations/china/item/asean-china-dialogue-relations (accessed on 18 September 2014).

40. 'India–China Bilateral Relations (Trade & Commercial Relations)', Embassy of India (Beijing, China), available at http://www.indianembassy.org.cn/DynamicContent.aspx?MenuId=3&SubMenuId=0 (accessed on 18 September 2014).

41. Jason Burke, 'India and China Announce Trade Deals during Xi Visit to Delhi', *The Guardian*, 18 September 2014, available at http://www.theguardian.com/world/2014/sep/18/india-china-trade-deals-xi-delhi (accessed on 18 September 2014).

42. 'India–Japan Relations', Ministry of External Affairs, Government of India, available at http://www.mea.gov.in/Portal/ForeignRelation/Japan_-_July_2014_.pdf (accessed on 18 September 2014).

43. 'India–Japan Relations'.

44. C. Raja Mohan, *Samudra Manthan: Sino-Indian Rivalry in the Indo-Pacific* (Washington, D.C.: Carnegie Endowment for International Peace, 2012).

45. C. Raja Mohan, 'India and Indonesia: A New Strategic Partnership', RSIS, 6 February 2011, available at http://www.eurasiareview.com/06022011-india-and-indonesia-a-new-strategic-partnership/ (accessed on 2 October 2016).

46. Pankaj K. Jha, 'India–Indonesia: Towards Strategic Convergence', IDSA Comment, 24 January 2011, available at http://www.idsa.in/idsacomments/IndiaIndonesiaTowardsStrategicConvergence_pkjha_240111 (accessed on 2 October 2016).

47. Michael Elliott, Zoher Abdoolcarim and Simon Elegant, 'Lee Kuan Yew Reflects', interview with *Time Asia Magazine*,

Singapore, 12 December 2005, available at http://www.singapore-window.org/sw05/051205t1.htm (accessed on 2 October 2016).

48. Ranjana Narayan, 'Modi Government to Give Greater Push to Look East Policy: Sushma', *Yahoo India News*, 24 August 2014, available at https://in.news.yahoo.com/modi-government-greater-push-look-east-policy-sushma-140619223.html (accessed on 18 September 2014).

49. Lee Kuan Yew, Minister Mentor, Lee Kuan Yew School of Public Policy, 4 April 2005.

50. Lee Hsien Loong, prime minister of Singapore, 3rd ASEAN Business and Investment Forum, 11 December 2005, available at http://www.nas.gov.sg/archivesonline/speeches/view-html?filename=2005121101.htm (accessed on 2 October 2016).

51. George Yeo, foreign minister, interview with *Lianhe Zaobao*, 7 October 2005.

52. See http://www.worldbank.org/en/country/china (accessed on 9 October 2016).

53. See http://asean.org/asean-gdp-grows-by-46/ (accessed on 9 October 2016).

54. Muni, *China's Strategic Engagement with the New ASEAN*, pp. 21, 132.

55. Ron Moreau and Richard Ernsberger Jr., 'Strangling the Mekong', *Newsweek*, 19 March 2001, Atlantic Edition, p. 26. For details of the Chinese dams, see Muni, *China's Strategic Engagement with the New ASEAN*, p. 84.

56. Andrew Selth, 1995, 'The Burmese Army', *Jane's Intelligence Review*, 7(11): 515.

57. Thayer, 'China Consolidates its Long-term Bilateral Relations with Southeast Asia'.

58. Andrew Selth, 'Burma: A Strategic Perspective', Asia Foundation Working Paper 13, May 2001 (originally presented at the conference on 'Strategic Rivalries in the Bay of Bengal: the Burma/Myanmar Nexus', Washington, D.C., 1 February 2001), available at http://indianstrategicknowledgeonline.com/web/burma%202001.pdf (accessed on 2 October 2016).

59. 'Pentagon Warns of China Threat', CNN, 17 July 2002, posted at 8:57 pm EDT (0057 GMT), available at http://www.cnn.

com/2002/WORLD/asiapcf/east/07/13/china.taiwan/ (accessed on 2 October 2016).

60. 'Pentagon Warns of China Threat'.

61. 'Singapore Unveils New Economic Plan', *International Herald Tribune*, 21 August 2001, p. 9.

62. 'Foreign Direct Investments to China and Southeast Asia: Has ASEAN Been Losing Out?' 2002, Economic Survey of Singapore, Third Quarter, available at http://unpan1.un.org/intradoc/groups/public/documents/APCITY/UNPAN010347.pdf (accessed on 2 October 2016).

63. 'Foreign Direct Investments to China and Southeast Asia'.

64. Rohit Sinha and Geethanjali Nataraj, 'Regional Comprehensive Economic Partnership (RCEP): Issues and Way Forward', *The Diplomat,* 30 July 2013, available at http://thediplomat.com/2013/07/regional-comprehensive-economic-partnership-rcep-issues-and-way-forward/ (accessed on 31 July 2015).

65. 'Enhancing Trade and Investment, Supporting Jobs, Economic Growth and Development: Outlines of the Trans-Pacific Partnership Agreement', Office of the United States Trade Representatives, 12 November 2011, available at https://ustr.gov/tpp/outlines-of-TPP (accessed on 31 July 2015).

66. Sean Mirski, 'The Trans-Pacific Partnership: China, America and the Balance of Power', *The National Interest,* 6 July 2015, available at http://nationalinterest.org/feature/the-trans-pacific-partnership-china-america-the-balance-13264 (accessed on 31 July 2015).

67. Obama quoted in John Garnaut, 'TPP Could Change the Story of a Rising China and a Declining America', *The Sydney Morning Herald,* 31 July 2015, available at http://www.smh.com.au/comment/tpp-could-change-the-story-of-a-rising-china-and-a-declining-america-20150730-ginnwq.html (accessed on 31 July 2015).

68. Jing-dong Yuan, *China–ASEAN Relations: Perspectives, Prospects and Implications for U.S. Interests* (Carlisle, Pennsylvania: Strategic Studies Institute, US Army War College, 2006), p. 15, available at http://www.strategicstudiesinstitute.army.mil/pdffiles/PUB735.pdf (accessed on 16 June 2008).

69. Thayer, 'China Consolidates its Long-term Bilateral Relations with Southeast Asia'.
70. See Caballero-Anthony, 'U.S.–Philippines Relations Post September 11'.
71. Amitav Acharya, 'ASEAN and Conditional Engagement', in James Shinn (ed.), *Weaving the Net: Conditional Engagement with China* (New York: Council on Foreign Relations, 1996), pp. 220–48.
72. Sujit Chatterjee, 'India, ASEAN Agree to Create Free Trade Area', *The Indian Express*, 9 January 2003, available at http://expressindia.indianexpress.com/news/fullstory.php?newsid=16537 (accessed on 2 October 2016).
73. Elliott et al., 'Lee Kuan Yew Reflects'.
74. Speech by George Yeo, Minister for Foreign Affairs, the Global Leadership Forum in Kuala Lumpur, 5 September 2005, available at https://www.mfa.gov.sg/content/mfa/overseasmission/wellington/press_statements_speeches/2005/200509/press_200509_4.html (accessed on 2 October 2016).
75. Speech by George Yeo.

# 6.

# China and India in the Emerging Global Order: Lessons from ASEAN

*H*as Asia been doing enough in leading the world opinion on how to manage, and in particular not to mismanage, the global challenges we face today, including that of terrorism, violence, and global injustice?' asked the Indian Nobel laureate Amartya

Sen at a forum in Bangkok in 2007.[1] Much has been said and written about the 'rise' of Asia, China, and India, but far less about Asia's, including China's and India's, contribution to global governance.[2] The founding leaders of China and India were preoccupied with bringing down colonial rule, protesting against Western dominance, asserting their sovereignty and equality, and, in many cases, demanding concessions and economic aid from the West. Hence, their ideas about international order were imbued with what might be called 'defensive sovereignty'. But if one takes the shift in world power to Asia as an incontrovertible fact or an irreversible trend,[3] then should we not expect their ideas about, and approaches to, international relations to change as well? Yet what are China and India doing to contribute to global governance and order?[4] Also, while as emerging global players China and India are supposed to lead Southeast Asia, it may be argued that they have much to learn from ASEAN.

Scholars of international relations usually speak of 'realism' and 'idealism' (which incorporates elements of liberalism) as the two alternative ways of describing the world views of states and leaders, as suggestive of their perspectives on global governance and order. Although these are theories of international relations, they also help understand and analyse the foreign policy of leaders and nations.[5]

Realists take international relations as a highly competitive game driven by considerations of national interest where war remains a constant possibility and genuine international cooperation highly improbable. Idealists/liberals are optimistic—believing that conflict can be mitigated through the pacific effects of economic interdependence, international institutions, and shared democratic governance. But these concepts, which derive from Western theory and experience, do not do justice to the 'complex' or eclectic (and quintessentially pragmatic) outlooks and approaches of Asian leaders. For example, India's Nehru was foremost among those nationalist leaders whose ideas about world order were eminently compatible with Wilsonian liberal internationalism. Myanmar's leader Aung San was a self-professed internationalist who championed economic interdependence and regional integration in Asia.[6] But Nehru's critics in Asia, such as the former foreign secretary of the Philippines Carlos Romulo, who once indirectly accused Nehru of being a 'starry-eyed idealist',[7] were not necessarily people who, as a realist might expect, dismissed regional and international cooperation. Romulo was actually an active champion of regional multilateral institutions. Realism, as some academic analysts argue, may well be the dominant mode of thinking among Asia's policymaking elite, although this has not prevented Asian states from engaging in multilateral cooperation at the global and increasingly *regional* levels, as the case of Singapore under Lee Kuan Yew attests.

India and China played very different roles in the post-war Asian order. Communist China took on the role of Asia's leading *revisionist* power. China, under the nationalist regime, started out as a conformist nation, but communist China was a different story. 'From its birth date,' writes Chinese historian Chen Jian, 'Mao's China challenged the Western powers in general and the United States in particular by questioning and, consequently, negating the legitimacy of the "norms of international relations".'[8]

By contrast, India's position may be best described as an *adaptive* one. Nehru rejected European-style power politics and was especially scathing of the realist prescriptions about international order which, as proposed in the 1940s by Nicholas Spykman, Winston Churchill, and Walter Lippmann, would have divided the world into a series of regional blocs, each under a great power's leadership (including one under India). Instead Nehru would propose what he called a 'world association' of states that recognized the essential equality of states. But

Nehru never went too far in his critique of Western dominance or in pushing for the creation of an anti-Western bloc in Asia, a fact recognized and appreciated by Britain (but not the US). He kept the tone of the ARC of 1947 (of which he was the chief organizer) or the Asian-African Conference in Bandung in 1955 (of which he was a co-sponsor) remarkably moderate. Nehru defended the UN and, for all his early championing of Asian unity and shepherding of communist China, he disagreed with Chou En-Lai at Bandung when the latter proposed a permanent regional association of Asian and African countries to serve China's need at a time when it was not recognized by the UN. Nehru's concept of 'non-involvement' (which later fused into the broader doctrine of 'non-alignment') was practically an adaptive extension of the Western principle of non-intervention at a time when the two superpowers were violating the doctrine with impunity.[9]

The predicament and position of Southeast Asian nations was closer to that of India than of China. They were willing to live within the existing system of international governance that preserved their independence. With the brief revisionist posture of Sukarno in the 1960s when he withdrew Indonesia from the UN and flaunted his own ideas about 'old established forces' (OLDEFOS) and 'new emerging forces' (NEFOS), and that of communist Vietnam in the 1970s and 1980s, Southeast Asian states have generally accepted the rules and norms of the international system, especially non-interference, diplomatic interdependence, and the sovereign equality of states. Myanmar's Aung San and U Nu exemplified this thinking in the early period, and later ASEAN spearheaded the emergence of a regional international society based on adaptations of these rules.

Ironically, in post-Second World War Asia, despite differences in the approach to Asian order, India's approach to economic development had more in common with socialist China than with democratic Japan. One offshoot of the divergent positions of Asia's major powers was that none would be able to lead an Asian regional organization. After the Second World War, nationalist China and Nehruvian India engaged in regionalism in a competitive way from 1947 to 1955 when Asia tried to develop a regional multilateral grouping. But neither would succeed, conceding the ground to a group of Southeast Asian countries who were suspicious of the bigger Asian powers' intention to lead the region. They—Indonesia, Malaysia, the Philippines, Thailand, and Singapore—formed ASEAN in 1967. ASEAN survived precisely because it was not led by any of the three great Asian powers. This failure of the major Asian powers to provide leadership in building viable regional institutions—and the resulting regionalist leadership of the ASEAN members—has since become a defining feature of Asian regional governance.

Have matters changed? The end of the Cold War, a general adherence to state-supported capitalist economic development, and the emergence of Asia-wide multilateral regional groupings like the ARF and the EAS, have effectively put an end to the revisionist–adaptive divide. Today the differences between China, India, and ASEAN countries over concepts and approaches to economic development are hardly fundamental. In foreign-policy terms, India, by abandoning Nehruvian non-alignment, and China similarly ditching Maoism have moved closer to Japan's conformist position. In this sense, all three Asian powers, China included, are best described as status-quo powers.[10] All have embraced ASEAN-led multilateralism in the region. Ironically, it was the US under the Bush Jr administration that seemed to be the least conformist power in relation to a world order and governance structure that it had played a central role in creating.

This apparent convergence of world views and approaches does not, however, mean that Asian powers share a common view of global governance and how to reform global institutions. Some argue that the simultaneous rise of India and China and their respective moves beyond non-aligned and socialist ideologies may actually mean greater competition rather than cooperation between them. In this view, India and China have become essentially similar players in the international system—both are aspiring great powers who are willing to assert their national interest, increase their power and influence in the world at large, and, when necessary, resort to the use of force in international relations. Realists see distinct prospects for an intensified security dilemma in the twenty-first century Asia, which is not unlike what Europe experienced in the late nineteenth and early twentieth centuries.

Moreover, there remain important areas of diversity in contemporary Indian and Chinese thinking on the relationship between democracy, regional stability, and international order. While Asian leaders have generally accepted the liberal view that economic interdependence is a force for peace and that international (including regional) institutions are useful if not powerful instruments for managing regional order, sharp divisions remain over the role of democracy—whether democracy promotes development or stagnation (the Lee Kuan Yew versus Fidel Ramos debate in the 1990s),[11] whether it is at all a suitable political arrangement for Asia, and whether it is a force of national and regional stability or a prescription for violence and disorder.[12]

In Asia, it is in China rather than in Japan or India that a good deal of conceptual thinking about the future of international order is taking place at official as well as academic levels. This is partly in response to the international community's doubts and misgivings about China's global role following its spectacular ascent—doubts that are less pronounced in relation to the role of Japan or India. Unsurprisingly therefore, Chinese thinking on international relations today is to a large extent an attempt to legitimize the rise of China as a fundamentally positive force in international relations.

China's initial conceptualization of the post-Cold War order was presented under the rubric of 'multipolarization'. Consider the following statement posted on the Chinese foreign ministry website in 2000:

> Since the end of the Cold War, the world has moved towards multi-polarity, and the international situation on the whole has become more relaxed. This is an objective tendency independent of people's will, reflecting the trend of the development of the present era. Multipolarization on the whole helps weaken and curb hegemonism and power politics, serves to bring about a just and equitable new international political and economic order and contributes to world peace and development.[13]

But the concept of multipolarization was dampened by the US victory over Saddam Hussein's Iraq in 1991 and the advent of the so-called 'unipolar moment'. This led some Chinese to modify their position by recognizing what they called 'uni-multipolarity'. At the same time, Chinese policy and academic discourse (the two are often inseparable) developed a common thesis about China's 'peaceful rise' (as an antidote to the 'China threat' thinking), thereby rejecting the view that the country's rise would trigger a power-transition dynamic that would lead to a war with the US and other 'status quo' powers.

China's attitude towards, and involvement in, global and Asian multilateralism has changed considerably, a change for which its Southeast Asian neighbours working through ASEAN can justifiably take some credit. To borrow Johnston's words, China is not only a 'status quo power' but also a 'social state'.[14] In Chinese academia, there are ongoing moves to develop a 'Chinese school of international relations' based partly on the historical (and benign) frameworks of the 'all under heaven' (*Tianxia*) concept, the tributary system, and the 'Chinese world order'.[15] The *Tianxia* concept, which stresses harmony (as opposed to 'sameness'—possibly to send a signal that China can be politically different but still pursues friendship with other nations),[16] is increasingly invoked by the Chinese leadership. Indeed President Hu Jintao has defined the objective of China's foreign policy as to 'jointly construct a harmonious world'[17] (though the present president Xi Jinping thinks that such a 'harmonious world' is too ideal compared to his 'Chinese Dream' philosophy).[18]

But while China has increased its *participation* in multilateralism and global governance, it has not offered *leadership*. This is explained in part by inexperience, fear of provoking a backlash from other powers, and the lingering impact of Deng Xiaoping's caution about Chinese leadership on behalf of the developing world.[19] Dongxiao Chen of the Shanghai Institute for International Studies points to a perception gap between how the world views China (as an emerging global power) and how China views itself (as a low-income developing country). Also at play are a desire not to sacrifice its sovereignty and independence for the sake of multilateralism and global governance, and the impact of domestic factors such as increasingly diverse interest groups, lack of sufficient institutional coordination for implementing international agreements, and limited integration between domestic and international considerations with regard to decision-making about issues of global governance. These factors, Chen argues, mean 'China would, at its best, be capable of playing "part time leader" in a selected way'.[20]

This ambivalence was demonstrated in China's recent reluctance to take the lead in allowing its ample financial resources to play a direct role in alleviating the impact of the global financial crisis. Hence the following argument from the former president Hu Jintao: 'The Chinese economy is increasingly interconnected with the global economy.... China's sound economic growth is in itself a major contribution to global financial stability and economic growth. This is why we must first and foremost run our own affairs well.'[21]

China, however, has been less reticent in assuming a regional leadership, as exemplified in its promotion of the Shanghai Cooperation Organization (SCO) and the idea of an East Asian community. But even here China has been a cautious exponent, backtracking in the face of resistance to any real or perceived effort on its part to drive the membership and agenda of the East Asian institutions.

What about India? Speaking to an annual assembly of overseas Indians in 2005, the then prime minister Manmohan Singh asserted that 'the 21st Century will be an Indian Century'. His prognosis was defined in economic and political terms: 'The world will once again look at us with regard and respect, not just for the economic progress we make but for the democratic values we cherish and uphold and the principles of pluralism and inclusiveness we have come to represent which is India's heritage as a centuries old culture and civilization.'[22] Although Singh refrained from trumpeting India as an emerging global power, Barack Obama, like Bush before him, did so more explicitly when he pledged America's support for India in realizing this goal during a visit to Delhi in November 2010.[23] Indian commentators and media have not been reticent either, although they may be happy to quote Western policymakers and analysts to make this point.[24] Arguably, media and policy talk about India as a global power is more cacophonous in Delhi than similar talk about China in Beijing.

India's policy of non-alignment has not been replaced by any broad organizing framework. In fact neither non-alignment nor Nehru has been formally and officially disavowed by India's post-Cold War governments. But in his 2003 book *Crossing the Rubicon,* Indian analyst C. Raja Mohan made a powerful case that India was reverting to a Curzonian geopolitics,[25] replacing the Gandhian world view that first made its appearance roughly a century ago, or the Nehruvian idealism that defined its foreign policy in the twentieth century. The Curzonian approach assumed Indian centrality in the Asian heartland and envisaged a proactive and expansive Indian diplomatic and military role in stabilizing Asia as a whole. The end of the Bharatiya Janata Party (BJP) government in 2004 might have slowed if not ended that transition, but Indian power projection in both the western and eastern Indian Ocean waters is growing, especially under the next BJP government under Narendra Modi which assumed office a decade later, reflecting a Mahanian rather than Nehruvian bent. It is partly driven by a desire, encouraged by the US and the Southeast Asian countries, to assume the role of a 'regional balancer' vis-à-vis China (whereas Nehru pioneered Asia's engagement of communist China). India, however, avoids any outright containment of China or offers of unconditional support to the US strategic framework vis-à-vis China.

Indian interest in advancing global governance is limited by its concern to advance its national power position in the international system that comes through high growth rates, infotech power, nuclear weapons capability, and space dreams (now a partial reality). Commenting on its stance on global issues ranging from nuclear non-proliferation, climate change, human rights, and corruption, veteran journalist Barbara Crossette calls India the country that gives 'global governance the biggest headache'.[26] India has a legitimate basis to feel that its contribution to global governance is being stymied by other powers, for example, the continuing resistance from the West (and China) to its desire to be recognized as a nuclear-weapon state (thereby joining the Nuclear Non-Proliferation Treaty on that basis). Like Japan, India has sought a permanent seat in the UN Security Council—a dream that seems destined to remain unfulfilled for some time despite the Obama administration's recent backing. It has done better through the G20 forum, but even there, there does not seem to be any obvious Indian ideas or imprint to inspire the reform and restructuring of the global multilateral order. Within Asia itself, India has returned to the fold of Asian regionalism, but in stark contrast to the Nehru era, India's role today is that of a follower rather than a leader. Its regional involvement is much stronger in its economic dimension than in its political and security one, even though it remains excluded from APEC.

Asia's role in global governance cannot be delinked from the question 'Who leads Asia?'. Historically, apart from their mutual rivalry, three factors have determined the issue of Asian leadership: political will, resource capacity, regional legitimacy and rivalry among Asian powers. In the immediate post-Second World War period, India had high legitimacy in Asia and was more than willing to lead, but was unable to do so due to a lack of resources. Japan's case was exactly the opposite; it had the resources (from the mid-1960s onwards) but not the legitimacy—owing to memories of its imperialism for which it was deemed to have been insufficiently apologetic by its neighbours—to be Asia's leader. Japan's involvement in regional leadership was deliberately low-key, cautious, and exercised mostly through development aid and promotion of ideas about regional economic cooperation, completely leaving aside the political–security domain. Looking at China then, it had neither the resources nor the legitimacy (since the communist takeover) or the political will (at the onset of the reform era) to be Asia's leader.

In Asia today, although China in an increasing manner and India to a lesser extent, have the resources to lead, they still suffer from a deficit of regional legitimacy deriving from past histories (that is, Japanese wartime role, Chinese subversion, and Indian diplomatic arrogance dating back to the Bandung Conference). China's recent foreign policy and strategic behaviour, especially in the South China Sea, is likely to accentuate its regional legitimacy deficit in Southeast Asia, while India has made considerable progress in repairing the damage to its image from its early post-war diplomatic style in the region. Moreover, their mutual rivalry prevents the Asian powers from assuming regional leadership singly or collectively. Hence regional leadership rests with a group of the region's weaker states: ASEAN. This is not entirely without merit or contribution. But while others laud ASEAN as a useful and influential voice in regional affairs, some doubt its ability to manage Asia—home to three of the world's four largest economies, four (excluding Russia) of its eight nuclear-weapon states, and its fastest growing military forces.

## Asia and the G20: An Uncertain Trumpet

The global economic crisis since 2008 has provided new opportunities for Asia to assume a greater role at least in global economic governance, especially through its participation in the G20. But the G20 was by no means an Asian idea[27] (Canada's former prime minister Paul Martin is credited for it, even though its composition—the crucial issue of who to invite—might have been decided by the US treasury officials and those of the Deutsche Bundesbank).[28]

But the G20 does have an Asian lineage. Four Asian members of the G20 attended the Bandung Conference—China (PRC), Japan, India, and Indonesia. The number increases to six if Saudi Arabia and Turkey are counted.[29] The Bandung Conference had several major and long-term implications for international order, chief among them being the genesis of NAM. It provided a powerful impetus for pan-African and pan-Arab movements led by Kwame Nkrumah (who was prevented by the British from attending) and Nasser (a star of the meeting but whose country is conspicuously not a G20 member) respectively. It advanced decolonization and symbolized the appeal of economic self-reliance in the Third World, thereby delaying the march of market-driven globalization that now underpins the G20's emergence.

But there are key differences. Bandung was an exclusively South–South event, whereas the G20 is a North–South forum. Bandung's focus was political, whereas G20's is primarily economic, at least to this date. Some of the key Bandung alumni in the G20 have themselves changed dramatically and irreversibly. For Japan, Bandung was the first foray into international diplomacy after defeat in the Second World War. It has emerged as a key player in Asia and the world. Bandung was communist China's debut on the world diplomatic stage. A poor and fledgling communist country, China then easily invited mistrust. India's Nehru did his very best (at the cost of his own image and India's influence) to project China as a constructive Asian neighbour rather than a communist mischief-maker and an integral member of the Sino-Soviet communist monolith, as the Eisenhower administration was doing its best to project. China is now the world's emerging superpower and a valuable and vital member of the global governance architecture. India, as noted, no longer professes Nehruvian non-alignment. It is no longer the leader of Asian unity; that task has long been ceded to ASEAN. Indonesia at Bandung was on the verge of sliding into authoritarianism; as a G20 member, it is held up as a shining example of Asian democracy. The global South is no longer led by the likes of Nehru, Nasser, or Nkrumah but by technocrats like (until recently at least) Manmohan Singh and Hu Jintao. The transition from firebrand ideologues like Mao and Sukarno to the introverted Singh and the former Indonesian president Susilo Bambang Yudhoyono signifies this shift within Asia.

India, China, and Indonesia continue to identify themselves as developing nations, and although China and India aspire to join the great-power club, their foreign-policy postures are shaped by the lingering normative legacy of their involvement in the Third World coalition. For example, India and China stake out positions on the global economy and ecology that are still framed in their predicament and perspective as developing nations. For them, national development goals take priority over complying with the West's demands for greener standards.

Whether the G20 will develop concrete institutional capacity or even emerge as a viable and permanent global institution sharing decision-making and agenda-setting powers with the G7 and the Bretton Woods institutions is far from clear. To cite Chinese expert Dongxiao Chen again, the G20 is not a group of like-minded nations, but one in which cooperation among the emerging powers is 'issue-based and specific interest-oriented'. The challenge to cooperation and coordination among these powers is stymied by 'the fact that the economies and trade interests among these emerging powers are more competitive than complimentary'.[30] Moreover, the G20 is a bit of an exclusive club, plagued by questions about its representativeness and legitimacy. According to two Indonesian analysts, although the G20's emergence as 'the premier forum for international economic cooperation', is 'historic ... from the perspective of global governance as well as the role of Asia in the global economy',

> there are many challenges that have to be dealt with first. Countries in the region have to showcase their abilities in sustaining high economic growth, maintaining political stability and working towards closer regional integration. An approach that relies on a politicised and formal structure will not suit the dynamics in a region which is economic growth-oriented and market-driven.[31]

Asia does not speak as one voice within the G20. On the issue of reforming global financial regulation, a key concern of the G20, the 'lack of a unified Asian voice' has made it easier for America and Europe to set the terms, sometimes at the expense of Asia's interests. For example, Lee Jang Yung, senior deputy governor of South Korea's Financial Supervisory Service, complains that Asian countries 'are facing significant challenges in meeting' the liquidity standards set under the Basel III framework.[32]

Nations represented at Bandung, including Nehru's India, Mao's China, and Nasser's Egypt, harboured no illusions about achieving a global great-power status, whether individually or collectively. All of Asia's G20 members aspire to be leaders of the world, not just of the region. Indeed they (even in the case of middle powers like Indonesia and South Korea) may be using the G20 to leapfrog Asia.

Asian approaches to the other major issue on the global governance agenda—climate change—are by no means shared or suggestive of an act of global leadership. China and India are leading the resistance to the demand for deeper level of cuts to carbon emissions. Both use the argument that as developing nations, they need more time before accepting slower growth rates (in both economic development and carbon emission) that Western nations are prepared to accept. Although at the 2010 Boao Forum held in China's Hainan Island, India's former environment minister Jairam Ramesh described cooperation between India and China on climate change and environment as 'one of the outstanding success stories of this bilateral relationship', he also conceded that the two countries 'might not be on the same page as far as emissions are concerned'.[33] To be sure, recent developments in the global climate negotiations, especially the US–China agreement and India's own flexibility that contributed to the Paris Agreement on climate change in December 2015, suggest a greater willingness on the parts of China and India to cooperate with the West at the multilateral level to reduce emissions. But their position remains defensive enough to fall short of fulfilling Amartya Sen's aforementioned desire to see Asia 'leading the world opinion on how to manage, and in particular not to mismanage, the global challenges we face today'.

Relations among the Asian G20 members remain competitive. China has not been supportive of the bids by India and Japan to acquire a permanent seat in the UN Security Council, even though such a development would be consistent with its own 'multipolarization' concept. This apparent contradiction has prompted some analysts to accuse China of seeking global multipolarity but regional unipolarity. At Bandung in 1955, there was the perception, exaggerated by Western media, of a Sino-Indian competition. Today there is similar talk of a China–India rivalry as well as competition between China and Japan, the latter being in no position to compete at Bandung. There is the danger that competition among the Asian G20 members could spill over into other parts of Asia, like Southeast Asia, similar to the Sino-Indian competition over African resources and markets, or competition among Russia, China, and Brazil over arms sales to African countries. In the meantime, countries left out of the G20 (for example, Singapore and Malaysia) are resentful of those who are savouring their new status in global affairs (for example, Indonesia).

While conceptions of international relations held by China and India are no longer a defensive or confrontational reaction to Western dominance, there remains a perceptible gap between their rise in terms of the traditional power indices of international relations and the requirements for global governance. The gap may be explained partly by resentment against Western resistance to their desire to increase their influence over global institutions commensurate with their rise in the global power structure. But whether a larger say over global institutions will yield a greater willingness on the part of Asian powers to go beyond their 'helping-others-by-helping-themselves' mindset is a fair guess. Also, there is hardly any question that intra-Asian differences and rivalries stifle Asia's bid to assume a greater share of the leadership in global governance.

The national power aspirations of China and India and their role as contributors to global governance need not contradict each other. The changing national-role conceptions, such as China's ideas about 'multipolarization' and 'peaceful rise' and India's seeming embrace of Curzon and Mahan at the expense of Gandhi and Nehru, do not translate into support for global governance. The obvious answer to Amartya Sen's question posed at the outset of this essay is that Asia is doing *more* than before, but this is still *far from doing enough*. And in this respect, they can learn some lessons from ASEAN.

## Lessons from ASEAN

What are the lessons of ASEAN regionalism? The key is its leadership style. David Rapkin argues that middle powers and weaker states that may lack material (military and economic) power can still play other kinds of leadership roles, especially those of 'entrepreneurial' and 'intellectual' leadership, in building international cooperation 'by establishing settings, framing issues and forming coalitions'.[34] Oran Young differentiates between three kinds of leadership: 'structural', 'intellectual', and 'entrepreneurial'.

> The structural leader translates power resources into bargaining leverage in an effort to bring pressure to bear on others to assent to the terms of proposed constitutional contracts. The entrepreneurial leader makes use of negotiating skill to frame the issues at stake, devise mutually acceptable formulas, and broker the interests of key players in building support for these formulas. The intellectual leader, by contrast, relies on the power of ideas to shape the thinking of the principals in processes of institutional bargaining.[35]

Leadership in and by ASEAN is not 'structural' or hegemonic or domineering, examples of which can be found in the US Monroe Doctrine in the Western hemisphere during the nineteenth and early twentieth centuries and Japan's concept of the Greater East Asia Co-Prosperity Sphere built around the Second World War, or Russia's conception of its 'Near Abroad' (including Ukraine, Caucasus, and Central Asia) and now the Eurasian Union. Such leadership relies heavily on the physical and material capabilities backed by the use or threat of use of sanctions and coercion. ASEAN's leadership style is better described as 'communitarian'.[36] It is flexible, shared, and pluralized. Indonesia, the largest ASEAN member in terms of population and the overall gross economy (not in per capita terms however), is often called the leader of ASEAN. But this would not be accurate. Indonesia's role in ASEAN has been likened to that of being in a 'golden cage'. Jakarta's restraint towards its smaller neighbours, such as Singapore and Malaysia, has led the latter to express a degree of deference to Indonesia as the 'first among equals' in ASEAN. There has been no war between Indonesia and its immediate neighbours since ASEAN was founded in 1967, just after Indonesia's war against Malaysia had ended. In reality, ASEAN has a plural leadership. Indonesia has mostly led on regional security issues, whereas Singapore has led on economic cooperation, and the Philippines in the area of human rights and civil-society engagement. In fact, the three countries were the proposers of the ASEAN Political-Security Community (APSC), ASEAN Economic Community (AEC), and the ASEAN Socio-Cultural Community (ASCC) respectively. ASEAN offers a direct contrast to the European or North American model and an alternative framework for regional cooperation. This is reflected in ASEAN's development of a process of regional interactions and cooperation, often called the 'ASEAN Way',[37] featuring informality, consensus-building, and non-confrontational bargaining styles that are often contrasted with the adversarial posturing, majority vote, and other legalistic decision-making procedures in Western multilateral negotiations.

For sure, ASEAN is not without flaws and limitations. But its style of leadership has made four major contributions to the Asian order. The first is its sheer endurance as Asia's only multipurpose regional organization, after the failed experiments in pan-Asian regional institution-building initiated by India and China. A second contribution is to keep its neighbourhood relatively stable. Although border skirmishes have occurred (notably between Thailand and Myanmar in 2001) and bilateral territorial disputes and political tensions persist (notably between Singapore and Malaysia), no ASEAN member has engaged a fellow member in a major armed confrontation since 1967. Third, ASEAN could take justifiable credit for bringing the decade-long Cambodia conflict, caused by the Vietnamese invasion and occupation of Cambodia in 1979, to the negotiating table and finally to a peace agreement. ASEAN's adversary in the conflict, Vietnam, is now a valued member of the organization. Further, as the Cold War ended, it was ASEAN that provided the platform for building wider regional institutions that would engage a rising China and the other major players of the Asia-Pacific region. Without ASEAN's neutral facilitating role, China might not have joined the ARF as the only official multilateral security forum for the Asia-Pacific region.

Moreover, among the many positives of ASEAN is the fact that it has been the primary vehicle of the socialization of both China and India into Asian cooperation. In the early 1990s, China was wary of regional multilateral cooperation. It viewed regional institutions like the ARF or ASEAN as ways for the region's weaker states to 'gang up' against Chinese interests and territorial rights. Yet China significantly revised its view of Asian regionalism and has now become a key player driving it.

Without engagement in this nascent regionalism, China would have had little option but to deal with its neighbours on a strictly bilateral basis, which would have given it far more leverage and coercive ability over its individual neighbours at a time of its rapidly expanding national wealth and power. In that event, China's re-emergence as a great power might have been much more rough and contentious. Many Chinese analysts agree that involvement in Asian regional institutions was a major learning experience for China in wider international cooperation. Moreover, Chinese participation in multilateralism encouraged its Southeast Asian neighbours, at least some of them, to argue against a policy of containment, as initially envisaged by the US after the end of the Cold War. Such an American policy, if undertaken in preference to either 'engagement' or 'hedging', would have stoked Chinese nationalism and evoked a more hardline stance towards its neighbours. Chinese cooperation on a host of transnational issues facing the region, such as the 1997 Asian financial crisis, the 2003 SARS pandemic, and its approach to the territorial dispute regarding the South China Sea might have been more uncertain and uncooperative.

Sceptics may see Chinese participation in regional multilateral institutions as little more than a 'time buying' tactic—that is, until such time as China is able to build up its economic and military muscle to show its true aggressive colours. They might also argue that China has not stopped dealing with its neighbours on a bilateral basis and that instead of acting as a follower of ASEAN's leadership in regionalism, China now or may soon want to lead them and mould them to its own advantage. Chinese desire to develop an East Asian community to the exclusion of the US, India, and Australia is said to be one clue to such an approach. There is thus but a thin line separating the Chinese charm offensive from a de facto Chinese sphere of influence.

But such scepticism can be challenged. Which country would totally eschew bilateralism in its foreign affairs? And which country, great power or not, wants to forsake aspiring to some sort of a leadership role in international cooperation, at least over some key issue areas? And while China may have initially made some strategic calculations about its interest in regional participation, it is not immune to the effects of socialization and learning fostered through the habits of dialogue and continuous interaction. Chinese policymakers are aware of the costs of switching from a policy of engagement to a posture of confrontation and the violation of the normative commitments that they have assumed by signing on to ASEAN's Treaty of Amity and Cooperation, or the Declaration on a Code of Conduct in the South China Sea. To be sure, such instruments are not enforceable, but their violation carries reputational and diplomatic costs that no major power, rising or sitting, can afford to ignore. Asian regional groups are not problem-solving or law-enforcing mechanisms but norm-making and socializing agents. In this respect, they do conform to the general model of international organizations, which generally lack coercive enforcement power but act as instruments of socialization and legitimation.

ASEAN was also the main vehicle for the re-entry of India into Asian regionalism. This happened at first in the economic arena, evident in India's gradual shift from economic nationalism and protectionism to trade liberalization and openness to FDI. This shift occurred haltingly and not just because of ASEAN, but the latter did provide a key stimulus, especially through negotiations over the ASEAN–India FTA. A related factor was India's hope for securing ASEAN's support in joining regional economic groupings in which ASEAN plays a key role, such as APEC and the RCEP. What is striking about India's membership in ASEAN, the ARF, and the EAS is that unlike the 1940s and 1950s, when India was the leading provider of Asian regionalist ideas and a key force behind Asian multilateral conferences (such as the ARCs of 1947 and 1949 and the Asian-African Conference of 1955), it is now following someone else's (ASEAN's) lead in regionalism.

One singular misconception about Asian regional institutions is that they are 'led' by ASEAN. ASEAN's role is better described as the hub and the agenda-setter. ASEAN's 'power' or 'leadership' is in reality a convening power and a normative and social leadership. Despite, or perhaps because of, lacking what might be called structural power (that is, the ability to compel or coerce) and material resources, ASEAN has used socialization and persuasion to engage not only other Southeast Asian and East Asian countries, but *all* the great powers of the current international order. Other contributions of ASEAN include keeping intra-Southeast Asian conflicts at a relatively lower level[38] and providing Cambodia, Vietnam, and later Myanmar a readymade forum to help them return to the international system after decades of self-destructive isolation. Anybody who says these developments were possible only because of sanctions by the Western countries has a poor understanding of Southeast Asian history and politics.

The principle of 'ASEAN centrality' is not an accident of history but rooted in past historical political conditions favouring Asia's weaker states in developing regional cooperation.[39] In other words, the 'ASEAN centrality' does not owe itself to the generosity of the big powers but to two other long-term factors. First, none of these great powers—including the US, China, Japan, and India—would be acceptable to the rest of the region as the sole driver of regionalism as each carries a baggage from the past, so to speak. Second, the two most important East Asian powers, China and Japan, do not find each other acceptable in such a role and the prospect of a Sino-Japanese rapprochement in the manner of the post-war Franco-German reconciliation, which will provide the strongest challenge to 'ASEAN centrality', does not appear likely in the immediate future.

The story of ASEAN is far from perfect. There are valid doubts about the ability of Asian regional institutions—led as they are by the relatively resource-poor ASEAN—to address the region's most serious conflicts (Korean Peninsula, India–Pakistan, South China Sea and cross-Strait) or cope with transnational challenges without a significant shift away from the region's prevailing neo-Westphalian mindset. Asia lags behind other regions in developing mechanisms for promoting human rights and democracy, and institutionalizing new global norms such as 'the responsibility to protect'. But a 'non-indifference' mindset and a 'responsibility-to-assist' principle may be emerging out of Asia's recent brush with a series of transnational threats, including the Asian Financial Crisis in 1997, the Bali terrorist attacks in 2001 and 2002, the SARS pandemic in 2003, the Indian Ocean tsunami in 2004, and Cyclone Nargis in Myanmar in 2008. This is an important, if as yet modest, shift from defensive sovereignty to responsible sovereignty. At the same time, Asian regional groups have contributed well to regional and global stability in engaging all the major powers of the world, including China (where they have arguably done a better job compared to the EU's and NATO's records in engaging Russia).

Although regionalism and globalism are sometimes seen as opposing forces, and despite the danger that the global-power aspirations of the key Asian nations might tempt them to neglect regional cooperation, Asian regionalism has the potential to pave the way for a more concerted and consequential Asian globalism and governance. This is not a mutually incompatible relationship. Asian regional institutions may not resolve all of the region's vexing security and economic challenges, but they may be useful as a potential avenue for tempering the hitherto singular and nationalistic efforts by individual Asian powers to claim their seat at the table of global decision-making bodies. Indeed while pursuing its engagement with global institutions and processes, Asia could do well by beginning its response to global problems at home, meaning, by solving them at the regional level, a strategy that is all the more justified because so many of the major global problems today—climate change, energy, pandemics, illegal migration, to name a few—have local Asian roots.

Asian regional institutions, formal and informal, are already responding to global issues, including climate change (ASEAN, APEC), financial volatility (Chiang Mai Initiative), and terrorism (ASEAN, the ARF, and a web of cross-cutting bilateral and subregional agreements). Much depends on whether Asian regional institutions can strengthen themselves with more robust financial stability and conflict-management mechanisms and move towards a more flexible view of state sovereignty to deal with transnational challenges—all big 'ifs'. But by engaging common issues of global governance at the regional level, Asian powers such as China and India can limit their intramural conflicts. By gaining experience in dealing with complex transnational issues, securing legitimacy from peaceful interaction with neighbours, and sharing leadership with the region's weaker states in managing the region's security and economic conflicts, Asia's emerging powers can derive from their regional interactions useful experience and expertise that could facilitate their substantive contribution to global governance from a position of leadership and strength.

There is much that China and India can learn from Southeast Asia. Instead of viewing it as a natural backyard for geopolitical competition, they should adopt ASEAN's approach of mutual restraint and accommodation through regional cooperation and legitimation. Without more regional legitimacy gained through restraint—admittedly, this is now more of a challenge for China than India—the global-power aspirations of both China and India will be seriously constrained.

# Notes and References

1. 'Eastern Influence Badly Needed', *The Bangkok Post*, 1 April 2007, p. 3.

2. Kishore Mahbubani's book *The New Asian Hemisphere* and other writings address the implications of Asia's rise for global governance. See Kishore Mahbubani, *The New Asian Hemisphere: The Irresistible Shift of Global Power to the East* (New York: Public Affairs, 2008); Mahbubani, *The Great Convergence: Asia, the West and the Logic of One World* (New York: Public Affairs, 2013). The literature on Asia's role in global governance has grown recently. See, for example, Srinivasa Madhur, 2012, 'Asia's Role in Twenty-first-century Global Economic Governance', *International Affairs*, 88(5): 817–33; Amitav Acharya, *The End of American World Order* (New Delhi: Oxford University Press, 2015); B.R. Deepak, 'India, China, and the Future of Global Governance', *The Diplomat*, 1 September 2016, available at http://thediplomat. com/2016/09/india-china-and-the-future-of-global-governance/ (accessed on 7 November 2016).

3. For a sceptical note on Asia's rise, see Pei, 'Bamboozled'.

4. I use the term 'global governance' to refer to 'collective efforts to identify, understand or address worldwide problems that *respect no national or regional boundaries and* go beyond the capacity of individual States to solve' (emphasis mine). This builds upon a definition offered by Thomas Weiss and Ramesh Thakur found in the *Definition of Basic Concepts and Terminologies in Governance and Public Administration* (New York: United Nations Economic and Social Council, 2006), p. 4.

5. Stephen Walt, 1998, 'International Relations: One World, Many Theories,' *Foreign Policy*, Special Edition: Frontiers of Knowledge (110): 29–32, 34–46.

6. 'I am an internationalist, but an internationalist who does not all [allow] himself to be swept off the firm Earth.' 'The one fact from which no nation, big or small, can escape is the increasing universal interdependence of nations.' See Aung San, *Burma's Challenge*, pp. 192–3. These remarks by Aung San are a far cry

from the self-imposed autarchy and isolationism of the military junta which came to rule the country.

7. Carlos P. Romulo, *The Meaning of Bandung* (Chapel Hill: University of North Carolina Press, 1956), p. 91.

8. Chen Jian, *Mao's China and the Cold War* (Chapel Hill: University of North Carolina Press, 2001), p. 10.

9. Acharya, *Whose Ideas Matter?*.

10. The question whether China is status-quoist or revisionist has attracted some debate. According to Randall Schweller, '[R]evisionist states value what they covet more than what they currently possess ... they will *employ military force* to change the status quo and to extend their values.' See Randall L. Schweller, 1994, 'Bandwagoning for Profit: Bringing the Revisionist State Back in', *International Security*, 19(1): 105. Alastair Iain Johnston defines status quo versus revisionist orientation in terms of participation in international (including regionally-based) institutions. See Alastair Iain Johnston, 2003, 'Is China a Status Quo Power?' *International Security*, 27(4): 11. In his view, China's growing participation in regional and global institutions (see Johnston, *Social States: China in International Institutions, 1980–2000* (Princeton, NJ: Princeton University Press, 2008]) is indicative of its status-quo orientation. China's recent assertiveness in the territorial disputes in the South China Sea and the East China Sea is fuelling suspicions that it is a revisionist power. In my view, China is better described as a status-seeker rather than a revisionist power, meaning, it seeks to enhance its own status within the existing international order with some modification than supplant it with one of its own design.

11. Fareed Zakaria, 1994, 'Culture Is Destiny: A Conversation with Lee Kuan Yew', *Foreign Affairs*, 73: 109–26; Kim Dae Jung, 'Is Culture Destiny? The Myth of Asia's Anti-democratic Values', *Foreign Affairs*, 73(6), available at https://www.foreignaffairs.com/articles/southeast-asia/1994-11-01/culture-destiny-myth-asias-anti-democratic-values (accessed on 26 September 2016).

12. Amitav Acharya, 2010, 'Democracy or Death? Will Democratisation Bring Greater Regional Instability to East Asia?', *The Pacific Review*, 23(3): 335–58.

13. 'China's View on the Development of Multi-polarity', embassy of the PRC in the Kingdom of Norway, 17 May 2004, available at http://www.chinese-embassy.no/eng/wjzc/gjzzhy/zgylhg/zzaq/t110857.htm (accessed on 2 October 2016).

14. See Johnston, *Social States*. See also Acharya, *Whose Ideas Matter?*.

15. Qin Yaqing, 'Why Is there No-Chinese IR Theory?', in Amitav Acharya and Barry Buzan (eds), *Non-Western International Relations Theory: Perspectives on and beyond Asia* (Abingdon: Routledge, 2010), pp. 26–50. On the Chinese world order, see Fairbank, *The Chinese World Order*.

16. Zhao Tingyang, *Tianxiatixi: Shijiezhiduzhexuedaolun* (The Tianxia System: A Philosophy for the World Institution) (Nanjing: Jiangsu Jiaoyu Chubanshe, 2005), translated for the author by Shanshan Mei; Yu Keping, 2007, 'We Must Work to Create a Harmonious World', available at http://china.org.cn/english/international/210305.htm (accessed on 2 October 2016). For a critical view, see William A. Callahan, 2008, 'Chinese Visions of World Order: Post-hegemonic or a New Hegemony?', *International Studies Review*, 10(4): 749–61.

17. Hu Jintao, 'Making Great Efforts to Build a Harmonious World with Long-lasting Peace and Common Prosperity', speech to the UN General Assembly marking the 60th anniversary of the establishment of the UN, 15 September 2005.

18. Zhai Kun, in interpreting Xi Jinping's style of new leadership as the 'Xi Jinping Doctrine' of Chinese diplomacy based on the president's new concepts, observes: 'The ideal of a "harmonious world" of the last leadership might be too high and faraway to reach. And the new leadership chooses a more simple, direct, popular, and clear way to talk to the world: you have your American dream, African dream, Latin American dream, etc. and I have my Chinese dream.' See Zhai Kun, 2014, 'The Xi Jinping Doctrine of Chinese Diplomacy', *China Focus*, available at http://www.chinausfocus.com/political-social-development/the-xi-jinping-doctrine-of-chinese-diplomacy/ (accessed on 31 July 2015).

19. Deng's words, often misquoted and misinterpreted, did not rule out Chinese leadership, but took a very cautious position. On 24 December 1990, Deng stated:

Some developing countries would like China to become the leader of the Third World. But we absolutely cannot do that—this is one of our basic state policies. We can't afford to do it and besides, we aren't strong enough. There is nothing to be gained by playing that role; we would only lose most of our initiative. China will always side with the Third World countries, but we shall never seek hegemony over them or serve as their leader. Nevertheless, we cannot simply do nothing in international affairs; we have to make our contribution. In what respect? I think we should help promote the establishment of a new international political and economic order.

See 'Seize the Opportunity to Develop the Economy', 24 December 1990, available at http://en.people.cn/dengxp/vol3/text/d1170.html (accessed on 2 October 2016).

Deng's dictum is derived from his assessment of China's limited capacity to lead and a fear of overreaching. See Wang Zaibang, 2010, 'The Architecture and Efficiency of Global Governance', in Alan S. Alexandroff, David Shorr, and Wang Zaibang, *Leadership and the Global Governance Agenda: Three Voices* (Waterloo: Centre for International Governance Innovation, 2010), p. 167, available at https://www.cigionline.org/sites/default/files/3_voices_0.pdf (accessed on 2 October 2016).

20. Dongxiao Chen, 'China's Perspective on Global Governance and G20', available at http://m.chinausfocus.com/article/1046.html (accessed on 10 November 2016). However, this does not mean that Chinese commentaries have been shy of referring to China's inevitable (re)emergence as a great power. China is also the world leader in doing 'comprehensive national power' estimates relative to other powers.

21. Frank Ching, 'China, Japan Can Help by Helping Themselves', *The Japan Times,* 11 November 2008, available at http://www.japantimes.co.jp/opinion/2008/11/11/commentary/china-japan-can-help-by-helping-themselves/#.V_C9DZN95sM (accessed on 2 October 2016).

22. 'PM's inaugural speech at Pravasi Bharatiya Divas', Mumbai, 8 January 2005, available at http://archivepmo.nic.in/

drmanmohansingh/speech-details.php?nodeid=60 (accessed on 2 October 2016).

23. 'US Supports India as Global Power: Obama', *Headlines India*, 8 November 2010, available at https://www.whitehouse.gov/the-press-office/2010/11/08/remarks-president-joint-session-indian-parliament-new-delhi-india (accessed on 2 October 2016). On a previous occasion, Obama had already described India as 'a leader in Asia and around the world' and as 'a rising power and a responsible global power'. See 'India Is a Rising and Responsible Global Power: Obama', *The Times of India*, 4 June 2010, available at http://timesofindia.indiatimes.com/india/India-is-a-rising-and-responsible-global-power-Obama/articleshow/6009870.cms (accessed on 2 October 2016).

24. See V.R. Raghavan, n.d., 'India and the Global Power Shift', available at http://www.delhipolicygroup.com/pdf/india_and_the_global_power_shift.pdf (accessed on 2 October 2016).

25. C. Raja Mohan, *Crossing the Rubicon: The Shaping of India's New Foreign Policy* (New Delhi: Viking Books, 2003).

26. 'The Elephant in the Room: The Biggest Pain in Asia isn't the Country You'd Think', 2010, *Foreign Policy*, available at http://www.foreignpolicy.com/articles/2010/01/04/the_elephant_in_the_room?page=0,0 (accessed on 6 June 2011).

27. For an 'official history' of the G20, see 'The Group of Twenty: a History', available at http://www.g20.utoronto.ca/docs/g20history.pdf (accessed on 2 October 2016).

28. Robert Wade, 2009, 'From Global Imbalances to Global Reorganizations', *Cambridge Journal of Economics*, 33(4): 553.

29. 'Asian' is not the preferred identity of either Saudi Arabia or Turkey today; certainly doubts are in order in Turkey's case given its fervent, if unrequited, wish to join Europe. The only Asian G20 member that had not taken part in Bandung was South Korea (neither Korea was invited). Australia, which shares with Turkey the problem of an ambivalent regional identity, did not even want to be invited to Bandung. South Africa was represented as an observer at Bandung by two members of the African National Congress. And two of the G20 members did their very best to sabotage the conference—the UK and the US. The UK feared

that Bandung might lead to increased pressure to relinquish its still considerable colonial possession in Asia and elsewhere, while the US feared a propaganda coup by communist China. Acting in concert, the two powers pressured their allies among the Bandung invitees—including Turkey, and also the Philippines, Pakistan, and Thailand—to frustrate not only communist China but also the 'neutralists' India and Indonesia who were running the show. They even supplied propaganda materials (in the form of 'background papers') telling allied nations what to say and what to do at the conference. See Amitav Acharya, 'Lessons of Bandung, Then and Now', *The Financial Times,* 22 April 2005.

30. Chen, 'China's Perspective on Global Governance and G20'.
31. Mahendra Siregar and Tuti Irman, 'G20 and the Global Agenda: A Bigger Role for Asia', available at http://www.eastasiaforum. org/2010/11/09/g20-the-global-agenda-a-bigger-role-for-asia/ (accessed on 2 October 2016).
32. 'Asia Regulators Say G20 Reform Driven by U.S., Europe', available at http://blogs.reuters.com/financial-regulatory-forum/ 2010/11/29/asia-regulators-say-g20-reform-driven-by-u-s-europe/ (accessed on 2 October 2016).
33. Anantha Krishnan, 'Climate Cooperation Changing India–China Ties, Says Jairam Ramesh', *The Hindu,* 9 April 2010, available at http://beta.thehindu.com/news/international/article392921. ece (accessed on 2 October 2016).
34. David Rapkin, 'Leadership and Cooperative Institutions', in Andrew Mack and John Ravenhill (eds), *Pacific Cooperation: Building Economic and Security Regimes in the Asia-Pacific Region* (St. Leonards, NSW: Allen and Unwin, 1994), p. 109.
35. Oran R. Young, 1991, 'Political Leadership and Regime Formation: On the Development of Institutions in International Society', *International Organization,* 45(3): 307. For further contributions to non-hegemonic leadership, see Andrew F. Cooper, Richard A. Higgott, and Kim Richard Nossal, *Relocating Middle Powers: Australia and Canada in a Changing World Order* (Vancouver: University of British Columbia Press, 1993).
36. Amitav Acharya, 1995, 'A Regional Security Community in Southeast Asia?', *Journal of Strategic Studies,* 18(3): 175–200.

37. The 'ASEAN Way' usually refers to a process and, although it has a cultural basis in the region, the term usually refers to a process of interaction combining traditional consensus-building methods and a more pragmatic approach to negotiations and dialogue. For more details, see Amitav Acharya, *Constructing a Security Community in Southeast Asia: ASEAN and the Problem of Regional Order,* third edition (Oxford and New York: Routledge, 2014).

38. Acharya, 'A Regional Security Community in Southeast Asia?'; Acharya, *Constructing a Security Community in Southeast Asia.*

39. Acharya, *Whose Ideas Matter?*.

# Conclusion: Alternative Visions of Asia

*T*his book is not a detailed history of Southeast Asia's relationship—whether bilateral or triangular—with India and China. The title or the theme of the book does not endorse a narrative about a strategic competition in which Southeast Asia balances its two neighbours by playing one against the other. Rather, it is a story about how the cultural and political encounters among the three have defined, and have the potential to redefine further, the future of Asia (or the Indo-Pacific, a currently fashionable term that may yet turn out to be a passing fad).

This book has a deliberate historical focus on developments from the post-war era to the Manmohan Singh era. Keeping it constantly updated is not only challenging but also detracts from the main goal of the book, which is to provide a background to the current events rather than an analysis of events as they unfold. It is a curtain-raiser rather than the main act on stage now. Its main value lies in helping to place the current developments in perspective. It serves as a benchmark against which changes—their degree and nature—may be judged. Too often, policymakers and policy analysts forget the past. There is a growing body of writing on India, China, and Southeast Asia, especially from a 'Look East' perspective. I myself have contributed to this debate elsewhere.[1] But I also feel that there is a need for a book that looks at the historical context.

The basic argument of this book is simple and straightforward. Although both China and India have influenced Southeast Asia—culturally, politically, and economically—for thousands of years, it was India that played an instrumental role in organizing regional cooperation of the postcolonial Asian nations, in which Southeast Asia was a major theatre of interaction.

I have also stressed on Asia as a region of diversity rather than one of any organic unity. At the same time, I have suggested the possibility of imagining and constructing Asia as a social project. But this could not have been done under the control or dominance of a single power, be it Japan, China, or India. It was left to a group of weaker states, ASEAN, to develop Asia's regional architecture. The ASEAN leadership means weak powers have disproportionate impact on regional architecture. This has helped to moderate great-power competition, including that between China and India in Southeast Asia. At the same time, Southeast Asia's desire not to be an extension of either China or India and to keep both of them engaged but without the privilege of ASEAN membership has been an important factor, perhaps more stabilizing than given credit for, in Asian security.

Much is happening that can challenge this pattern. In conclusion, I focus on a few of these keeping in mind the alternative visions of Asia as discussed in Chapter 2, although by no means in a detailed or exhaustive manner.[2] The intention here is not to predict the future but to examine how the recent and ongoing developments may alter the encounter between the three and bring about a different image of Asia and pattern of Asian interaction and order than what has been the case so far. They may even challenge the basic argument of the book, but this challenge is itself indicative of the book's usefulness as a benchmark against which present and future developments may be studied.

The key development challenging this book's argument is the simultaneous rise of China and India. The latter is moving faster, of course, but both are on the move. Turning to China first, this book has argued against taking the prospects for a Chinese regional hegemony too seriously. But China is not only expanding its military power in the South China Sea and the Indian Ocean—the two maritime flanks of Southeast Asia—but is also building its economic and diplomatic leverage through initiatives such as One Belt, One Road (OBOR), the Maritime Silk Road, and the AIIB. Moreover, China is reigniting the talk of 'Asia for Asians'. It remains to be seen whether this slogan keeps faith with the emancipatory and universalist visions of pan-Asianism offered by Rabindranath Tagore, Sun Yat-sen, Okakura Kakuzo, and Nehru or becomes another version of the imperial pan-Asianism championed by Japan during and before the Second World War.[3] If the latter is the case, it will alter the political landscape of Asia profoundly for the worse, even if it will be resisted by others including India and most, if not all, Southeast Asian nations.

I think a Chinese hegemony over Asia or even Southeast Asia, especially the coercive Monroe Doctrine-type, is impossible. And there is no indication that China itself wants this to happen. A more benign version of Chinese hegemony, which relies on economic aid, investment, and market access as well as diplomatic support in return for loyalty to China in a manner akin to the old tributary system,[4] may seem more likely, but is also implausible. However, this is something that should be monitored and responded to by its neighbours, because it will be bad news for Southeast Asia. If it materializes, it will certainly cover at least parts of Southeast Asia, including some of the states involved in the South China Sea conflict.

As for India, it has moved from 'Look East' to 'Act East' under Prime Minister Narendra Modi. This may seem mere policy rhetoric, but at least in the security arena, India has pushed its military presence and deployments with a noticeably greater focus on Southeast Asia and East Asia than ever before. This is not a rerun of the Chola expeditions against Srivijaya in the eleventh century AD. But it may be the most significant Indian military interaction with Southeast Asia since the Second World War when the Indian forces under the Allied South East Command of Lord Louis Mountbatten (before he became the last viceroy of India) fought against the Japanese occupation of Southeast Asia. Add to this India's new diplomatic activism in Asia. The India–US joint strategic vision for the Indian Ocean announced in January 2015 and S. Jaishankar's statement that India seeks to be a 'leading power', not just a 'balancing power', point to a greater willingness on the Modi government's part to play a proactive security role in Asia.[5]

Against this backdrop, what is the place of Southeast Asia in my 'East of India, South of China' narrative, which lies at the core of what Chapter 1 has described as Regionalist Asia? ASEAN was created in 1967 when China and India were both 'down and out' in so far as their diplomatic engagement with Southeast Asia was concerned. Neither country was an economic power of consequence. India was too preoccupied with its domestic problems and its rivalry with Pakistan. China was mired in domestic upheavals of the Cultural Revolution. Both powers were too distracted to exert any serious influence on Southeast Asia after the 1955 Bandung Conference. And the Sino-Indian War of 1962 not only humiliated India at least before Southeast Asia, but, contrary to the views of some, it was hardly a political victory for China in the eyes of Southeast Asia. It actually enhanced the fear of China, rather than the respect the Chinese premier Chou En-Lai had earned for his country at Bandung.

The sidelining of both China and India created the space for the smaller and weaker Southeast Asian nations to build up their diplomatic framework without either of them. Southeast Asia got the autonomy it craved for. The most tangible outcome of Southeast Asia's coming of age as a region was ASEAN. And despite its troubles and limitations, ASEAN has not only survived but also progressed during the past decades as Asia's pre-eminent regional organization.

Today both China and India are well and truly back in the game. Where does it leave Southeast Asia? The issue to me is not that Southeast Asia will come under either Chinese or Indian (far less likely) dominance, as some geopolitical pundits fear. This is a non-issue. For a variety of reasons, especially the role of countervailing powers such as the US, the structure of economic interdependence (rather than dependence), the difficulty of either China or India exercising significant control over the maritime domains of Asia (and the region is predominantly a maritime strategic theatre), we can dismiss the prospect of an overarching hegemony of a single nation—whether China or India—over Asia, including over Southeast Asia as a whole.

Hegemony in Asia is not a given. This book has provided much evidence of the forces that work against hegemony. Asia is more anti-hegemonial than the stereotype of the region in the West takes it to be, presenting it as the alter ego of Westphalian Europe. I also doubt that a two-power condominium or a Chindia could emerge and operate as an order-management device in Southeast Asia. While relations between China and India are unlikely to be wholly competitive, they are even less likely to be wholly cooperative to permit the emergence of a much talked about Chindia that might leave Southeast Asia thoroughly marginalized.

Southeast Asia is also unlikely to come under the dominance of an Asian great-power concert, whereby the region's major powers join hands to manage not only their mutual relationship but also the affairs of the region as a whole. The model of such a concert that is often invoked by the pundits is the European Concert that emerged from the Congress of Vienna in 1814–15. It was an ideological front of Europe's conservative powers against the tide of the revolutionary fervour sweeping Europe. It functioned as a great-powers club for half-a-century managing Europe's security issues. Thanks to the collective hegemony of the great powers, the weaker and smaller nations of Europe had little say over their own affairs. But this is a wholly different era. The great powers of Asia that may form the core of such a concert, a ChiJIA (China–Japan–India–America), share no common ideological ground. The rivalry between China and the other three great powers also militates against a ChiJIA. International norms such as non-intervention and equality of states are much more entrenched today than in nineteenth-century Europe. They favour Southeast Asia's quest for autonomy from collective great-power subjugation.

So the chances are that Asia will not turn into a hegemonic region, whether under any single Asian power or a collective-hegemony framework. The more relevant issue is whether

Southeast Asia can retain its autonomy from a competitive relationship between China and India that is also shaped by the involvement of other major powers such as Japan and the US. This is a more serious and plausible challenge for Southeast Asia and one it must guard against.

For Southeast Asia to retain its autonomy—which is *the single most important contribution it makes to the Asian regional order*—the region and ASEAN (in whatever form it continues) has to stay united, speak in one voice, and act multilaterally on contentious issues such as the South China Sea dispute. Southeast Asian countries have to keep in mind the essential lesson of Bandung, that neither China nor India can shape Southeast Asia's destiny as they might have done in the past.

The fear of those who believe Asia will come under a hegemonic order of a single Asian nation, be it China, India, or any other power, or even a collective hegemony of a Chindia or a ChiJIA concert, is as misplaced as the hopes of those who think Asia will become a region of unity. Asia will remain a region of diversity, and building regional order will depend on both its stronger and weaker nations. Here, Southeast Asia's encounter with simultaneously rising China and India will be pivotal.

In the days of the sailing ship, Southeast Asia, as the meeting point of the two monsoons, was the crucial link in the India–China and hence East–West trade and cultural encounters. Today some analysts think it risks becoming a theatre of China–India rivalry. This book argues that the prospect for Southeast Asia retaining its autonomy and identity is best served if it continues its historic position as a meeting place for the cultural, economic, and ideational currents from the two civilizations, rather than taking sides in the emerging major-power rivalry in the region. By playing the role of a bridge rather than that of a buffer between China and India, Southeast Asia will make a crucial contribution to the peace and well-being of Asia and the world in the twenty-first century.

## Notes and References

1. Amitav Acharya, 2014, 'Power Shift or Paradigm Shift: China's Rise and Asia's Security Order', *International Studies Quarterly*, 58(1): 158–73.
2. For a sophisticated realist view of how India–China rivalry might shape the future geopolitics of the Indo-Pacific region, with implications for Southeast Asia, see Raja Mohan, *Samudra Manthan*.
3. See the discussion on the alternative visions of Asia in Chapter 2.
4. Kang, 'Getting Asia Wrong', pp. 57–85. For a contrarian view, see Amitav Acharya, 'Will Asia's Past Be its Future?' *International Security*, 28(3): 149–64.
5. 'India Wants to be a Leading Power Rather than Just a Balancing Power', *The Wire*, 20 July 2015, available at http://thewire.in/2015/07/20/india-wants-to-be-a-leading-power-rather-than-just-a-balancing-power-6903/ (accessed on 10 October 2016).

# Index

# About the Author

**Amitav Acharya** is Distinguished Professor in International Relations and the UNESCO Chair in Transnational Challenges and Governance at the School of International Service, American University, Washington, D.C., USA. His major publications on Southeast Asia include *Constructing a Security Community in Southeast Asia: ASEAN and the Problem of Regional Order* (2001), *The Making of Southeast Asia: International Relations of a Region* (2013), and *Whose Ideas Matter?: Agency and Power in Asian Regionalism* (2009). He is the former president (2014–15) of the International Studies Association. His Twitter handle is @ AmitavAcharya.